The Feast of the World's Redemption

The Feast of the World's Redemption

EUCHARISTIC ORIGINS AND CHRISTIAN MISSION

John Koenig

TRINITY PRESS INTERNATIONAL
Harrisburg, Pennsylvania

Trinity Press International, P.O. Box 1321, Harrisburg, PA 17105

Trinity Press International is a division of the Morehouse Group.

Cover art: *The Last Supper,* S. Apollinare, Ravenna, Italy.
Scala/ArtResource, New York.

Cover design: Kirk Bingaman

Library of Congress Cataloging-in-Publication Data

Koenig, John, 1938-
The feast of the world's redemption : Eucharistic origins and Christian mission / John Koenig.
p. cm.
Includes bibliographical references and index.
ISBN 1-56338-274-1 (pbk. : alk. paper)
1. Lord's Supper – Biblical teaching. 2. Missions – Biblical teaching. 3. Jesus Christ – Historicity. 4. Bible. N.T. – Criticism, interpretation, etc. 5. Lord's Supper – History – Early church, ca. 30-600. 6. Missions – History – Early church, ca. 30-600. I. Title.
BV823.K633 2000
234′.163 – dc21

99-058730

Printed in the United States of America

00 01 02 03 04 05 06 10 9 8 7 6 5 4 3 2 1

TO MY FATHER AND MOTHER

Almighty God . . .

We bless you for our creation, preservation, and all the blessings of this life; but above all for your immeasurable love in the redemption of the world by our Lord Jesus Christ; for the means of grace, and for the hope of glory. And, we pray, give us such an awareness of your mercies, that with truly thankful hearts we may show forth your praise, not only with our lips, but in our lives, by giving up ourselves to your service. . . .

From *The Book of Common Prayer (1979)*
The General Thanksgiving, Morning Prayer, Rite II

CONTENTS

PREFACE

Most of us who call ourselves Christians are known to celebrate some form of ritual meal. Depending on our church affiliations, we call this rite the Lord's Supper, Holy Communion, the Eucharist, the Mass, or perhaps the Love Feast (*agape* in Greek). We disagree among ourselves a good deal about the meanings of our meals. We differ, for example, on whether or not we should call them "sacraments" and whether or not they should occupy a central place in our worship each Sunday. Yet on one point we find ourselves in almost total agreement: we all tend to link the meals we celebrate directly to Jesus of Nazareth.

This usually means that we think of them as deriving from Jesus' distinctive activities at table (especially his eating with tax collectors and sinners and his washing of the disciples' feet), or from his last supper with his closest followers, his postresurrection appearances in a variety of meal settings, or some combination of these. The great majority of Christian believers today would probably want to extend this consensus even further by affirming that the celebration of our rituals allows us in some manner to dine with Jesus, to receive his presence in our sharing of bread and wine.

But what exactly do we do when we eat and drink with Jesus? Traditionally, we have answered that question along the following lines: we take into ourselves bodily the forgiveness and eternal life Jesus has won for us; we remember his great acts, especially his dying and rising, and participate in them anew; we express our hope for his reappearance when God's kingdom comes in its fullness. We also declare our unity as members of Christ's body and act to build one another up in it. Thus we seek nourishment for our personal and corporate faith, and a maturing strength to love as Jesus did.

The study of eucharistic origins presented here supports all these traditional meanings. But the main point of the study lies elsewhere, for in it I explore dimensions of the church's earliest meal rituals that seem to have suffered eclipse among many Christians through the centuries. I am referring to those features of "eucharistic meals" (the best term, I think, for describing the New Testament table rituals as a whole) that have to do with the church's mission, with its special tasks in God's ongoing redemption of the world. In other words, I concentrate on how these first table liturgies served to define and fuel the outreach ministries of Jesus' disciples and then became such ministries in themselves.

I do not try to define "mission" in a comprehensive way at the outset but rather to highlight its major dynamics in the common life of the earliest churches. As far as meals are concerned, we can locate them on a missionary spectrum, one end of which represents liturgies held with an eye toward bringing more people to faith in Jesus. At the other end are celebrations that placed more emphasis on the self-offering of believers for new ministries of witnessing by word and action. All along the spectrum, however, table rituals were understood by participants as contributing to God's restoration of the whole created order, with their own praise and thanks playing a vital role.

The missionary quality of the New Testament meals is hardly my own discovery. Those acquainted with literature in this area will quickly recognize how dependent I am on seminal works like Alexander Schmemann's *For the Life of the World* (1963); J. G. Davies's *Worship and Mission* (1966); and Geoffrey Wainwright's *Eucharist and Eschatology* (1971). Where I think I have moved beyond these works a little is to provide a firmer exegetical grounding for some of their chief hypotheses and, perhaps, to reflect more on the implications of such results for the worship life of the contemporary church. I have also argued, more intensively than my predecessors, that the missionary thrust of the earliest church's table worship goes back to Jesus' own actions at the last supper. Here I enter directly into the current debate over what we can know about the historical Jesus and his self-consciousness as messiah.

As far as I can tell, the missionary dimensions of the church's eucharistic rituals are not of primary concern to most Christians today, not even to those who take chief responsibility for organizing the church's most public activities. Contemporary writings by missiologists give scant attention to the role of the eucharist, and studies of the eucharist by liturgical specialists often have little or nothing to say about mission. Scholarly explorations of ritual meals and of mission in the New Testament tend not to bring the two together. I know of some happy exceptions to this general picture, especially in the World Council of

Churches' *Baptism, Eucharist and Ministry* document of 1982. Other examples of twentieth century thinking on the issue that seem to me to be moving in the right direction can be found in chapter 6. But on the whole it is probably fair to say that today's churches have not made the best use of their meal liturgies for mission — at least not by New Testament standards.

One more preview of my results may prove useful here. In chapters 4 and 5 I offer some findings that came as a surprise to me. I believe I have shown there that we can identify in our New Testament writings far more references and allusions to eucharistic meals than commentators typically note. In fact, I suspect that most churches of the New Testament period regarded eucharistic meals as a normal part of their Sunday worship *and* of their missionary activity. If these positions hold up to critical response, some church groups today who maintain a high view of the New Testament's authority may want to rethink their worship patterns. On the other hand, those of us who already stress the importance of the eucharist in our Sunday services will not necessarily feel comforted by my study, partly because it challenges us to incorporate into our meal rituals the regular practice of what the New Testament calls "spiritual gifts." I think we all have something to learn from this study, and I put myself first in line since I am quite sure I have not told the whole truth about our eucharistic mission as Christians, and perhaps not even the best part of it. May the conversation continue.

Many thanks are due to those who encouraged me in this project, above all to Elisabeth Koenig, Professor of Ascetical Theology at the General Seminary, my spouse and dearest companion. Professor Richard Corney, also at General, stands out for his willingness to read and respond to an early draft of chapter 1. Much of the work on this volume came to completion during a sabbatical leave that Elisabeth and I enjoyed in the last six months of 1998, and for which we thank the Board of Trustees of the seminary. We chose as our sabbatical site Berkeley, California. There we lived at the Berkeley Presbyterian Mission Homes, a small international village of bungalows and apartments presided over by its director, the Rev. Dr. Ted Crouch. Both Ted and his wife, Alice, extended gracious hospitality beyond our expectations. A large group of people associated with Berkeley's Graduate Theological Union welcomed us warmly. They included Dean Margaret Miles and the Rev. Dr. Owen Thomas, her spouse; Professor Mark and Brenda Lane Richardson (who are now with us at General); and Professor Emeritus Charles McCoy. From the Church Divinity School of the Pacific we remember with pleasure Dean Donn Morgan and Alda Marsh Morgan; Academic Dean Arthur Holder and his spouse, Sarah; Professors L. William Countryman and Louis Weil. The people of St. Mark's Church, and especially their rector, the Rev. Robin Clark, offered us a parish home away from home. Dr. Michele Chase, practitioner in the Taoist healing art of Chi Nei Tsang, gave us much inspiration. Generous financial support for the sabbatical leave came from the Conant Fund for teachers in seminaries of the Episcopal Church and from the Episcopal Evangelical Education Society.

Back on the East Coast, I want to pay special tribute to Sarah Johnson, who worked with me as an editorial assistant during the last year and half of the book's progress. Her expertise and natural interest in the topic proved tremendously helpful. Sincere gratitude goes also to my editors at Trinity Press International, Harold Rast and Laura Hudson; to Trinity's director of marketing, Debra Farrington; and to John Eagleson, who set this type. All four provided good cheer and wise counsel at just the right times.

Thinking once more of Berkeley, I applaud whoever decided to make the cafeteria at the Alta Bates Medical Center on Ashby Avenue into a welcoming public space. Sometimes I took early breakfasts there — it was just half a block from our bungalow — and typically I carried along some materials from the evolving book. Over coffee, toast, and eggs I puzzled out the meaning of notes I had taken, scribbled new ones onto cards, and occasionally wrote a few draft pages. The new shift of the hospital staff came on duty at 8 a.m., so my companions in the main dining area tended to be nurses, doctors, and other medical personnel. Often they gathered together into boisterous, joking groups; but sometimes I caught sight of them alone and quiet, exhausted from the night's work. A few patients, dressed in bathrobes, came down from the upper floors. More frequently I identified the families of patients, usually by their worried looks. Some had probably kept long vigils with loved ones in crisis. And then there were the street people, three or four of them regulars who sipped coffee and dozed, escaping the morning chill. Nobody bothered them. As I worked and ate, I reflected on how the eucharist was not unlike this gathering since it also brings together all sorts and conditions of humanity.

At the same time, though, it surpasses our hospital breakfasts by reaching out even to those who can't or won't come. And the embrace it offers works for redemption—no matter what. I wondered if my brothers and sisters at table would be able to hear that message as good news. I continue to hope so, because this book is for them, too.

J.K.

Epiphany, 2000
Chelsea Square
New York City

The Feast of the World's Redemption

CHAPTER ONE

VISION AND PROMISE AT THE LAST SUPPER

TAKING INTO VIEW the whole span of the church's art, architecture, music, and forms of worship through the centuries, one would have to conclude that the vast majority of Christians have traced their chief ritual meal to a last supper hosted by Jesus for his disciples on the night of his arrest. Paul's account of this supper, as well as those occurring in Matthew, Mark, and Luke, are most easily read as founding events, an interpretation that finds expression in Justin Martyr's description of Christian meal liturgies taking place about 150 C.E.:

> As we have been taught, the food which has been made into the Eucharist by the Eucharistic prayer set down by [Jesus], and by the change of which our blood and flesh is nourished, is both the flesh and blood of that incarnated Jesus. The Apostles, in their Memoirs which they produced, which are called Gospels, have thus passed on that which was enjoined upon them: that Jesus took bread and, having given thanks, said, "Do this in remembrance of me; this is my body." And in like manner, taking the cup and having given thanks, he said, "This is my blood." (First Apology 128)[1]

This same direct linkage of the church's worship at table with the last supper appears in an Egyptian church order of about 215 C.E. that has come to be known as the Apostolic Tradition of Hippolytus (see 394a). These two patristic passages have done much to shape the eucharistic liturgies of both the Eastern and Western branches of Christianity.

That is not to say, however, that all Christians everywhere have regarded the bread and cup words attributed to Jesus at the last supper as an indispensable formula for celebrating their table rites. The farewell dinner narrated in John's gospel contains no such words, and neither do the instructions for holding eucharistic meals set forth in the early Christian tractate Didache, which is usually dated about the end of the first century C.E. Emboldened by this evidence and by new perspectives on how Paul and the synoptic evangelists composed their last supper accounts, some twentieth-century scholars have asked whether the final meal Jesus shared with his disciples (everyone agrees that one had to be chronologically last) was really so important after all, and whether at that meal the historical Jesus uttered anything close to the words passed on to us by Paul, Matthew, Mark, and Luke. Because the present study is dedicated to determining how, if at all, the first-century church's meal liturgies impinged upon or emerged from its missionary activity, we need to address this new line of scholarly reasoning early on. If we conclude that there was no last supper, as this has been traditionally understood, we shall have to look elsewhere for data that may help us discern links in the experience of the earliest disciples between their Lord's call to mission and their celebration of ritual meals.

Was There a Last Supper?

The question we are posing here focuses on whether Jesus, in sensing that a decisive action against him by the authorities was imminent, elected to speak and act symbolically at what he foresaw as a final meal in the company of his disciples. Also implied in our question is the issue of whether such words and actions, if they actually took place on a single occasion, were meant by Jesus as a special disclosure of his role in God's plan that would help to encourage his followers when they were forced to deal with his absence. Since the dawning of critical biblical scholarship in the eighteenth century, the majority of its practitioners have answered with at least a qualified yes to our question and its subquery.[2]

Now, however, some outspoken members of the much-publicized Jesus Seminar want to challenge this consensus in a very pointed manner. Because truth is never a simple matter of majority rule, we need to examine the skeptical views of these scholars with an open mind, ascertaining, if we can, the extent to which they provide us with new evidence or with new perspectives on old data that will require major reinterpretations of the last supper narrative found in our synoptic Gospels and Paul's First Letter to the Corinthians.

The issue has wide-ranging consequences. On the one hand, I am confident that the church could more than survive a high-probability result of historical criticism that Jesus never held an intentional last supper with his disciples. On the other hand, for most Christians around the world the transformation of thoughts, feelings, and images of faith forced by such a basic change in the traditional story of Jesus would come at a high price. A. N. Wilson, the celebrated British novelist and biographer who recently renounced Christianity for a militant form of agnosticism, seems most disillusioned by what he takes to be the established fact that Jesus himself played no part at all in founding the church's eucharist.[3]

What exactly are the positions of contemporary scholars who doubt the historicity of the last supper? John Dominic Crossan takes the boldest stance. In his recent *Jesus: A Revolutionary Biography*, he asserts:

> What Jesus created and left behind was the tradition of open commensality [Crossan's term for Jesus' unusual practice of eating with marginal people and social outcasts] . . . what happened was that, after his death, certain Christian groups created the Last Supper as a ritual that combined that commensality from his life with a commemoration of his death. It spread to other Christian groups only slowly. It cannot be used as a historical event to explain anything about Jesus' own death.[4]

Another member of the Jesus Seminar, Marcus Borg, offers this more cautious assessment of the traditional Christian view:

> We do not know if Jesus in fact held a "last supper" with his disciples at which elements of the meal (bread and wine) were invested with special significance. The stories of a last supper in the gospels may be the product of the early community's embryonic ritualization of the meal tradition [i.e., "open commensality"] rather than a historical recollection of the last night of Jesus' life. There seems, in this instance, no way of moving beyond "not knowing."[5]

Borg's way of formulating the issue here appears to indicate a shift on his part toward a more thoroughgoing skepticism. In an earlier work, *Jesus, A New Vision,* he writes: "the details of the [last supper] story have been affected by the liturgical practice of the church. That Jesus held such a final meal does seem historically likely, however."[6]

Perhaps the most nuanced and comprehensive theory of how the last supper story found its way into our New Testament documents is set forth by a third member of the Jesus Seminar, Bruce Chilton. Chilton argues that the historical Jesus, for a short period of time that followed upon his protest action in the temple (Mark 11:15–19), hosted a series of distinctive meals for his disciples. During these meals, which were private, he spoke words over bread and wine much like our traditional words of institution at the eucharist ("This is my body. . . . This is my blood"). However, Chilton insists that Jesus did not think he was effecting a supernatural change in the elements or establishing a sacrament for a future church. Nor did he have it in mind to symbolize his approaching death. Even so, Jesus' words came across as quite radical in their context; for what he meant by them was that this bread and this wine, as blessed by him, now constituted both his own and his disciples' proper sacrifice to God, a sacrifice that was to replace the offering of animals in the temple cult.[7] On Chilton's hypothesis, one or more of Jesus' disciples betrayed his secretive practice to the authorities, who understood it to be a blasphemous redefinition of Torah commandments relating to the purity of sacrificial offerings. This meal practice of Jesus, when combined with what some officials understood to be offensive behavior on his part in the temple itself (Mark 11:15–19), caused a group within the priestly hierarchy to arrest him and turn him over to the Romans for execution.

Chilton theorizes that soon after Jesus' death and the event we now call the resurrection, some of his disciples, in bringing to mind the revisionist meals their master had held just prior to his arrest, idealized one of them (which may or may not have been literally the last), thus causing its symbolic meaning to expand. Then, Chilton thinks, a circle of believers with Peter at its center initiated a regular memorializing of this "last supper" in the early Jerusalem worship assemblies but modified it through liturgy so that it became a covenant meal rather than a substitute for temple sacrifices. This new, deradicalized understanding allowed the infant church to participate in the temple cult (see Acts 2:46ff.), despite the fact that Jesus himself had challenged its efficacy.[8] Subsequent changes in the meaning of the supper, all of which (Chilton argues) deviate from Jesus' original intention in the several distinctive meals just prior to his arrest, came about through innovations wrought by Jesus' own brother James, the apostle Paul, and the writers of the Gospels. Altogether, Chilton identifies five stages of development in the ritualization of the last supper within the period of the New Testament writings.[9] This scenario is an impressive one and will require careful evaluation by the scholarly community.

Before revisiting a more traditional interpretation of the last supper, we need to take a close look at the four New Testament texts that describe a final meal during which Jesus spoke symbolic words over bread and wine (see the table on page 10). Three of these, we see, occur in the synoptic Gospels: Matthew, Mark, and Luke. The three accounts are probably related to one another in a manner that is usually called "literary dependency," with Mark serving as the basis for both Matthew and Luke. The fourth text, written in the early 50s C.E. (and therefore the earliest), comes from Paul's First Epistle to the Corinthians.[10]

Readers are urged to spend a little time studying these passages, noticing especially where they agree with one another and also where — quite frequently — each one provides a unique wording. Conservative scholars tend to emphasize similarities in the texts and try, whenever possible, to determine which portions of a given text might represent the very words of the historical Jesus, or at least something close to them. Scholars at the other end of the spectrum, even when they assume a historical last supper, typically regard attempts to recover original wordings as an exercise in futility. From their point of view, too much liturgical development has taken place in the New Testament tradition to permit such precise reconstructions.

Can we, however, point to some strengths in the more

Table of Passages

Matt. 26:26–29	*Mark 14:22–25*	*Luke 22:17–20*	*1 Cor. 11:23–25*
[26]Now as they were eating, Jesus took bread, and blessed, and broke it, and gave it to the disciples and said, "Take, eat; this is my body." [27]And he took a cup, and when he had given thanks he gave it to them, saying, "Drink of it, all of you; [28]for this is my blood of the covenant, which is poured out for many for the forgiveness of sins. [29]I tell you I shall not drink again of this fruit of the vine until that day when I drink it new with you in my Father's kingdom."	[22]And as they were eating, he took bread, and blessed, and broke it, and gave it to them, and said, "Take; this is my body." [23]And he took a cup, and when he had given thanks he gave it to them, and they all drank of it. [24]And he said to them, "This is my blood of the covenant, which is poured out for many. [25]Truly, I say to you, I shall not drink again of the fruit of the vine until that day when I drink it new in the kingdom of God."	[17]And he took a cup, and when he had given thanks he said, "Take this and divide it among yourselves; [18]for I tell you that from now on I shall not drink of the fruit of the vine until the kingdom of God comes." [19]And he took bread, and when he had given thanks he broke it and gave it to them, saying, "This is my body, which is given for you. Do this in remembrance of me." [20]And likewise the cup after supper, saying, "This cup which is poured out for you is the new covenant in my blood."	[23]For I received from the Lord what I also delivered to you, that the Lord Jesus on the night when he was betrayed took bread, [24]and when he had given thanks, he broke it, and said, "This is my body which is for you. Do this in remembrance of me." [25]In the same way also the cup, after supper, saying, "This cup is the new covenant in my blood. Do this, as often as you drink it, in remembrance of me."

conservative approach? I think we can, especially when we apply a good dose of common sense to our assessments of the available evidence. The place to start is with Paul's version of what he calls the "Lord's Supper." The apostle tells his readers that the ritual meal tradition he has previously handed over to them, probably when he founded the congregation in about 51 C.E., was received by him "from the Lord" (11:23). This almost certainly means to Paul not a personal message from the historical

Jesus, whom he had never met, nor a direct revelation to him from the risen Christ, but words spoken by Jesus to his first disciples, who then passed them on to other believers, Paul included. We can accept this explanation as the most plausible one because the words "received from" and "handed on" represent technical terms in the early church, taken over from Judaism, for describing the transmission of important sayings through a chain of teachers and prophets.[11] A parallel passage is found at the beginning of the early rabbinic tractate *Pirke Aboth* ("Sayings of the Fathers"): "Moses received Torah from Sinai and delivered it to Joshua, and Joshua to the Elders, and the Elders to the Prophets, and the Prophets delivered it to the Men of the Great Synagogue" (1:1).

But where and when did Paul receive the last supper tradition that appears in 1 Corinthians? He could have learned something about it already during his days as a persecutor of the believers in Jerusalem, not long after Stephen's death (Acts 7:58–8:1; 9:13, 21).[12] Alternatively, he might have encountered this material as part of a table liturgy celebrated by the congregation of Jesus' followers in Damascus that he joined at the time of his conversion (Acts 9:19; see also Gal. 1:17). However, the best-documented occasion for an early transfer of the last supper tradition is Paul's initial trip to Jerusalem following his conversion. In his Epistle to the Galatians the apostle notes that this event took place "after three years" (1:18), which in Jewish reckoning could be considerably less than three full years, by analogy with Jesus' resurrection "after three days" (Mark 10:34). Paul's first journey to Jerusalem as a believer included a visit to Cephas (the

Aramaic name of Peter), with whom he stayed for fifteen days. During that same visit Paul also met "James the Lord's brother" (Gal. 1:18–19). It is virtually inconceivable that these two prominent leaders failed to share with their guest of more than two weeks the Jerusalem church's foundational worship practices, especially table rituals associated with the life of Jesus. And this is exactly how Paul conceives of the Lord's Supper: it is an observance deriving, at least in part, from the last meal held by "the Lord Jesus" with his disciples "on the night when he was betrayed" (11:23).[13]

To be sure, one might argue, with Crossan, that there was no last supper tradition in Jerusalem for anyone to pass on to Paul since this fictitious story arose only later in the church's history, among unnamed believers. But here we must simply appeal to the court of common sense. Paul was personally acquainted with Peter and James, and he wrote to the Corinthians in part to nurture good relationships between them and the believers in Jerusalem (1 Cor. 16:1–4). Would Paul, under such circumstances, really want to remind his readers of a meal tradition that supposedly originated in Jerusalem on the eve of Jesus' arrest but which he knew to be inauthentic? The answer must surely be no.[14]

If, as many scholars now think, Paul's conversion took place only a year or two after the crucifixion, for which the most probable date is 30 C.E., then the time of his visit to Peter would be 35 at the latest and 33 at the earliest.[15] Obviously, even this spectrum of dates allows for some development in the Jerusalem meal practice. Peter and his supporters might have already done what Chilton theorizes: that is, fabricate a last supper event for the purpose of grounding and regularizing the church's worship at table in a way that was compatible with temple worship. But how likely is this? We must consider it to be extremely unlikely for at least two reasons. First, there were plenty of eyewitnesses to Jesus' last days actively participating in the earliest Jerusalem congregation. Could Peter really distort recent history in such a manner while these original disciples just stood by and said nothing? Second, it is hard to understand why the creation of a last supper ritual would be of much help to the infant group of believers when they were already drawing upon rich memories of the communal meals that had occurred throughout Jesus' ministry. Why not base the community's regular order of meal worship on these, as true icons of continuing life with the master?[16] In fact, public knowledge of a last supper story like the one found in our synoptic Gospels and 1 Corinthians would almost certainly create problems for the earliest believers in their Jerusalem environment, not solutions. On any interpretation, words like "This is my body" and "This is my blood" are provocative (see John 6:52–59) and would provide those who wished to suppress the church's witness with powerful negative evidence. Why fabricate such words (Crossan) or highlight them by inventing a dramatic last supper narrative (Chilton) that inevitably called to mind Jesus' execution as a criminal? To do so would be to further endanger the Jerusalem congregation, closely watched as it was by the very authorities who had precipitated Jesus' trial.

It seems far more probable that a form of the last supper narrative, based on a real event and containing troublesome words by the historical Jesus over bread and wine, is just what Peter handed on to Paul not more than five or six years after the crucifixion. Most likely, Peter did this because the story conveyed his own sharp memory and that of his sister and brother disciples of what had actually transpired at Jesus' final meal with a select group of them.

In fact, we have access to another, quite different, body of evidence supporting the view that the historical Jesus celebrated a last supper closely resembling the one transmitted by Paul and the synoptic evangelists. This data, compiled from details of Jesus' Galilean ministry and his days in Jerusalem just prior to the crucifixion, has led most interpreters to conclude that it would be quite natural and "in character" for Jesus to host such a final meal. We can present the relevant data in summary form because most of its components are not hotly disputed, although their full implication for our understanding of the last supper has not always been recognized.

1. Virtually all interpreters of the New Testament now agree that Jesus centered his proclamation and his most characteristic activity on what he called the kingdom of God.

2. Most students of the New Testament these days also conclude that Jesus looked forward to some future fulfillment or completion of the kingdom, probably in a renewed creation that would be brought to perfection by God rather than by human efforts. E. P. Sanders has termed this complex of ideas and beliefs "Jewish restoration eschatology," and he locates Jesus squarely within it.[17] Some contemporary scholars, like Borg and Crossan,

deny that the historical Jesus ever held such a literal view of the world's final transformation, but sound historiography pushes us in the direction sketched out by Sanders.[18]

3. It is a striking fact that a great number of images in Jesus' talk about the kingdom have to do with eating and drinking. No other group of metaphors comes close to this predominance. Here are a few examples from statements attributed to Jesus of how the kingdom resembles or is closely associated with a meal:

a. Blessed are you poor, for yours is the kingdom of God. Blessed are you who are hungry now, for you will be filled [in the kingdom] (Luke 6:20f.).

b. Your kingdom come. Give us this day our daily bread (Luke 11:2f.).

c. Many will come from east and west and will eat with Abraham, Isaac and Jacob in the kingdom of heaven (Matt. 8:11; see also Luke 13:28f.).

d. The kingdom of heaven may be compared to a king who gave a wedding banquet for his son (Matt. 22:2).

e. Then the kingdom of heaven will be like this. Ten bridesmaids took their lamps and went to meet the bridegroom [for the wedding feast] (Matt. 25:1; see v. 10).

The preceding sayings are thought by most scholars to preserve genuine words of Jesus. To this group can be added others with a high claim to authenticity in which the kingdom, though not specifically mentioned, is present by implication as a feast. One of these is the parable of the prodigal son (Luke 15:11–32); another is Jesus' ironic complaint that when he, the Son of Man, came eating and drinking in the communal meals of his ministry, certain righteous people took great offense at his behavior: "They say, 'Look, a glutton and a drunkard, a friend of tax collectors and sinners!' " (Matt. 11:19).[19]

Attentive readers can see where this kind of evidence is taking us. If Jesus engaged in a distinctive set of meal practices (which everyone acknowledges), and if he spoke a lot about how his ministry disclosed or anticipated God's kingdom banquet, then we must consider it altogether characteristic of him, as his public ministry drew to a close,[20] to hold a final meal with his disciples that included words about the feastlike quality of the kingdom.

And this is just what we find in the synoptic last supper prediction of Jesus that he will drink wine at a future meal in the perfected kingdom (Mark 14:25; Luke 22:18; Matt. 26:29 adds the phrase "with you"). Paul, in 1 Corinthians 11, does not transmit this saying; but he probably knew some form of it, for his own commentary on the supper, which emphasizes that whenever believers partake of it they "proclaim the Lord's death until he comes" (v. 26), seems to echo Mark 14:25. Indeed, for Paul, this second coming of the Lord (*parousia* in Greek) means nothing other than the complete establishment of God's kingdom on earth (1 Cor. 15:24–28). When viewed as a whole, the evidence cited above adds up to a probable intention on Jesus' part to celebrate a final supper that would help his followers keep their kingdom hopes alive, despite an impending separation between him and them.

But we can say more on this point. Even the most skeptical scholars are willing to grant that Jesus was at least a prophet in his own self-understanding and that of his contemporaries. As a prophet he could be expected, like Isaiah and Ezekiel of old, to enact his messages symbolically on some occasions. And this he did. Perhaps the most visible of these enactments, which continued throughout his public ministry, was his traveling about with twelve chosen disciples. The number itself is highly charged, for within the framework of Jewish restoration eschatology it would have excited hopes for a reassembling of Israel's twelve tribes, most of whom had been lost to other cultures through the centuries by assimilation. This vindication of Israel's chosenness, many thought, would occur in a glorious time at the end of conventional history.[21] Then, God's covenant faithfulness to the Jewish nation would be openly demonstrated to the whole world (see Is. 25:6–9). Jesus' own proclamation of a future kingdom, precisely in the company of his twelve followers, must have fanned such expectations. This electric atmosphere, which pertained especially during the Passover festival, forms the necessary context for evaluating data that might shed light on the historicity of the last supper.

Jesus' symbolic activity appears to have increased during the final days of his life, which should not surprise us if we posit that he had some special purpose in journeying to Jerusalem for Passover with a substantial group of followers. The four-gospel tradition portrays Jesus, with his twelve disciples and a number of others, staging a dramatic entry into the city. Christians now refer to this event as Palm Sunday, although none of the Gospels specifies that it happened on the first day of the week. What all four of them do tell us is that Jesus' ride into the city on a donkey marked the beginning of a short period of time, just before Passover, that was to culminate in his execution. E. P. Sanders draws upon what we know about the traditional practices of Jewish pilgrims who traveled to Jerusalem for this annual high feast and estimates that the period described in our Gospels was in fact about a week. He also concludes that the account of Jesus' riding on a donkey is historically probable.[22]

In sharp contrast, scholars associated with the Jesus Seminar object that what we have in the passion narrative as a whole is a collection of mythical accounts that bears little relationship to real history. John Dominic Crossan, for example, considers it "most likely that those closest to Jesus knew almost nothing about the details of the event [i.e., his death]. They knew only that Jesus had been crucified, outside Jerusalem, at the time of the Passover."[23] Presumably, this radical thesis applies also to the time period just before Jesus' arrest, although Crossan does concede that on one occasion, possibly near Passover, Jesus acted symbolically in the Jerusalem temple and his disciples were aware of it.[24] Overall, Crossan takes an exceedingly skeptical approach to the historicity of the passion narrative. He estimates that only about 20 percent of the events referred to in it are based on actual occurrences; the others were manufactured by the post-Easter church.[25]

This extreme view has been effectively countered in Raymond Brown's magisterial two-volume work, *The Death of the Messiah.* There Brown shows, through painstaking exegesis and common sense, that most elements in our gospel accounts of Jesus' arrest, trial, and execution have some factual basis, even though they are often elaborated upon in the retelling. Brown begins his treatment of the passion narrative with Jesus' prayer in Gethsemane (which he takes to be historical). Thus he offers no explicit interpretation of the last supper story that immediately precedes the narration of the prayer. But by analogy we can surmise that the same respect for factuality prevailing in the accounts of the later events of Jesus' last week would be present in the earlier ones as well. Brown himself hints at this.[26]

What we have, then, is an interrelated set of historically probable actions on Jesus' part during the time just prior to his arrest:

1. He entered Jerusalem on a donkey, perhaps intending to fulfill a prophecy from Zechariah ("Lo, your king comes to you; triumphant and victorious is he, humble and riding on a donkey, on a colt, the foal of a donkey"; 9:9).

2. He visited the temple, creating a major disturbance there because at least some of those present thought that his words and actions were meant to predict the sanctuary's destruction.[27]

3. At a last meal with his disciples, he spoke unusual words over bread and wine, some of which ad-

> dressed the anxious hopes of his followers for a restoration of Israel's fortunes in a future kingdom of God.[28]

All of these actions seem to disclose a lively expectation by Jesus that God was doing something decisive through him.

When we reflect upon the breadth and diversity of the evidence outlined above, we should entertain no serious doubts about the essential historicity of the last supper.

What Jesus Foresaw

As we move forward now in our study of the last supper, we may accept it as probable that some form of the words "This is my body" and "This is my blood" were spoken by Jesus at the meal. We shall look more closely at variations on these words and their possible meanings below. Here, however, we do well to examine what is probably the least familiar passage in the synoptic accounts of Jesus' last meal, least familiar because it plays no prominent role in the extant eucharistic liturgies of our Western churches. I refer to Mark 14:25 and its parallels in Matthew and Luke.

Apart from scholars associated with the Jesus Seminar, most students of the New Testament today accept the core of this triple tradition as an authentic saying of Jesus. But we need to consider the reasoning they use so that we can appreciate the full force of these synoptic words within the context of the last supper.[29]

Mark 14:25	*Matt. 26:29*	*Luke 22:18*
[25]“Truly, I say to you, I shall not drink again of the fruit of the vine until that day when I drink it new in the kingdom of God.”	[29]“I tell you I shall not drink again of this fruit of the vine until that day when I drink it new with you in my Father’s kingdom.”	“Take this and divide it among yourselves; [18]for I tell you that from now on I shall not drink of the fruit of the vine until the kingdom of God comes.”

Mark, with Matthew following him, puts Jesus’ predictive saying just after the words of institution. Luke, who may know the saying from two sources, Mark and his own special fund of tradition,[30] places it before the bread and cup words. Regardless of this inconsistency, however, the statement itself is firmly anchored in the tradition. Paul, as we have noted, echoes the futuristic part of it in 1 Cor. 11:26. Moreover, the Didache, in which the word “eucharist” is used for the first time on record to identify the church’s chief ritual supper, offers these directions for celebrating it: “And concerning the Eucharist, hold Eucharist thus. First concerning the cup, “We give thanks to thee, our Father, for the Holy Vine of David thy child, which [vine] thou didst make known to us through Jesus thy child; to thee be glory forever” (9:1–2).

The Vine of David referred to here is probably a messianic vine that was expected by some Jews of the first century to produce grapes for the superior wine of the kingdom (see Is. 25:6f.; Zech. 8:12; 9:16f.).[31] Certain Qumran authors, for example, seem to have understood the “choice vine” referred to in Gen. 49:11 as a feature of the renewed creation that would greet the Davidic messiah when he came to claim his throne.[32] In all probability, the prayer of thanks over the cup in Didache 9:1f., drawing upon an unspecified revelation made "through Jesus," evolved from a version of our synoptic "fruit of the vine" saying.

Can we draw some reasonable conclusions about which gospel formulation of this saying is the earliest, while conceding at the outset that no one of them necessarily conveys Jesus' exact words? I believe we can. The choice is almost certainly between Mark 14:25 and Luke 22:18 because Matthew's wording "with you" is what members of the early church wanted to hear from Jesus and could well have been added in the retelling of the last supper story under the influence of their Lord's resurrection presence. The Marcan and Lucan verses are really about Jesus himself, not the church's participation in the kingdom banquet as his table companions. Therefore these versions are likely to be more original. It is harder to decide which of the two presents us with greater historical accuracy, but the evidence seems to tip slightly in favor of Mark's wording.[33]

We have already established that it would be in character for Jesus, at a final meal, to speak about a future kingdom feast. An earlier prophecy of his, asserting that many people will come from east and west to dine with Abraham, Isaac, and Jacob "in the kingdom" (Matt. 8:11; Luke 13:28–29), could be said to lay the groundwork for Mark 14:25. But this prophecy, in turn, is almost certainly based on Jesus' knowledge of Is. 25:6–8 and Zech. 8:7f., 19–23.[34] It will be useful to examine these passages and keep them in mind for future reference:

> On this mountain the Lord of hosts will make for all peoples a feast of rich food, a feast of well-aged wines, of rich food filled with marrow, of well-aged wines strained clear. And he will destroy on this mountain the shroud that is cast over all peoples, the sheet that is spread over all nations; he will swallow up death forever. Then the Lord God will wipe away the tears from all faces, and the disgrace of his people he will take away from all the earth.... (Is. 25:6–8)

> Thus says the Lord of hosts: I will save my people from the east country and from the west country; and I will bring them to live in Jerusalem.... Thus says the Lord of hosts: The fast of the fourth month, and the fast of the fifth, and the fast of the seventh, and the fast of the tenth, shall be seasons of joy and gladness and cheerful festivals for the house of Judah.... Many peoples and strong nations shall come to seek the lord of hosts in Jerusalem, and to entreat the favor of the Lord. Thus says the Lord of hosts: In those days ten men from nations of every language shall take hold of a Jew, grasping his garment and saying, "Let us go with you, for we have heard that God is with you." (Zech. 8:7f., 19–23)

Here we are looking at streams of Jewish tradition that must have fed more or less constantly into Jesus' consciousness and decision making.

What, specifically, does Jesus reveal about himself and his future in his kingdom saying at the last supper? Some scholars believe that he is taking a vow of abstinence, renouncing something dear to him in order to focus more acutely on his vocation in the face of a crisis. That is possible. But John Meier probably comes closer to the truth in labeling Mark 14:25, with its oracular introduction, as a "promise/prediction/prophecy of what Jesus will not do in the immediate future (drink wine at a festive meal) until some future event occurs (the day on which he drinks it new in the kingdom of God)."[35] In other words, Jesus' primary intent is to speak about himself in the end time, which will come before he is able to hold another meal with his disciples that involves wine. The prospect here is mostly a joyful one, and is almost defiant. The vision that gives rise to Jesus' prophecy has to do chiefly with God's world-redeeming abundance, and of himself savoring the great feast in the perfected kingdom.

If, as we must suppose, Jesus sensed that the end of his public ministry was imminent and that imprisonment or death waited in the wings, then the prospect announced in Mark 14:25 is best understood as his experience of commendation by God in the light of all that he as God's servant had accomplished up to the present moment. Our textual evidence does not require us to posit that Jesus at this moment saw himself feasting as one who had died and come to life again, although Matt. 8:11 obviously pictures the final banquet with resurrected saints in attendance.

At the last supper Jesus probably believed that the final establishment of the kingdom was soon to appear, but precisely how and when that happened he would have to leave up to God (Mark 13:32). The most we can say is that the feeling tone of Jesus' prayer in Gethsemane strongly suggests that he finally considered his own suffering and death more probable than God's intervention to prevent it. If that is so, we might then read the same tone back into Mark 14:25 and agree with John Meier that the saying is a "veiled reference to his death."[36] Until we consider other evidence, however, we should treat Meier's thesis as a possibility rather than a probability. In any case, the prophecy shows that Jesus expected a period of time, commencing with the last supper, during which he would not drink wine in a festive manner.

So the two earliest forms of what scholars have come to call Jesus' "eschatological prospect" (i.e., Mark 14:25 and Luke 22:18) both focus primarily upon his own destiny and not that of his disciples. Thus they indicate that he was thinking here mostly about his own special vocation as God's agent at the dawning of the kingdom. But that vocation obviously had a corporate dimension. Jesus knew himself as the one who had begun to reassemble the twelve tribes of Israel. He was their leader, and so now he would also be their pioneer and forerunner into the kingdom. An element of the vicarious is already present in Mark 14:25 because even though Jesus does not speak explicitly of a reunion with his disciples in the perfected kingdom, he discloses his future to them as a host and master who has chosen them as companions. Confused as they were, the disciples surely perceived that Jesus, who had called them together for this solemn meal, was speaking of his future for their sake.

What we have just outlined, I believe, represents a minimalist reading of Mark 14:25 in the light of what we know about Jesus' ministry as a whole. I think we can say more. Because Jesus clearly reflected on the final coming of the kingdom and on his own role at the kingdom banquet, we should probably assume that he also knew about traditions in Judaism according to which God's coming abundance was linked with a messianic ruler and a luxuriant vine. Does it not make perfect sense that Jesus, speaking the words of Mark 14:25, saw himself as the Davidic king referred to in Gen. 49:10–12, who, "binding his foal to the vine, and his donkey's colt to the choice vine . . . washes his robes in the blood of grapes"?

In their context these verses from Genesis form part of an extended prophecy by the patriarch Jacob to his sons, the founders of Israel's twelve tribes. (See Matt. 8:11, where Jesus explicitly mentions Jacob as one of the expected guests at the future kingdom banquet.) Verses 10–12 of the Genesis passage occur in the section devoted to the future of Judah, Jacob's fourth-born son. It is the longest section of the prophecy, probably because Judah — the words "Jew" and "Judea" derive from this name — was the most important tribe left in the Holy Land after the Babylonian exile that ended in 586 B.C.E. The priestly scribes who produced the final form of Gen. 49:10–12 in the postexilic period would have highlighted Judah's role not least because the great king David, one of Israel's chief models for the messiah, came from this tribe. In the New Testament, Jesus is pictured as a lineal descendant of David (see the early confession in Rom. 1:4), and Raymond Brown believes this claim to be historically probable.[37] Here is the whole prophecy spoken to Judah:

> 8“Judah, your brothers shall praise you; your hand shall be on the neck of your enemies; your father’s sons shall bow down before you.
> 9Judah is a lion’s whelp; from the prey, my son, you have gone up. He crouches down, he stretches out like a lion, like a lioness—who dares rouse him up?
> 10The scepter shall not depart from Judah, nor the ruler’s staff from between his feet, until tribute comes to him; and the obedience of the peoples is his.
> 11Binding his foal to the vine and his donkey’s colt to the choice vine, he washes his garments in wine and his robe in the blood of grapes;
> 12his eyes are darker than wine, and his teeth whiter than milk.

It is easy to see how these verses could be understood, as they were at Qumran, to foretell a Davidic messiah.

What is the relationship between the wine and the messianic ruler? Verses 10–12 do not literally state that the ruler described will drink the new wine produced by the “blood of grapes,” but his act of washing his garments in it probably envisions a triumphant revelry that would include imbibing. Claus Westermann must be correct in judging that verse 12 has to do with a redness of the eyes that results from wine consumed, as in Prov. 23:29–30.[38] Indeed, the Palestinian Targum, a collection of Aramaic paraphrases of the Hebrew scriptures that may have circulated in an embryonic oral form during the first century, tries much too hard to avoid the impression that the royal figure of Gen. 49:12 has overdrunk.[39] The Greek Septuagint version of Gen. 49:12 that was current in Jesus’ day actually reads "glazed are his eyes from wine," which means that inebriation was considered by many to be the proper interpretation of the Hebrew verses.

It is hard to avoid the conclusion that in the words of Mark 14:25, on the last night of his public ministry, Jesus was alluding to his own messianic identity, perhaps with an ironic twist. Earlier, during his Galilean ministry, some had denounced him as "a glutton and a drunkard" (Matt. 11:19). Now, in a vision shaped by Gen. 49:10–12, Jesus saw himself embodying their accusations to the nth degree. He would not only sit at table with Abraham, Isaac, and Jacob in the kingdom of God; he would lead the feasting — ecstatically and with God's blessing! However, given Jesus' rejection during his ministry of the triumphalism found in popular expectations of the Davidic messiah's advent (see Mark 10:35–45; 12:35–37), we must suppose that his vision simply bracketed out features of verses 10–12 that would have fed such hopes. His prophetic focus was on the festal celebrating of the messiah, not on the subjugation of his enemies.

Another striking fact about Mark 14:25 deserves mention at this point. Nowhere in our New Testament documents do their authors assert or even imply that Jesus' prophecy at the last supper reached its fulfillment in meals involving the risen Christ.[40] Stories about such post-Easter meals occur in Luke 24:13–43, John 21:1–23, and the longer ending of Mark (16:9–18). Luke also alludes to a period of forty days during which Jesus' disciples "ate and drank with him after he rose from the dead" (Acts 10:41). But in none of these accounts do we receive the faintest impression that Jesus and his followers were celebrating the final establishment of the kingdom. Furthermore, we find no reference in any of these passages to a drinking of wine on Jesus' part. He eats fish in Luke 24:42–43 and may have joined the disciples in drinking some liquid on other occasions — Acts 10:41 hints at the possibility. But wine as such does not enter into the picture. Nor do any of the New Testament references to daily church meals, or to what Paul calls the Lord's Supper, suggest that in them the kingdom has finally come and is being celebrated by the risen Jesus and his followers with a drink from the fruit of the vine. This refusal to equate church ritual with the feast of the perfected kingdom also holds true in the Didache, where the following words of a prescribed eucharistic prayer occur: "Remember, Lord, thy Church, to deliver it from all evil and to make it perfect in thy love, and gather it together in its holiness from the four winds to thy kingdom which thou has prepared for it" (10:5; see also 9:4). Here the compiler of the Didache may be drawing on Matt. 24:31, and in any case he understands the kingdom to be future. As in the New Testament, no attempt is made to show that prophecies uttered by Jesus about the kingdom feast are coming to fulfillment in the church's meal liturgies.

This altogether consistent picture of nonfulfillment, which runs counter to the church's hope, provides additional support for our conclusion that Mark 14:25 contains something very close to the real words of Jesus. The church might have profited by erasing this prophecy from the gospel tradition since it could be used by enemies to argue that Jesus was mistaken about the kingdom's imminence. Alternatively, our New Testament writers might have developed some pictures or stories of Jesus' eating and drinking with his disciples "in the kingdom." But neither of these options was exercised. We must assume that Mark 14:25 persists in our New Testament documents chiefly because a large number of early believers were convinced that Jesus actually spoke such words.

This perspective on Jesus' prophecy at the last supper also means that however the earliest believers experienced his resurrected presence in their ritual meals, and whatever he may have said to them on such occasions, the One they encountered was not totally with them, not in the final, festal sense of the kingdom's perfection. Built into their eating and drinking was a profound longing for his abiding presence at the great feast still to come.[41] Indeed, Jesus' earliest followers must have sensed their risen Lord yearning for them, too, in the full communion of the kingdom banquet.[42] Even at the beginning of the church's corporate worship, when Jesus sometimes appeared to his disciples at table, he and they met one another from opposite sides of the resurrection. In different ways he and his followers all remained servants of the kingdom yet to come, still on their way to the culmination of God's redemptive plan (see 1 Cor. 15:20–28).

Sharing the Messiah's Destiny

We have established the likelihood that Jesus spoke words on the order of "This is my body. . . . This is my blood" over the bread and wine at his last meal with the disciples. Paul probably received a version of these words from Peter in Jerusalem no later than 35 C.E. We have also noted that on any interpretation words of this sort must have troubled mainstream Jews. Understood as a surrogate for animal sacrifices in the temple (Chilton's theory), the sayings would have offended all those who considered the existing system of purity to be still valid. Understood as a reference to Jesus' sacrificial offering of himself, shared by means of eating and drinking, the words were open to charges of cannibalism. John 6:52ff. reflects some such objection to the early church's meal practices. When the fourth evangelist observes that "the Jews then disputed among themselves, saying 'How can this man give us his flesh to eat?' " the meaning is probably "How dare he (and the church) conceive of such a thing?"

All of us know about provocations like this that play upon our strong convictions. We become most agitated when we believe that the symbols we treasure are being debased — as, for example, when national flags are flown upside down or displayed in the wrong colors. And yet deep symbolizations do change, especially in liturgical contexts. Rabbi Lawrence Hoffman has argued that quite apart from developments in Christian meal practices during the mid first century, some Jews had simultaneously begun to think of the Passover bread (matzah) as a symbol of salvation, thus going beyond what we know about its role in the feast from the Hebrew Bible. According to Hoffman, it was this interpretation that allowed Jewish leaders, with relative ease, to substitute the matzah for the lamb in their Passover seders (liturgies) once the temple's destruction in 70 C.E. rendered impossible the ritual slaughter of animals. Post-70 Jews would not have drawn on the emerging eucharistic symbolism of Christians to shape their practices. Instead, argues Hoffman, they relied upon traditions about the matzah that were operative in the Jewish mainstream prior to 70.[43] The point here is that Jesus' words about the bread being his body, however offensive they sounded, would have been understood by at least some Jews as a salvational reference to the Passover lamb. Hoffman concludes that Jesus' last supper words over the bread "spoke directly to the Jewish context of his listeners."[44]

The kind of meaning for Jesus' bread words that is being set forth here would be quite possible even if, as many scholars now think, Jesus' last supper was not a Passover seder as such.[45] Probably the best date to posit for this final meal is the night before what we now call Maundy Thursday, with the latter understood to be the official eve of Passover.[46] But even such a dinner (still on Thursday, according to the Jewish practice of marking a day's beginning at sunset) would partake of the Passover atmosphere and allow for its symbols to dominate.

Hoffman also proposes (though he does not argue the case in detail) that first-century Jews could have understood wine drunk during the Passover week as a salvation symbol. In the biblical story of Passover it was the blood of the paschal lamb, smeared on the doorpost that spared families from death to their firstborn (Ex. 12:21–27). But Hoffman also notes that the Bible refers to the "blood" of grapes; and here he cites, without comment, Gen. 49:11 ("Binding his foal to the vine and his donkey's colt to the choice vine, he washes his garments in wine and his robe in the blood of grapes"). Readers will recall that we have taken just this prophecy to be the major force field operative in Jesus' messianic vision of himself at the kingdom feast (Mark 14:25).

What exactly did Jesus say over the cup at the last supper? Paul's version of the tradition, the earliest in most particulars, reads "This cup is the new covenant in my blood" (1 Cor. 11:25). We note that no simple equation exists here between cup/wine and blood. Mark, on the other hand, has "This is my blood of the covenant" (14:24), and so does Matthew (26:28). Luke, by contrast, follows Paul's wording (22:20). All four versions of the cup saying make use of the term "covenant," which suggests that this is a good place to start in attempting to establish what Jesus actually said about the wine.

Scholars have sometimes balked at attributing the use of the word "covenant" to the historical Jesus at the last supper. This is partly because the word's appearance in our New Testament accounts of the supper takes two quite different forms (Mark/Matthew vs. Paul/Luke) and partly because in none of our four gospels does Jesus so much as mention the covenant prior to the last supper narrative. But this second difficulty is not so weighty as it appears, for Jesus' calling of the twelve provides strong testimony to God's covenant relationship with Israel, and so does the centrality of the kingdom motif in his words and actions. Jesus proclaimed the covenant in many ways without actually using the word. Indeed, this practice of symbolizing Israel's unique bond with God, instead of naming it outright, is common in the Jewish literature of Jesus' day. There too the actual term "covenant" occurs infrequently, and yet it is always present as a leitmotif.[47]

It would be altogether natural for a solemn occasion like the last supper to call forth Jesus' utterance of the word, especially since the Passover story concerning God's deliverance of Israel was prominent in the minds of those attending.[48]

As for the discrepancy between "my blood of the covenant" (a direct reference to Ex. 24:8) and "the new covenant in my blood" (which points to the future covenant envisioned in Ez. 31:31–34), it is substantial and probably indicates that at least one of our phrases, or some part of it, did originate in the early church as an interpretation of Jesus' words over the wine. Perhaps both phrases are reworkings of what Jesus actually said. But even if that is true, we do not have to go so far as Chilton in theorizing that the very notion of covenant was first inserted into Jesus' last supper discourse by Peter, after the resurrection. Again, the presence of Jerusalem eyewitnesses would militate against such an innovation.

What is the likeliest course of development for our two phrases? Robert O'Toole, following a number of other scholars, makes the cogent observation that the Pauline words over the cup from 1 Corinthians ("This cup is the new covenant in my blood"; 11:25) are not parallel to the blunt and straightforward sentence "This is my body."[49] We may take it to be a general rule that as eucharistic liturgies evolve, more parallelism tends to occur (as in Mark and Matthew), which means that the Pauline words are probably more original. In addition, they do not directly equate the cup or its contents with blood, which makes them more sensitive to Jewish injunctions against drinking that vital fluid.[50]

But what about the word "new"? It makes good sense to understand this adjective as a post-Easter interpretation of Jesus' words based on Jer. 31:31ff. ("I will make a new covenant with the house of Israel and the house of Judah. . . . I will put my law within them, and I will write it on their hearts") in conjunction with Ezek. 36:26f. ("I will remove from your body the heart of stone and give you a heart of flesh. I will put my spirit within you, and make you follow my statutes"). This modification of the cup saying would have occurred early, as a result of the church's Pentecost experience. We can imagine Peter in Jerusalem telling Paul something like this about Jesus' words over the wine: "He spoke of the cup as 'the covenant in my blood'; but because he has sent us the Holy Spirit, he must have meant also the new covenant foreseen by Jeremiah." Paul accepted this interpretation and passed it on to the Corinthians in his version of the last supper words.[51] Mark and Matthew retained the more accurate verbalization of Jesus' saying in this case ("covenant" rather than "new covenant") but shaped it into a balanced liturgical formula ("This is my body. . . . This is my blood of the covenant"). The fact that Mark keeps the word "covenant" at all argues for its secure place in the tradition. If he had felt free to make his formula completely parallel, he would have dropped "of the covenant." But he did not, probably because all narratives of the last supper known to him included it.

We can be reasonably confident, then, in positing that what the historical Jesus said at table with his disciples on the night of his arrest included words very close to the following:

1. This [bread] *is* my body.
2. [The wine in] this cup *is* the covenant in my blood.
3. Truly I tell you, I will never again drink of the fruit of the vine until that day when I drink it new in the kingdom of God.

The bracketed words were probably not spoken by Jesus but represent the meaning he wished to convey. The two italicized verbs that appear in our English and Greek translations would not have occurred in Jesus' original Aramaic. Obviously, since the last supper was a real meal, Jesus said a lot more than the sentences presented above, including, almost certainly, some words of blessing or thanksgiving over the bread and wine. But all three of the statements listed above express what we can know about his mind and his special purposes with a high degree of probability, given the nature of our sources.

What did Jesus wish to communicate to his disciples through statements about his body and blood? What was he drawing them into by inviting them to consume bread and wine sanctified with his words? In trying to determine the meaning for Jesus of his sayings, we should proceed backward from Mark 14:25. Jesus pointed to his body and the covenant in his blood as one who knew himself to be messiah-designate, as Israel's forerunner and pioneer into God's kingdom at the end of days. He would lead the feasting at God's great banquet for Israel. Not only the resurrected saints of the Jewish people but also those still living on the final day would be there. Some of these would be united with their ancestors in the twelve reassembled tribes, probably under the leadership of Jesus' own disciples.[52]

Prior to this final feasting, however, a painful separation between God's messiah and his followers must take place, a separation occasioned by nothing less than the offering up of Jesus' life. There is really no satisfactory alternative to this interpretation of the bread and cup words, given the Passover atmosphere of the meal in which the matzah almost certainly stood for the ritual lamb and in which Israel's covenant hopes were asserted to be somehow confirmed or fulfilled "in" (i.e., by means of) Jesus' blood. A slim possibility existed that Jesus' offering of himself would not end in death, for God could always intervene at the last moment. But no memory of this prospect has been preserved in our last supper narratives, and it is hard to imagine Jesus articulating anything of the sort once he had spoken the definitive bread and cup words. John Meier is probably right that Mark 14:25 constitutes an intentional reference on Jesus' part to his impending death.

Most likely, the disciples' eating and drinking of symbolic elements did not yield a clear meaning for them on this last confusing night. If they did understand something of what their master was getting at, we can guess that they felt no great joy in consuming elements linked to his sacrificial body and blood. For Jesus, however, the disciples' physical participation in this meal meant that they were now joined in a unique way to his destiny, which is what he had wanted from the beginning of his ministry and now desired most strongly as his messianic vocation came into clearer focus. Separation and death loomed, but this supper was a solemn pledge that both would be transcended in the kingdom.

What about the offense of cannibalism? That Paul and the synoptic Gospels, still in a Jewish orbit, would be able to show Jesus connecting bread and wine with his body and blood in such a direct manner must mean that the verb "is" (absent in Aramaic but present in the Greek) meant something other than simplistic identification. Jewish sensibilities, including those of Jewish believers, would not have allowed for a medieval doctrine of transubstantiation. At the last supper, Jesus' disciples almost certainly avoided a cannibalistic interpretation of their actions.

Can we say more about Jesus' personal conceptualization of his messianic role as this is expressed in his last supper words? The connection he made between Israel's covenant and his blood must have evolved at least in part from the Exodus 24 story of God's granting the Torah to Israel. Here is the relevant text in full, including a dramatic incident that occurred immediately after the covenant's ratification:

> Then [Moses] took the book of the covenant, and read it in the hearing of the people; and they said, "All that the Lord has spoken we will do, and we will be obedient." Moses took the blood [of oxen previously slain] and dashed it on the people, and said, "See the blood of the covenant that God has made with you in accordance with all these words." Then Moses and Aaron, Nadab and Abihu, and seventy of the elders of Israel went up, and they saw the God of Israel. Under his feet there was something like a

> pavement of sapphire stone, like the very heaven for clearness. God did not lay his hand on the chief men of the people of Israel; also they beheld God, and they ate and drank. (24:7–11)

If we accept that Jesus not only saw himself as Israel's messiah but also expected to suffer death, is it not natural to suppose that he reflected upon scenes like this from the scriptures, which combine the leadership of Moses (a figure held by some to be a messianic prototype), the blood of the covenant, and a worshipful eating and drinking in God's presence? For Jesus, this passage must have served to unite both himself and his followers with Israel's past and future. From his point of view, the visionary meal hosted by God for Moses and Israel's elders offered a preview of the kingdom banquet.[53] His own last supper, then, would have functioned as a necessary link between the events of Exodus 24 and that final banquet. But Jesus also believed that if this ultimate flowering of God's covenant was to reveal itself before the whole world, thereby bringing human history to its fulfillment, his blood would have to flow.[54]

But here a word of caution is in order. The nature of our evidence does not allow us to argue that in his planning of the last supper Jesus had already formed a perfectly clear picture of himself as the lamb of the God who takes away the sins of the world (John 1:29). Surprisingly, only one of our four last supper narratives (Matt. 26:28) mentions the forgiveness of sins in connection with Jesus' words over the cup; and this reference turns out to be suspect because Matthew as author is particularly interested in forgiveness.[55] The phrases "for many" (Mark) and "for you" (Paul and Luke) are more general and therefore less likely to have been added by the early church. But even if they were, the vicarious element in Jesus' vocation that they convey is already present in Mark 14:25. There Jesus was probably signaling that he thought of himself in the role of a forerunner-martyr, though not necessarily a sacrifice for sin. His death as God's anointed, as one who most emphatically did not deserve to die, would be taken up into the divine purpose as a ransom to free Israel from all forms of bondage so that the whole people of God, past and present, could assemble in their twelve tribes for the great banquet.[56] The "covenant in my blood" means for Jesus that God's faithfulness will now reveal itself in its most complete form because of his self-offering as messiah. The disciples who eat and drink at Jesus' last supper will share his destiny in a special way by leading Israel into the enjoyment of God's consummate goodness.

Presence and Promise for All

If we are mostly right in the analysis presented above, Jesus' presence at the last supper was intentionally and foundationally messianic. Christological consciousness was not something first imposed upon Jesus by the early church as the result of its resurrection experiences and reflections upon scripture. Instead, it was a central feature of Jesus' life (at least toward the end), a sense of vocation that he articulated to his disciples on the night of his arrest and carried with him into his death. This means that the last supper was not so much a farewell meal — though it has those qualities — as a salvation event in which God's gracious plan for Israel was freshly and definitively revealed and into which the disciples were enlisted, more deeply than ever before, by their ritual eating and drinking.

We must conclude then that the historical Jesus himself believed his messianic presidency at the last supper to be transhistorical. That is, the covenant and the kingdom disclosed in Jesus' words at table linked him uniquely with Israel's past and future. Moreover, this space-time convergence of God's redeeming work in and through the messiah was being mediated to Jesus' followers in a most physical manner. They could not have understood very much of the divine focusing upon them during the supper itself. They were unable to clarify their special mission to Israel until some time after the resurrection, when the Spirit came upon them in power. But the roots of that mission, as they eventually discovered, lay in this meal, this ritual that had made them privileged partners in the messiah's sacrifice even before it happened and would later require their own sacrifices in the messiah's service.

Jesus' presence at the last supper is the presence of a messiah on the move. He goes from the meal to his arrest and death; but more important, he presses toward the kingdom. Later, when the church began to commemorate this supper on a regular basis, it did not forget that its meetings with the resurrected Jesus in the bread and wine continued to be with a traveler on his way, with one continuing to labor in every time and place for the kingdom fulfillment of all God's promises (1 Cor. 11:26;

15:20ff.). Meanings associated with rest and peace soon found their way into the eucharist, but the primal experience at the church's earliest communal meals was one of sharing Jesus' energy for the perfection of God's reign.

Jesus' presence at the last supper was shaped both by his vision of God's abundance and his willingness to sacrifice himself. We tend to accent the latter because Jesus' "institutional" words point to it and because his death followed so rapidly upon the meal's completion. But it is God's abundance, foreseen in Mark 14:25 and implied in the use of the word "covenant," that provides the real basis for Jesus' self-giving, both in the supper itself and in the events that followed soon afterward. Jesus knew and treasured the prophecy transmitted in Is. 25:6–8, where God's final purpose for Israel and for the world is depicted in terms of a feast: "On this mountain [Zion in Jerusalem] the Lord of hosts will make for all peoples a feast of rich food, a feast of well-aged wines, of rich food filled with marrow, of well-aged wines strained clear. And he will destroy on this mountain the shroud that is cast over all peoples, the sheet that is spread over all nations; he will swallow up death forever."

This hope had guided Jesus' behavior during the whole course of his ministry, especially in his practice of eating with sinners and outcasts. Now, at the last supper, a sharpened vision of God's cosmic feast in the perfected kingdom empowered him to complete his self-offering. Only by means of this personal act, Jesus believed, could God's messiah open the doors of the banquet hall to Israel and the nations. But the feast itself was already there. Jesus could see it, and it drew him forward.

Here we should say one more thing about the role of the disciples on that fateful night. Surely not much could have been expected of them, confused and afraid as they were. Some were probably spoiling for a final battle with the forces of evil (Luke 22:49f.; John 18:10f.); all were likely to have been troubled. Yet Jesus considered the presence of his distraught followers indispensable to God's purposes. They must be there to join in this final symbolization of his messianic vocation prior to the cross itself. We cannot be sure about how long or in what manner Jesus expected the disciples to "carry on" in his absence. The resurrection and Pentecost would provide more clarity about what they were to do, but on this night their chief calling was simply to witness and join the messiah's great act of self-giving by means of ritual. Paul did not invent early Christian convictions about the necessity of "sharing... his sufferings by becoming like him in his death" (Phil. 3:10). Most likely, the apostle was articulating an experience of the first disciples that had become, through their early commemorations of the last supper, a normative feature of their self-understanding (see Mark 10:39; 1 Cor. 11:26). The presence of Jesus' disciples at this final meal enlarged them and deepened them more than they could possibly know at the time.

What the last supper offered then was a bodily sharing, through Jesus' messianic presidency, in God's covenantal redemption of the world. The foundational message of the supper is one of promise nearing fulfillment. This meaning comes through most clearly in the prophecy of Mark 14:25, where Jesus envisions his own celebration at the kingdom feast. But the very atmosphere of the supper is communal, and so therefore is the hope it conveys. Jesus prophesies and goes on his way to the cross for his disciples, for Israel, and ultimately for the whole world. This means that Jesus' utterances over the cup really imply some form of the phrase "for many" (Mark 14:24), whether or not he actually expressed himself just that way. The presence of Jesus and the promise of God for all humanity belong together — always. But it is the last supper, coming to mind repeatedly in the communal meals of the earliest believers, that most powerfully and consistently presents this redemptive connection. As we shall see, the first ritualizations of the supper function in a decisive way both to define and to fuel the church's emerging mission.

CHAPTER TWO

FEASTS OF THE CHURCH'S FOUNDING

In setting out to explore the meals that are most closely associated with the founding of the church, we are already begging a few questions. First, of course, we need to ask what the earliest church was—and whether there was only one. This means, primarily, finding out how Jesus' confused group of disciples, unnerved by the arrest and execution of their master, came to think of themselves as a continuing community with an urgent mission. Second, we have to inquire into what it means to *found* a church. Since Jesus did not establish an organizational structure for his followers (beyond promising them special places in the reassembled tribes of Israel at the kingdom banquet and granting a certain primacy to Peter, James, and John),[1] it behooves us to learn as much as possible about how and when the first orderings of their common life emerged. Finally, we have to decide whether we can in fact focus upon a particular group of meals that are properly designated as feasts of founding. Is there something quite unusual about the eating and drinking of the church-in-becoming that distinguishes it, say, from what we know about mainstream Jewish practice or from the communal meals at Qumran? The answer to this last question, as proposed below, comes down strongly on the affirmative side. And that answer has much to do with what we shall discover about how earliest believers experienced the presence of the resurrected Jesus.

The First Communities

Usually we think of a single "earliest church," namely, the Jerusalem community described for us in chapters 1–8 of Acts. That is certainly the view that Luke advances. For him, there is a fairly simple continuity between the group of men and women who followed Jesus up to the time of the crucifixion and the congregation of disciples who became the church in Jerusalem shortly after the resurrection. All of the resurrection appearances Luke records take place within Jerusalem and its suburbs. That includes the experience of Cleopas and his companion on the road to Emmaus, since the two disciples are reported to have made their way back to the city on foot from the scene of their meal with Jesus, toward nightfall, in just a few hours (24:28–33). The fourth evangelist supports Luke's general schema by providing two accounts of appearances to the disciples in Jerusalem: one on the evening of the resurrection when Thomas is absent (John 20:19–23; see the parallel in Luke 24:36–43) and another, one week later, with Thomas present (John 20:26–29).

The problem with taking this composite sketch as an altogether accurate record of what happened is that according to Mark and Matthew the first resurrection appearances to the disciples seem to occur in Galilee, all parts of which are a few days' walk from Jerusalem (see Matt. 28:16–20; Mark 16:7). These narratives, of course, are countered by a Matthean story of Jesus' appearance to "Mary Magdalene and the other Mary" in Jerusalem (Matt. 28:9f.) and by the Johannine account of an appearance to Mary Magdalene alone just outside the tomb (John 20:11–18).

To complicate matters further, both Paul and Luke know of an individual appearance to Peter, who was probably separated from the other disciples during some part of the period bounded by Jesus' arrest and the Sunday morning we now call Easter (Luke 24:34; 1 Cor. 15:5). But in none of our sources do we find a discrete narrative account of this appearance. Paul lists a series of self-disclosures by the risen Jesus in what may be a kind of creedal formula: "he appeared to Cephas, then to the twelve. Then he appeared to more than five hundred brothers and sisters at one time, most of whom are still alive, though some have died. Then he appeared to James [the brother of Jesus], then to all the apostles. Last of all, as to one untimely born, he appeared also to me" (1 Cor. 15:5–8). This list looks chronological, but we cannot be certain that the various events follow in strict sequence. Paul is the only New Testament witness who writes of an appearance to "more than five hundred" disciples, so we can say virtually nothing about its character or location.

Two final observations should be made about the New Testament accounts of Jesus' postresurrection appearances. First, John records not only the pair of appearances to disciples in Jerusalem noted above but also a later one, by the Sea of Galilee, to a smaller group of followers, one of whom is later identified as the Beloved Disciple (21:1ff.). Second, Luke believes that Jesus revealed himself to his disciples with some regularity and typically at table during a forty-day period following the resurrection (Acts 1:3–4; 10:41; see also Mark 16:14–18).

There seems to be no way of bringing all this information together into one harmonious picture. Although many have tried, we do best simply to admit that there is much we do not know about how, when, and where the risen Jesus revealed himself during the earliest period of regroupings on the part of his disciples. There could well have been more appearances than those cited in stories from the Gospels and Acts, or in Paul's list. What remains highly probable, however, even from the standpoint of secular history, is that appearances of some kind did take place both in Jerusalem and in Galilee and that differing groups, as well as individuals, experienced these revelations.

An additional fact, and a quite remarkable one when we stop to think about it, is that despite many variations in the New Testament accounts, we have no evidence from any first-century document that the people referred to in our sources as eyewitnesses used their experiences to establish separatist movements in competition with the major group of disciples that eventually became the church in Jerusalem. Somehow, despite their differences, these earliest believers were able to agree that it was the same Jesus who had appeared to them all and that he wished them to unite in their witness to his resurrection. Although factions and quasi denominations arose in the church quite early, they did not define themselves on the basis of disagreements over who had seen Jesus first or longest or most clearly. Nor were such groups characterized by denunciations of their opponents for falsely claiming to have seen the Lord.

Taking all of this data into consideration, we should adopt the working hypothesis that the corporate identity of those who first saw the risen Jesus emerged only gradually during the earliest months and in at least two geographical locations, namely, Jerusalem and Galilee.[2] At the beginning, gatherings of eyewitnesses and those who believed their testimony must have been devoted largely to expressions of amazement, mutual support, and worship. Some of the earliest witnesses, including a number of women who followed Jesus, probably remained in Jerusalem throughout the entire formative period (see Matt. 28:1; Mark 15:40f.; Luke 22:55f.). Certain of Jesus' Galilean disciples, we may guess, chose not to accompany him on his final pilgrimage to the holy city, and resurrection appearances to them in their homeland might only have strengthened their conviction that they should remain there. Still other disciples, including Peter and some of the original twelve followers, spent time in Galilee during a portion of the fifty days after Passover but eventually returned to Jerusalem, where they took up residence as a community. Luke's belief that the twelve did not leave the environs of Jerusalem at all prior to Pentecost (Acts 1:6–21) is probably inaccurate given the strong tradition of Galilean appearances.

In none of these, however, does Jesus *order* his disciples to depart from Galilee for the holy city. They probably used their reason and enthusiasm to make this decision.

Almost certainly Jesus' ministry had prepared them to expect a final, kingdom-perfecting action on God's part in Jerusalem. Jesus' vision of the kingdom, as related at the last supper (Mark 14:25), is consistent with that expectation. Remembering their master's promise and believing that the general resurrection of the kingdom had begun with his own triumph over death, they probably concluded that they themselves must now initiate the reassembling of Israel's twelve tribes in Jerusalem. The first resurrection appearances probably fed a conviction among Jesus' disciples that their master was to play the central role in this cosmic drama. At the very least his followers would have seen him as their special welcomer into the imminent kingdom banquet. His prophetic words at the last supper, now invested with huge authority by his resurrected state, would have established this belief almost beyond doubt. In all likelihood, the disciples were also moving even at this early stage toward the corporate conviction that Jesus must be, as he himself had implied in his last symbolic actions, the royal messiah of Israel.

Not long after the community of the resurrection began its life together in Jerusalem, something very much like the Pentecost event narrated in Acts 2 must have occurred. This is highly probable for at least two reasons. First, while a number of the resurrection appearance stories contain commands by Jesus regarding what the disciples should now do (Matt. 28:18–20; Luke 24:46–49; John 20:22f.; 21:18ff.; Acts 1:8), the directives are quite general and provide no details as to how they ought to be implemented. In other words, what was *heard* from the risen Jesus did not amount to a practical mission agenda.

Luke is probably right in citing a corporate memory of the early witnesses that Jesus' chief message to them had to do with their waiting for "power from on high" (Luke 24:49; Acts 1:8).

Second, just as Luke's Pentecost story claims, some dramatic change must have taken place among the disciples in Jerusalem after the resurrection. Otherwise they could not have functioned as an articulate band of missionaries, clearly proclaiming their master's messianic identity in the very place where he had been executed for merely symbolizing it. This obviously required uncommon courage. Luke calls the force that emboldened these missionaries to Jerusalem the Holy Spirit. Here he must be drawing upon early and reliable witnesses, for how else could the power deemed responsible for belief in Jesus' messianic lordship and for courageous speech on his behalf acquire this name in so many of our New Testament documents?

The literary evidence here is overwhelming and deserves a moment of our reflection. A short list of passages referring to the conversion and/or missionary functions of the Holy Spirit would include Matt. 3:11, Mark 13:10f., Luke 11:13, John 20:12f., Acts 1:8, and many other places; references to a common experience of the Spirit in virtually every Pauline and post-Pauline epistle; Heb. 2:4, 1 Pet. 1:2, 2 Pet. 1:21, 1 John 4:2, Jude 19–20, Rev. 2:7, and several other places. The most natural way of reading this data is to accept the traditional view that an extraordinary outpouring of the Spirit shaped the self-understanding of believers at a very early stage.

Paul writes most extensively on the Spirit as creator of the believer's identity in Christ (see 1 Cor. 12:3, 13;

Gal. 3:1ff.; 4:6; and Rom. 8:9–17); and he clearly does so on the assumption that he is building upon a universal experience among believers. In all probability Paul himself received the Spirit at his baptism (Acts 9:17–19) and spoke of that event with Peter during his first trip to Jerusalem as a believer. We find no evidence whatsoever in the New Testament against the well-documented view that manifestations of the Spirit typically accompanied a person's turning to Jesus as Messiah and/or baptism into his name. The best explanation for this common testimony remains an overpowering event or set of events in Jerusalem very similar to the Pentecost story transmitted to us in Acts 2.[3]

To what extent are we justified in using the word "church" (*ekklesia* in Greek; *qehala* in Aramaic) to describe the first communities that took shape in Galilee and Jerusalem? As for the group(s) in Galilee we have nothing to go on apart from a passage in Matthew's gospel where Peter, in the "district of Caesarea Philippi" confesses Jesus to be Messiah and hears his master respond with the words, "You are Peter, and on this rock I will build my *ekklesia*" (16:18). But here the word "church" could have been introduced into the Matthean story when his gospel was being composed sometime in the 80s. Among the gospel writers, he alone places the term on Jesus' lips.

A similar caution has to be exercised with regard to Paul's insistence that believers in "the churches of Judea" did not know him by sight for some years following his conversion (Gal. 1:22) and with regard to the apostle's confessions that prior to his conversion he had persecuted "the church of God" (1 Cor. 15:9) or "the church" (Phil.

3:6). All of these statements were written by Paul in the 50s, so they may tell us no more than that *ekklesia* was the favored term in Greek *at this time* for local communities of believers and for regional networks of such communities. Curiously, nowhere in his letters does Paul specifically identify the congregation in Jerusalem as an *ekklesia.*

Even in Acts itself Luke does not use the word "church" to depict the community of the holy city until 5:11. The term "Way," which is often thought to be a self-description of what Jesus' followers preached and practiced shortly after the resurrection, does not turn up until Acts 9:2, in the first account of Paul's conversion. Instead, when Luke recounts the Jerusalem congregation's earliest days, he refers to their corporate identity only with personal words like "brothers [and sisters]" (1:15), "witnesses" (2:32), and "believers" (2:44; 4:4). From chapter 6 onward, he also calls them "disciples," and by this time the term clearly refers to all followers of Jesus, not just the 120 or so who experienced the Pentecost outpouring.

When we consider the whole range of our evidence, we find it supporting our initial guess that some time was required for Jesus' first followers to designate themselves as a *qehala* or *ekklesia.* It was not that the earliest groups had no corporate identity, but this derived much more from their common experience of Jesus than from the feeling that they were sociologically unique within Judaism. Accordingly, if we want to speak of a *church founding* in these first days, we must understand it as a series of encounters with the risen Jesus, along with experiences of the Holy Spirit as a force sent by Jesus (see especially Acts 2:33; Rom. 8:9; John 20:22). For the sake of simplicity, we may use the word "church" to designate all groups of believers after the resurrection, but we should do so with some reservations. Even by the 50s, when Paul wrote, *ekklesia* may not have been the favored self-designation of the Jerusalem congregation.

But we also need to avoid an opposite danger. It would be unwise to collapse what our New Testament sources tell us about the earliest gatherings of post-Easter followers into the simplistic modern term "Jesus movement." That expression, while popular in many scholarly circles today, does not convey what is most distinctive about such gatherings, namely, that they were shaped above all by Jesus' resurrection and by the Spirit, that they began very early to proclaim his messiahship, and that they tended to establish a common life in specific localities, the most prominent of which was Jerusalem.

The Earliest Meals

How, as a component of the various founding events that gave believers their first intimations of corporate identity and purpose, should we understand their meal practices? We may begin to answer this question by observing that the two kinds of meals held during the earliest days would have been (a) daily gatherings by eyewitnesses to the resurrection appearances and people associated with them; and (b) occasions of eating and drinking in which the risen Jesus himself was felt (or seen) to be present. To some extent, (a) and (b) must have overlapped. The New Testament offers three long narrative accounts of the risen Jesus joining his disciples for a meal: the Emmaus story (Luke 24:13–35); the gathering of the eleven and their companions in Jerusalem later that night where Jesus ate a piece of broiled fish (Luke 24:36–49); and the breakfast hosted by Jesus for some of his disciples beside the Lake of Galilee (John 21:1–23). To these narratives we may also add a vignette from Mark's longer ending in which Jesus "appeared to the eleven themselves as they were sitting at the table" (Mark 16:14). The two Johannine stories of Sunday evening gatherings in Jerusalem (20:19–29) might be construed as meal settings, although this is not explicitly stated. More specific (but frustratingly brief) references to postresurrection meals with Jesus occur in Acts 1:4 and 10:41.

Finally, we should mention here a passage from the church father Jerome in which he cites a (probably) second-century work called the Gospel of the Hebrews. Apparently quoting from that gospel, Jerome writes:

> [T]he Lord . . . went to James [his brother] and appeared to him. For James had sworn that he would not eat bread from that hour in which he had drunk the cup of the Lord until he should see him risen from among them that sleep. And shortly thereafter the Lord said: Bring a table and bread! And immediately it is added: He took the bread, blessed it and brake it and gave it to James the Just and said to him: My brother, eat thy bread, for the Son of man is risen from among them that sleep.[4]

We can see that this story is partly dependent upon language from our canonical gospels. Still, it may contain some independent information about the individual appearance to James that Paul mentions so briefly in 1 Cor. 15:7.

Although we cannot establish that any one of the appearance stories cited above is factual in all its particulars, it would be foolish to ignore the widespread conviction on the part of early believers that some of their postresurrection meals involved a visible and tangible communion with Jesus. In preaching to the centurion Cornelius, Luke's Peter puts it this way: "God raised him on the third day and allowed him to appear, not to all the people but to us who were chosen by God as witnesses, and who ate and drank with him after he rose from the dead" (Acts 10:40f.). Here "church founding" and meals come very close together.

In this context we need to reflect more extensively on the deeply human dimensions of what probably happened at these earliest meals. We have previously suggested that almost all the first gatherings of Jesus' followers after the resurrection were marked by expressions of amazement, mutual support, and worship. We may now add that the emotional note most frequently sounded, especially at meals, would have been one of rejoicing (Luke 24:41), with its expression in worship as praise and thanksgiving to God. This would be the case whether or not the risen Jesus himself was visibly present, for the joy of his ministry meals would have been recalled, and the benedictions typically recited at Jewish meals would now be enlarged with expressions of the disciples' resurrection faith.

But more somber chords were struck as well. After all, Jesus had just *died* — terribly, painfully, and shamefully.

This could not be forgotten and was surely pondered almost continuously, especially in light of the master's solemn references to his body and blood at the last supper. Yet there is nothing in any of our biblical or extrabiblical sources to indicate that verbal communications from the risen Jesus "explained" his death to the disciples in a full or satisfying manner. All of our data lead to the view that the disciples had to struggle for some years over the meaning of Jesus' death, as well as the real possibility of their own.[5] To the degree that the last supper story occupied a major place in their consciousness during this period (and it obviously did, given the fact that an early version of it was transmitted by Peter to Paul not later than 35 C.E.), this struggling would have come to regular expression in the church's developing table liturgies.

But there was surely another dark side to the earliest meal settings, especially when Jesus himself appeared. We must recall that most of the male disciples had denied or abandoned their master during the period of his arrest and trial. The point here, well explicated by Rowan Williams, is that encountering Jesus as the risen one, especially in the intimate context of a common meal, would inevitably stir up bitter feelings of remorse among some of Jesus' closest followers.[6] Two New Testament stories spell this out in the case of Peter. One is the postbreakfast conversation between the risen Jesus and Peter by the Lake of Galilee. When Jesus asks Peter for the third time, "Simon . . . do you love me?" thus forcing him to relive the third denial of his master, he is said to be "grieved" (21:17). That, we can imagine, would be putting it mildly. A second story, probably a variation on the Johannine account just mentioned (but placed by Luke early in his narration of Jesus' ministry), gives us the following picture: "When Simon Peter saw it [a huge catch of fish resulting from obedience to Jesus' directions about where to cast the net — as in John 21:4–8], he fell down at Jesus' knees, saying, 'Go away from me, Lord, for I am a sinful man' " (5:8). In its Lucan setting, there is nothing to provoke this extreme response from Peter. But if we place the story in a postresurrection context, just prior to a meal hosted by Jesus, Peter's feelings of guilt and unworthiness become quite understandable.[7]

We can also detect an element of remorse in the Emmaus story, for while the two disciples involved are astonished by the self-disclosure of their guest-host in his breaking of the bread, what they actually say to each other at this moment is: "Were not our hearts burning within us while he was talking to us on the road, while he was opening the scriptures to us?" (Luke 24:32). In other words, the fact that the stranger accompanying them turned out to be Jesus required them first of all to confront their own foolishness and lack of faith (vv. 25–27). The incomparable holiness of Jesus' appearance exposed them to the searing light of judgment. Williams writes:

> [T]he resurrection meals, for John and Luke alike, echo specific occasions of crisis, misunderstanding, illusion and disaster. [The disciples] "recover" not only the memory of table fellowship, but the memory of false hope, betrayal and desertion, of a past in which ignorance and pride and the rejection of *Jesus'* account of his destiny in favor of power des-

> tinies of their own led the disciples into their most tragic failure, their indirect but real share in the ruin of their Lord. Yet Jesus, even as he sees their rejection taking shape, nonetheless gives himself to his betrayers in the breaking of the bread [at the last supper]. The resurrection meals restore precisely that poignant juxtaposition of his unfailing grace and their rejection, distortion and betrayal of it.[8]

We need to add only a few points of commentary here. In all probability, Williams's interpretation of the Johannine and Lucan data provides an accurate insight into what really happened during at least some of the post-resurrection meals. It was not just reflection on the part of the evangelists many years later but the actual experience of eyewitnesses that gave rise to these self-incriminating stories.[9] Moreover, such feelings of pain and guilt, while not felt equally by the disciples (e.g., by the women who remained close to Jesus all the way to his death), would obviously serve to stamp their memory of the last supper and their faithlessness in Gethsemane upon all the ritual meals of the Jerusalem community. Every time they commemorated Jesus' death and resurrection at meals, these first followers would also recall his abundant mercy to them (see, e.g., Luke 22:31–34).

Kingdom and Messiah

What can we say about the place of the kingdom in the earliest postresurrection meals? It is an arresting fact that no appearance story and no description of the earliest communal meals includes a specific word from Jesus about the *basileia.* Luke does tell us that Jesus "presented himself alive to [the disciples] by many convincing proofs . . . speaking about the kingdom of God" (Acts 1:3). But he gives no details regarding the content of what Jesus said. Similarly, just prior to the ascension, Luke shows us the disciples asking their master whether "this is the time when you will restore the kingdom to Israel" (Acts 1:6). But the disciples' question receives only an indirect answer: "It is not for you to know the times or periods that the Father has set by his own authority" (1:7). Again, when the two disciples en route to Emmaus express their anguish about the death of their master in kingdom-like language ("we had hoped that he was the one to redeem Israel"; Luke 24:21), the Jesus Incognito who accompanies them makes no direct response to this. Nor does he speak to any such concern when he reveals himself in the breaking of bread.

Whatever conversations may have taken place on this matter during the initial period of the appearances, the hopes of believers for an imminent and physical restoration of Israel were not at all diminished. The Spirit's coming in force at Pentecost probably heightened their expectations. Paul, in writing the letter we call 1 Corinthians (about 53 C.E.), expressed his conviction that Jesus' return, and with it the final coming of God's kingdom, would occur in his own lifetime (15:23–24, 51–52). This means that the apostle's interpretation of what believers are doing in the Lord's Supper ("For as often as you eat this bread and drink the cup, you proclaim the

Lord's death until he comes"; 11:26) links the meal ritual to a highly charged view of the future. Along with other early believers, Paul was accustomed to praying the Aramaic sentence "Maranatha" (16:21; see also Rev. 22:20), which literally means "Our Lord, come!" and almost certainly represents a petition addressed to Jesus that he would return to complete his kingdom work (see 1 Cor. 15:24–28). This very prayer also occurs in the Didache, precisely at the end of a eucharistic liturgy and in conjunction with a reference to the future kingdom that seems derived from the Lord's Prayer:

> Remember, Lord, thy church to deliver it from all evil . . . and gather it together in its holiness from the four winds to thy kingdom which thou hast prepared for it. For thine is the power and the glory forever. Let grace come and this world pass away. Hosannah to the God of David. If any man be holy, let him come! If any man be not, let him repent. Maranatha. Amen. (10:5–6)

Although no New Testament text clearly witnesses to the employment of the Our Father or the Maranatha prayer in a ritual meal, the passage cited above suggests that this usage existed in some groups of believers during the composition of our canonical writings.

In any case, we should assume that Paul's view of the Lord's Supper as an eschatological feast, anticipating the kingdom, almost certainly coincided with what the earliest believers in Jerusalem thought about their ritual meals. Peter himself had passed on Jesus' words over the bread and wine to Paul, probably with commentary; and the two had met again, not many years prior to the writing of 1 Corinthians, at a council of apostolic leaders (including James) that produced substantial agreement on missionary efforts to the Gentiles (Gal. 2:1–10; Acts 15). This agreement must have been based on a more or less common understanding of the immediate future.

By way of summary, we can say that there is no evidence against, and much evidence for, the view that meals connected with experiences of the risen Jesus fanned the hopes of believers for an imminent completion of God's redemptive work.[10] What these meals did *not* turn out to be, at any stage of development discernible to us in the first century, were fulfillments of Jesus' prophecy that he would "drink of the fruit of the vine...new in the kingdom of God" (Mark 14:25). When Jesus was felt (or actually seen) to be present with the disciples at table, he joined them as a pioneer and perfecter of something not yet finished, as one still laboring to bring about the full abundance of God's rule.

Is it appropriate, then, to characterize the first meals of the postresurrection believers as "messianic"? We should note at the outset that among the many New Testament appearance stories, only two, both recorded in Luke 24, show Jesus proclaiming his messianic identity. And this he does rather obliquely by instructing the disciples in how to read the scriptures:

> "Was it not necessary [Jesus asks them] that the messiah should suffer all these things and then enter into

> his glory?" Then beginning with Moses and all the prophets, he interpreted to them all the things about himself in the scriptures. (24:26f.; see also the close parallel in 24:44–46, which occurs at a meal with the eleven)

These scenes hint at a progressive learning about Jesus' role in God's plan rather than an instantaneous comprehension of the whole truth (see also Acts 1:3). Indeed, nothing in the extant records of pre-Christian Judaism requires the conclusion that a prophetic figure raised from the dead should be ipso facto acknowledged as God's messianic ruler.

But here again we have to look at the larger picture of Jesus' ministry, especially the events surrounding his death. Some of his own followers (and enemies) did apparently discern a claim to messianic identity by Jesus in the last week of his life. Such views were based chiefly on Jesus' symbolic entry into Jerusalem and his protest action in the temple. Moreover, in chapter 1 we have argued that the last supper itself contains evidence of Jesus' own messianic self-understanding, especially in his personalized references to Gen. 49:10–12 and Zech. 9. Although allusions like these might not have been picked up by the disciples on that perilous night, they would have been recalled very soon afterward in the light of the resurrection. In particular, post-Easter meals must have stimulated reflection on everything Jesus had said and done at table during his last night of freedom. Indeed, the event of Jesus' death itself, with the title affixed to his cross by Roman officials ("This is the king of the

Jews"), could now be understood, thanks to the resurrection, as God's own proclamation to the people.[11] From the human side of things, we can see that the "raw material" for producing early confessions of Jesus' messiahship by his disciples was substantial. Worship at table would have offered a natural setting for such confessions.

At this same early period we can posit speculation by the disciples about how Jesus' status as God's Anointed One now altered or displaced the military understandings of mission associated in the popular mind with the end-time coming of a Davidic ruler. Here we should ponder a matter that is obvious enough to the sensibilities of faith but is seldom taken up in critical examinations of how church "doctrine" developed. If Jesus thought of himself as messiah before his death, considered himself vindicated in that understanding by the resurrection but also found his (human) comprehension of messiahship enlarged by God's miraculous endorsement, would he not do his best to communicate this new knowledge from the very moment he rejoined his disciples? If he did do so, then the earliest post-resurrection meals, both those involving Jesus' visible presence and those at which he was remembered or awaited as one close at hand, would have been *at least* "messianic" as far as the disciples were concerned. Jesus' followers must have felt that precisely at these meals they themselves were being drawn inexorably into their master's redemptive work of the end-time. A common partaking of bread and wine associated with Jesus' body and blood could only have strengthened the disciples' sense of vocation.

Liturgical Forms of Presence

Here we need to focus more closely on the second category of meals noted above, namely, those during which Jesus was not actually seen by believers. Such gatherings would have been the most numerous by far in the life of the earliest communities, even during the initial period when resurrection appearances were still occurring. Can we speak, also with regard to such meals, of Jesus' *presence?* If we appeal to a Jewish understanding of memory and hope, according to which events of the past are re-presented through ritual in a very palpable manner — the Passover seder itself being a prime example — then we can answer affirmatively. Even when it was not yet commemorated in a formal manner, the last supper would have been recalled and reflected upon at the earliest daily meals.[12] Verbalizations of this surely brought a heightened awareness of Jesus' person and work into the community's eating and drinking. When we consider as well the disciples' expectation that their master might literally appear at any moment to instruct them further or to introduce the kingdom in its final form, we have to say that virtually every meal in those early days was permeated by Jesus' presence.

Any references to the Lord's bread and cup words at the last supper, no matter how they were interpreted, would have enhanced this sense of presence. Larry Hurtado notes that although

> we cannot say with full assurance that some form of "Lord's Supper" was always part of Christian

> worship gatherings in the earliest decades, . . . some such Christ-centered meal was in all likelihood a familiar and normal aspect of corporate Christian religious life.
>
> [Thus] we have indication of the reshaping of monotheistic devotion involved in early Christianity and [an] example of a devotional innovation for which we do not have a parallel in Jewish groups of the time. Common meals, yes, as at Qumran. But meals devoted expressly to celebrating and perhaps communing with God's heavenly "chief agent" are not found in the records of ancient Jewish devotion.[13]

Hurtado carefully refrains from applying his judgment specifically to the earliest years of the Jerusalem community. But if we excise from his words the terms "Christian" and "Christianity," which were not employed as self-definitions among the first believers in Palestine, then the preceding passage may well give us an accurate characterization of the church's meals in the very first days after the resurrection.

What we are theorizing is that devotion to the risen Jesus as Messiah and Lord, especially when this was articulated through prophecies, hymns, and prayers inspired by the Spirit given at Pentecost, presupposed his active presence. These acts of worship would not be restricted to meals, but they would typically occur in such settings. Thus, when we read in Acts that the Spirit-filled believers devoted themselves to the "breaking of bread" (2:42) and "day by day" continued this practice in their homes "with glad and generous hearts, praising God and having the good will of all the people" (2:46f.), we should assume that they felt Jesus to be among them, even when they could not literally see him.[14]

Here we must posit a major event that exerted great influence on the way Jesus' presence was experienced not only among believers in Jerusalem following the initial period of resurrection appearances but also among new disciples outside the holy city. This was a decision by Jerusalem leaders to commemorate the last supper in a particular liturgical manner and on a regular basis. We cannot determine exactly when this development occurred, though one plausible theory has it that the earliest ritualization took place on or near the first anniversary of Jesus' death, sometime during the feast of Passover when expectations for a definitive act of redemption on God's part ran high.[15] Forms of an annual messianic Passover (*pasach*) continued in many churches throughout the first and second centuries.[16] It might well be that the chief impetus for this new table ritual came from the words attributed to Jesus in 1 Cor. 11:24–25 ("Do this . . . in remembrance of me"). If these words were not spoken by the historical Jesus at the last supper — the affirmative view still has its supporters[17] — they probably came to the earliest congregation through a prophet who delivered them as a command from the risen Christ. In either event, Paul considers the words a part of the tradition he inherited (11:23), probably from Peter not more than five or six years after the crucifixion. Peter himself must have played a vital role in the first commemoration liturgy.[18]

However the earliest commemorations of the last supper had their origin, some such ritual quickly became a foundational element of the church's worship life. By the mid-50s, when Paul wrote 1 Corinthians 11 — and probably much earlier — a meal presupposing the recollection of the last supper words he had learned from Peter was taking place with regularity. The phrase "as often as you eat this bread and drink this cup" (11:26) suggests frequent celebrations with some kind of set liturgy. So do references to the cup and table of the Lord in 1 Cor. 10:16–22, where a regular table ritual is assumed, and the present tense of the participle *synerchomenoi* (11:18, 20, and 33), which literally means "in your repeated comings together [to eat]." Some exegetes argue from 1 Cor. 16:2 ("On the first day of every week each of you is to put aside and save whatever extra you can so that collections [for Jerusalem] need not be taken when I come") that the Lord's Supper was celebrated each Sunday in the Pauline churches. By itself this text does not prove a weekly rhythm because we cannot be positive that it refers specifically to a table ritual, or even to congregational worship at all. However, a parallel reference by the apostle to a collection of money for Jerusalem that took place in Macedonia does argue for *some* type of worship setting also in Corinth. In 2 Cor. 8:1–5, Paul is holding up to his readers a sterling example of generosity on the part of Macedonian believers:

> We want you to know, brothers and sisters, about the grace of God that has been granted to the churches of Macedonia; for during a severe ordeal of affliction, their abundant joy and their extreme poverty have

> overflowed in a wealth of generosity on their part. For as I can testify, they voluntarily gave according to their means, and even beyond their means, begging us earnestly for the privilege of sharing in this ministry to the saints — and this, not merely as we expected; they gave themselves first to the Lord and, by the will of God, to us.

This corporate self-giving "to the Lord" almost certainly points to a time of common worship during which the collection for Jerusalem was initiated. A natural conclusion would be that Paul wants the Corinthians to behave in a similar manner at their regular worship gatherings, namely, on Sundays. The question then is whether or not 1 Cor. 16:2 also presupposes a ritual supper.

There are good grounds for supposing that the Corinthian church usually met together in full assembly no more than once a week. Because of the church's diverse membership, which included a number of slaves and women who had little control over their personal schedules (1 Corinthians 7), leaders of the congregation would have found it difficult, if not impossible, to arrange more frequent meetings for all believers. If assemblies of the whole church typically took place on Sunday, which seems likely, then at least some of these must have included celebrations of what Paul calls the Lord's Supper (1 Cor. 11:18, 20–34).

But a Sunday supper, according to the usual Jewish reckoning of time, could take place anytime after sundown on Saturday, thus making possible what a number of scholars have termed an "extended Sabbath."[19]

For Jewish believers, this arrangement would permit the continued observance of a decalogue commandment (beginning on Friday evening at sundown and followed by a Saturday of rest and worship), plus an honoring of the day on which Jesus was raised from the dead (beginning after the sundown that ended the Sabbath). Possible references to such a liturgy occur in John 12:1–8, where an evening meal with Jesus at the home of Lazarus is said to take place "six days before the Passover," that is, sundown on Saturday, and Acts 20:7–12.[20] The early-second-century Epistle of Barnabas also contains a passage that is best read as a description of an extended Sabbath practice by believers: "The present sabbaths [says God] are not acceptable to me, but that which I have made, in which I will give rest to all things and make the beginning of an eighth day, that is the beginning of another world." The writer then continues: "Wherefore we also celebrate with gladness the eighth day in which Jesus also rose from the dead" (Barn. 15:8–9).

Here two questions arise. First, did such an extended Sabbath exist prior to Paul's contact with the Corinthians? Second, if it did, would Paul have commended this practice to Gentiles? As for the first question, it seems likely that extended Sabbaths would have come into use quite early among groups of Jewish disciples, for most of whom faith in Jesus as Messiah did not preclude Torah observance. Fundamental to this observance was Sabbath keeping, which stood at the heart of Jewish family life. We cannot know whether Peter urged the practice of an extended Sabbath upon Paul when he first transmitted Jesus' bread and cup words to him, but the possibility certainly exists. Paul's ministry in Antioch (roughly 39–49 C.E.), where groups of Jewish believers ate communal meals together with Gentile believers (Gal. 2:11–14), would have been a natural setting for the wider development of Sabbath extensions because these allowed Jews to retain a practice central to their faith without imposing the whole day's obligations on Gentiles. Peter, who visited the church in Antioch and ate with Gentiles there before messengers from James persuaded him to desist (Gal. 2:12), would presumably support such liturgies. Indeed, it is possible that extended Sabbaths had already been introduced as the tradition of Jerusalem by the Antiochene church's Hellenist Jewish founders, or by Barnabas, himself an early member of the Jerusalem congregation (Acts 4:36f.; 11:19–26). We cannot claim certainty on these matters, but the likelihood is that Paul knew about extended Sabbaths before he came to Corinth.

If so, did he then commend this practice to the believers in Corinth, most of whom were Gentiles? That seems more than plausible when we consider how strongly Paul felt about building cordial relationships between members of his Gentile congregations and the mother community in Jerusalem (Rom. 15:25–32; 1 Cor. 16:2f.; 2 Cor. 8–9; Gal. 2:9f.). Granted, we find no hint in the apostle's writings that he wished to impose Sabbath keeping upon Gentile converts. But if Paul knew that mixed churches like Antioch, as well as the Jerusalem congregation itself, were in the habit of commemorating the last supper at communal meals after sundown on Saturday, he might well have encouraged his Gentile churches to embrace this custom, thereby creating a worldwide *koinonia* at the Lord's Table. It is probably no accident that Paul uses the Jewish phrase *mia sabbatou* (literally "[day] one of Sabbath") to name the time when the Corinthians should regularly add to their collection of money for believers in Jerusalem (1 Cor. 16:2). On the whole, it seems best to conclude that Saturday night was the normal time for Corinthian believers to gather as a whole church — and to celebrate the Lord's Supper.[21]

Can we say more about why the Jerusalem congregation, at an early stage, might have adopted an extended Sabbath that included a commemoration of the last supper? First, we should dispose of one improbable hypothesis. Bruce Chilton is not convincing when he argues that the last supper story was artfully melded into the Jerusalem community's daily meals by a Petrine group of disciples so as to produce a "covenantal sacrifice of sharings" that brought the table practices of believers into line with existing temple worship.[22] In fact, the sacrificial worship taking place in the temple was probably never felt by most leaders of the Jerusalem congregation to be fundamentally at odds with what Jesus had taught them.[23] Thus they had no need of creating meal practices that would soften Jesus' critique of the temple.

To be sure, the first disciples knew that Jesus had taken a prophetic stand against some temple practices. But they also expected him to return soon, in the vanguard of God's final redemptive action, and therefore believed that the temple would be properly cleansed or (if necessary) created anew at that time. Until then, they felt they could take part in the sacrificial worship of the people with a good conscience. Indeed, they found these assemblies useful, for inside the temple precincts they were able to reach large numbers of worshipers with the good news of Jesus' resurrection (Acts 3–5). There is no real evidence that Peter or anyone else manipulated the community's meals in the manner posited by Chilton. Indeed, we have no data to suggest that the *daily* meals of the Jerusalem congregation were ever shaped, liturgically, by the bread and cup words found in our New Testament accounts of the last supper.[24] A priori, the daily use of wine by believers with limited resources is highly improbable.

But should we then conclude that believers in Jerusalem were the first to combine commemorations of the last supper with the practice of extended Sabbaths, thus establishing weekly celebrations of this rite on Sunday as the norm? Such a view seems likely in that these early Jewish disciples of the Risen One needed to seize every liturgical opportunity they could for explaining, both to themselves and to the population of the holy city, how the death of Jesus *as messiah* signaled the climax of God's redemptive acts on Israel's behalf. This was not at all clear to the first group of disciples themselves, and our New Testament accounts of Jesus' resurrection appearances contain no detailed information on the matter. By contrast, Jesus' words at the last supper could be understood, after Easter, as a discourse by *the Messiah himself* on his sacrificial death for Israel and its decisive role in the final establishment of God's kingdom. Now it could be seen that Jesus' utterance over the wine ("this cup is the covenant in my blood") interpreted his self-offering as a unique extension of the covenant administered through Moses. In addition, following the Holy Spirit's advent at

Pentecost, believers could discern the beginnings of the new covenant predicted by Jeremiah (31:31–34). Sabbath sundowns presented the perfect liturgical time for such blendings of old and new. In these weekly commemorations of the last supper, Israel's past, present, and future could manifest themselves as a holy and seamless garment. In fact, these last supper rituals at the end of the Sabbath probably functioned as forums for the teaching and baptism of new believers.

In what sense did the earliest weekly commemorations of the last supper mediate the presence of Jesus? An insight by R. H. Fuller, though intended as a description of the church's eucharistic practice at a later stage, may well clarify what was understood to be happening in the first ritualizations of the meal at Jerusalem:

> [I]t is not enough to talk about the Christ event [Fuller's term for the whole passion-resurrection complex]. This event must become by God's action a renewed reality in the midst of the congregation. That is what happens in the breaking of bread. Like baptism, this is an action of the church.... But... just as in baptism [it] is met and crossed by the action of God which makes present his redemptive act in Christ. This is the meaning of the promise "This is my body... This is my blood." Body and blood here denote not "substances" but event—the event of God's redemptive act in Christ. We might speak of "transeventualization" rather than "transubstantiation" as being what happens in the Eucharist.[25]

For the early believers in Jerusalem, weekly commemorations of Jesus' last supper must have provided a unique entryway into God's continuing redemption of all times and spaces. In these meals the feast of the kingdom was almost there, so close that it could be seen prophetically and tasted in the bread and wine. But Jesus himself was present too as God's viceroy, laboring on both sides of the kingdom threshold, drawing his followers into God's reign and at the same time pulling it toward them by words of promise and the power of the Holy Spirit. (Mark 14:25; Rom. 14:17; 1 Cor. 15:20–28, 45). And this vocation he was exercising specifically as the crucified Messiah who had offered up his life for God's saving purposes.

Here we must emphasize again the Holy Spirit's activity in guiding the Jerusalem community through prophecy into liturgical innovation and scriptural study.[26] Perhaps the very first commemoration of the last supper came about through the hearing of a prophetic command from the risen Jesus to "Do this for my memorial" (1 Cor. 11:24–25; Luke 22:19). In addition, prophetic interpretations of the bread and cup words that highlighted their vicarious intent ("for many"; "for you") might have entered the ritual at this stage. Even images of Jesus as the paschal lamb (1 Cor. 5:7; John 1:36; Rev. 5:6ff. et al.) could have made their way into liturgies of commemoration during the earliest period, especially if the Johannine dating of the crucifixion (John 19:31–37) is correct. As for the bread and the wine themselves, it was not a matter at this point of their *containing* or *becoming* Jesus. Instead, when the elements were blessed, shared, and consumed in the course of some reference to dominical words from the last supper, they served to make Jesus known among the worshipers as an active and powerful presence.

Feasting and Mission

Can we spell out in more detail the relationship between the earliest community's meals and its central task of proclaiming Jesus' messiahship? The word "mission" serves well enough to describe what believers did by way of response to Jesus' resurrection and the advent of the Holy Spirit. But what about "feasting"? Usually we think of that term as depicting a surfeit of food and drink at table, so we might hesitate to use it in connection with the extended Sabbaths of the first believers. Nothing in the Acts of the Apostles gives us reason to suppose that believers in Jerusalem enjoyed much more than the basics when it came to physical nourishment. No multiplication of loaves and fishes is remembered. Instead, Luke gives us the impression that church members expected an equitable distribution of limited resources (see Acts 2:45; 4:35; 6:3, where the Greek word *chreia* stands for "something lacking" or a "necessity").

And yet Luke also indicates that a deep and lively sense of abundance permeated the first community's daily life. If this was historically true, then we have to imagine that most gatherings for meals would have been experienced as celebrative, whether or not the food and drink provided met our modern standards for feasting. In addition, we must guess that on at least some occasions believers did all they could to memorialize in their own meals their master's well-known love of eating and drinking (Matt. 11:19). Largesse at table would symbolize the kingdom banquet proclaimed in Jesus' name (see Mark 14:25). Extra provisions are most likely to have appeared in rituals commemorating the last supper, for these required the use of wine and, as signs of congregational unity, would tend to stimulate generous sharing among groups larger than basic family units.

Here it will be useful to review some stories of the abundance that Luke considered foundational to the first community's life in Jerusalem. Having done this, we can then make some judgments about the historical value of these vignettes and, where warranted, incorporate them into our reconstructions of the meals held by early believers. In describing the days immediately after Pentecost, the author of Acts tells us that

> those who welcomed [Peter's Pentecost] message were baptized, and that day about three thousand persons were added. They devoted themselves to the apostles' teaching and fellowship, to the breaking of bread and the prayers. Awe (*phobos*) came upon everyone, because many wonders and signs were being done by the apostles. All who believed were together (*epi to auto*) and had all things in common; they would sell their possessions and goods and distribute the proceeds to all, as any had need. Day by day, as they spent much time together (*homothymadon*) in the temple, they broke bread at home (*kat'oikian*) and ate their food with glad and generous hearts, praising God and having the good will

> of all the people. And day by day the Lord added to their number those who were being saved. (2:41–47)

Then Luke adds:

> ...many of those who heard the word believed; and they numbered about five thousand.... Now the whole group of those who believed were of one heart and soul, and no one claimed private ownership of any possessions, but everything they owned was held in common. With great power the apostles gave their testimony to the resurrection of the Lord Jesus, and great grace was upon them all. There was not a needy person among them, for as many as owned lands or houses sold them and brought the proceeds of what was sold. (4:4, 32–34; see also 5:12–26, 42)

In Luke's view, trials of church members before the Jerusalem Sanhedrin (4:1–22; 5:12–42), plus an act of deception on the part of the two believers Ananias and Sapphira (5:1–11) and an inner-community dispute about the equity of daily food distributions to the needy (6:1–6) represented, at most, temporary setbacks for the congregation. The narrative in Acts makes clear that all these incidents ended with more vigorous missionary efforts than ever on the part of believers.

With good reason, then, C. K. Barrett can refer to the Jerusalem congregation's "success and popularity," and even to its "prosperity" — as seen through the eyes of Luke.[27] But we have to ask whether Luke's account is anything more than an idealized portrait of church origins, a nostalgic look back at the good old days that never were. Many contemporary scholars hold exactly this position, understanding Luke to be a literary-theological artist instead of a historian.[28] Barrett himself, however, along with a number of other investigators,[29] argues that the idealized portraits in Acts do not necessarily distort history. In commenting upon 2:42 ("They devoted themselves to the apostles' teaching and fellowship, to the breaking of bread and the prayers"), Barrett states his case as follows:

> That [this verse] is not misleading appears at once if negatives are inserted: they ignored the teaching of the apostles, neglected the fellowship, never met to take a meal together, and did not say their prayers. This would be nonsense. The idealizing is in the participle *proskarterountes* ["devoted themselves"] and that Luke did not intend it to be understood as unmarked by exceptions is shown by his story of Ananias and Sapphira (5:1–11). There is no ground for doubting the outline of Luke's account; if he had not given it we should doubtless have conjectured something of the kind.[30]

S. Scott Bartchy also posits the essential historicity of Luke's record in the early chapters of Acts. Building upon an overview of kinship practices in first-century Mediterranean cultures and then focusing on a particular case of this in the common ownership of goods at Qumran, Bartchy concludes that

> in Acts 2:42–47 and 4:32–5:11, Luke uses language that echoes Greek utopian hopes to describe the actual meeting of human needs among the Jewish Christians in the Jerusalem house-churches by means of their pervasive acts of sharing, which Luke believes had indeed happened. Such sharing would have been expected in any well-functioning kin group. . . . To support his goal of moving the members of Christian house-church congregations in his own time toward increased sharing of their goods (and awareness of themselves as a kin group), Luke relies . . . on the earned reputation and honor of the first Christians in Jerusalem as a powerful motivation for a change in their attitude and praxis regarding possessions.[31]

With these quite commonsense observations, Barrett and Bartchy warn us to think twice about dismissing Luke as a novelist who creates events in the early church's life at will in order to illustrate his theological concerns.

Material from the Pauline epistles lends additional support to Luke's portrait of the abundance experienced by believers in Jerusalem during the earliest period. From Gal. 2:10 we learn that in about 50 C.E., at the apostolic council in Jerusalem, James, Peter, and John asked the visiting Paul to "remember the poor" in their community. What this seems to mean is that the congregation of the holy city, having cared for its neediest members with internal resources (Acts 6:1–6), then fell upon hard times. Paul responded to the three leaders' request for help by seeking to organize monetary contributions from the Gentile congregations he had founded. Much of 2 Corinthians 8–9 consists of an appeal to the Corinthians to make good on their earlier pledge to join the relief effort. But in this very section Paul also makes clear that his readers should not consider the Jerusalem community a passive and impoverished recipient of welfare aid:

> [I]t is a question of fair balance between your present abundance and their need, so that their abundance may be for your need, in order that there may be a fair balance. . . . Through the testing of this ministry you glorify God by your obedience to the confession of the gospel of Christ and by the generosity of your sharing with them and with all others, while they long for you and pray for you because of the surpassing grace of God that he has given you. (8:13f.; 9:13–14)

The basic idea here seems to be that believers in Jerusalem can and will enrich the Corinthians with their spiritual wealth even as they receive monetary help from them.

For the apostle, such abundance was no mere rhetoric. Instead, he saw it as a powerful reality consisting of gifts bestowed by the Holy Spirit and transmitted through the human agency of intercessory prayer. Paul believed that the first congregation was still exercising its original vocation as fountain and source of God's Pentecostal outpouring. To be longed for and prayed for by these believers was to grow in grace in quite tangible ways. The apostle articulates such a conviction in Rom. 15:26–27, where he reports that believers in Macedonia and Corinth have completed the assembling of a relief package for Jerusalem and then adds: "They were pleased to do this, and indeed they owe it to them, for if the Gentiles have come to share in their spiritual blessings (*tois pneumatikois*), they ought also to be of service to them in material things." Here the "spiritual blessings" referred to should probably be understood as charismatic gifts for ministry (Rom. 1:11; 12:1–8). These were known to have originated in Jerusalem, from which they then spread to new believers throughout the empire. Fundamental to Paul's mission was an urging of his congregations to honor the first believers as special channels for God's empowerings through the Spirit.

The full range of evidence cited above makes it probable that Luke's sketch of common life in the first years of the Jerusalem church is accurate in its broad outlines. At a minimum we can assume that the earliest believers experienced themselves as extraordinarily blessed and gifted with the power of the Spirit. This atmosphere of abundance must have manifested itself often in thanksgivings at meals, especially in weekly commemorations of the last supper where Jesus' allusion to the banquet of the kingdom (Mark 14:15) would be highlighted. Feasting, then, does in fact become the appropriate term for many of the first community's eating and drinking rituals.

We conclude with three observations on how occasions of feasting by the earliest believers were likely to have served them in their missionary outreach to the inhabitants of Jerusalem. First, meals of celebration proved foundational for the shaping, renewing, and expression of the community's corporate identity. As a congregation of the resurrected Jesus, the first believers found that much of what they experienced as his presence with them, whether in memory, hope, infillings of the Spirit, or actual visions, occurred during meal liturgies. If we posit that members of the congregation met for daily meals shaped by their faith, *plus* regular Sabbath dinners and Saturday evening commemorations of the last supper, then people who came into contact with them could hardly fail to notice this zeal for communal eating and drinking and would begin to wonder what it signified.

The most public activities of the first believers were preaching and healing. But curious inquirers would soon discover that underlying these was an attitude of praise that emerged most typically at meals (Acts 2:46f.). Such a dynamic would soon become evident to anyone who bothered to ask members of the church a few questions or visit one of their house gatherings.[32] Commenting upon the Pentecost experience of the Jerusalem believers, John V. Taylor writes: "In a new awareness of [the risen Lord] and of one another, they burst into praise, and the world came running for an explanation."[33] This sequence of events was almost certainly replicated in exchanges with visitors at the community's meals.

Second, some occasions of feasting probably became the typical settings for baptism, with ensuing manifestations of the Spirit that confirmed new members in their corporate identity (Acts 2:38). House liturgies involving such phenomena help us to make sense of what would otherwise seem to be a self-contradictory account by Luke of the early community's missionary stance:

> Now many signs and wonders were done among the people through the apostles. And they were all together in Solomon's Portico [inside the temple precincts]. None of the rest dared to join them, but the people held them in high esteem. Yet more than ever believers were added to the Lord, great numbers of both men and women. (Acts 5:12–14)

Luke's point is that believers occupied a definable physical space in the temple (probably on the north side of the Court of Women), the boundaries of which were honored by their brother and sister Jews. The "high esteem" in which people held these believers was probably generated by respect for the signs and wonders that were being accomplished through them, especially healings (3:1–10; 5:15f.). We may guess that that respect also included an element of fear ("none of the rest dared to join them"). Yet the latter was counterbalanced by a desire on the part of some for closer association with this group that claimed to be a radically new incarnation of God's redemptive love for Israel. Sympathetic observers could take a step closer to the church by visiting its house gatherings and joining, at some level, in its distinctive worship at meals. During assemblies like these new believers might be "added to the Lord" on the spot through baptism (see Acts 8:36; 9:17–19; 10:44–48).

Finally, if John Taylor is right in proposing that for believers in Jesus Christ "the heart of mission is communion with God in the midst of the world's life,"[34] then we gain yet another perspective on how the meal practices of the first believers shaped their outreach to the inhabitants of Jerusalem. Commemorations of the last supper would have been the most natural settings for followers of Jesus to experience, interpret, articulate, and embody what they meant by communion with God. For interested Jews who came to visit, these meals assumed the character of a welcoming to deeper participation in God's redemption of Israel through Jesus and the holy spirit. And so the church's first table worship on Sundays continued its master's intention at the last supper to enlist Israel decisively in his royal calling. At once numinous and mundane, Jesus centered and traditionally Jewish, the last supper commemorations of the earliest believers served to channel the promise and power of God's imminent kingdom into daily life. The emerging church in Jerusalem owed no small part of its missionary vigor to its liturgies of messianic feasting.

CHAPTER THREE

EUCHARISTIC MEALS AND MISSIONARY BOUNDARIES

IN THIS CHAPTER we shift our attention from the meal practices of the first Jerusalem congregation to those of the expanding church. We shall expect to find diversity in table worship and its nomenclature as the church spreads into various Gentile cultures. But we shall also discern common themes, and we shall argue that the term "eucharistic meals" serves us well as a phenomenological description of the first-century church's chief table liturgies. With regard to possible relationships between meals and mission, we must focus particularly on Paul's writings since the apostle provides more firsthand information about congregational rituals and outreach activities than any other New Testament writer. In chapters 4 and 5 we shall discover that much of what Paul tells us directly on these matters can be inferred for the churches to which the other New Testament documents were written.

Trends and Terms

Much remains obscure in the development of ritual meal practices among believers from the first years of the Jerusalem church to the writing of Paul's epistles. But one thing is certain: the progressive decision by Jewish followers of Jesus to accept Gentiles as full members of the broader church must have played a major role in the shaping of meal liturgies associated with the presence of the Risen One. By no later than the forties some groups of believers consisted largely of Gentiles (1 Thess. 1:9f.),[1] and others, where a Jewish majority prevailed, welcomed Gentile followers of Jesus (Acts 11:19–21; Gal. 2:11f.). No doubt a number of congregations continued to admit only Jews as full members, but given the openness of synagogues to Gentile visitors, we should imagine that all who showed sympathy for the religious traditions of Jewish believers in Jesus would have been allowed to attend and participate in at least some parts of their worship. Jerusalem disciples, living with the threat of sporadic persecution by priestly officials (Acts 3–9), must have occupied the more conservative end of the spectrum. In the holy city, believers were particularly vulnerable to charges that their counterparts in other locales were diluting Jewish identity by partaking of common meals with unclean Gentiles.

Nevertheless, a council held in Jerusalem and usually dated about 50 C.E. is reported to have confirmed the equal status of Gentile believers (see Gal. 2:1–10; Acts 15:1–35). In Luke's account of the meeting, James, the brother of Jesus, acts as presiding officer, and the mind of the council is delivered in his words:

> Therefore I have reached the decision that we should not trouble those Gentiles who are turning to God

> [by requiring circumcision], but we should write to them to abstain only from things polluted by idols and from fornication and from whatever has been strangled and from blood. For in every city, for generations past, Moses has had those who proclaim him, for he has been read aloud every sabbath in the synagogues. (Acts 15:19–21)

This pronouncement probably alludes to requirements that were already in place for Gentiles participating in the worship life of diaspora synagogues. It is clear that two of the three rules of abstinence enjoined here help to clear the way for a full sharing in communal meals. According to Luke, the words of James produced broad agreement among those in attendance at the council, and a further decision was made to communicate this consensus, via letter, to the mixed community of Jewish and Gentile believers in Antioch (15:22–35).

Paul himself refers to a meeting in Jerusalem that dealt with the question of whether or not Gentile believers would have to undergo circumcision, and most scholars equate this event with the one narrated by Luke. But in Gal. 2:1–14, where Paul recounts his version of the meeting, no mention is made of any moral or ritual restrictions placed upon Gentile converts. Instead, Paul stresses the features of the agreement that pertain to his own missionary efforts: "and when James and Cephas [Peter] and John, who were acknowledged pillars, recognized the grace that had been given to me, they gave to Barnabas and me the right hand of fellowship, agreeing that we should go to the Gentiles and they to the circumcised" (Gal. 2:9). Thus, even if we agree that Luke and Paul are talking about the same meeting, we have to concede that certain discrepancies exist in the two accounts. But this should not surprise us, given our own experiences with widely varying descriptions of a single event by eyewitnesses. Historically speaking, we must regard it as probable that the Jerusalem council's decision meant somewhat different things to different people.

In light of these developments, we can now move more directly toward our objective in this chapter, which is to sketch out how the ritual meals of believers up to and including the time period reflected in the Pauline correspondence (roughly 34–60 C.E.) both shaped their sense of mission and were shaped by it. As in chapters 1 and 2, we shall give special attention to the role of the risen Jesus in directing the outreach activities of his disciples. But before we can shift our investigation into high gear, we have to clarify a few terms that occur in the relevant biblical passages (and one important term that does not).

Finding words or phrases that accurately describe the diverse meal practices of the church in the period prior to 60 C.E. presents a challenge. Many scholars have chosen to use Paul's term "the Lord's Supper" for this purpose, but that phrase really occurs only once in the New Testament, in 1 Cor. 11:20. Technically, it may be applied only to what the apostle and the Corinthians knew as the type of ritual that they themselves practiced. We may guess that the term *kyriakon deipnon* (which means an evening meal "consecrated to the Lord" or "in honor of the Lord")[2] was used rather broadly in the Pauline mission field, but we cannot be sure. Perhaps the nomenclature was current among members of the community at Antioch, where Paul served as one member of a leadership team (Acts 13; Gal. 2). But the same could be said of the phrases "table of the Lord" and "cup of the Lord" (1 Cor. 10:21). Our evidence is simply too meager for sweeping conclusions. Since the apostle does not claim that any of these three terms occurred in the supper tradition inherited by him "from the Lord" (i.e., from the first Jerusalem believers), we should refrain from using them to describe the earliest meals held in Palestine.

A better candidate for those rituals is "the breaking of bread" or *he klasis tou artou* (Acts 2:42; see also 2:46; 20:7,11, where the verbal clause "to break bread" occurs to describe meals among believers; and 27:35, where Paul, as a prisoner on a ship headed for Rome, gives thanks to God and breaks bread at the beginning of a ritual meal). Apparently, "breaking of bread" was not a standard Jewish designation for a full meal, but only for the ritual act that initiated it.[3] What seems to have happened is that the early believers in Jerusalem took up this typical description of a meal's commencement and applied it to their entire liturgy of eating and drinking. It might have come into regular church usage to commemorate the distinctive blessings and gestures with which Jesus inaugurated meals during his ministry. This is suggested by the fact that in the Emmaus story what triggers a recognition by the two disciples of their risen Lord is the special way in which he blesses, breaks, and distributes bread (Luke 24:30f., 35). C. K. Barrett concludes that "*he klasis tou artou* is probably an old traditional Christian term, antedating the Pauline development [of the Lord's Supper terminology]."[4]

We can also be reasonably certain that prior to the time 1 Corinthians was written (about 53 C.E.) the "breaking of bread" nomenclature had become synonymous, in some groups of believers, with what Paul calls the Lord's Supper. The apostle's rhetorical question, "The bread that we break, is it not a sharing (*koinonia*) in the body of Christ?" (1 Cor. 10:16), clearly describes the same commemorative meal that he refers to a few verses later in chapter 11.[5] This equation seems also to be assumed in Acts 20:7, 11, where Luke tells of a stopover in Troas by Paul and his companions on what proves to be the apostle's last journey to Jerusalem. In this passage, which may represent an eyewitness account and presupposes that the visitors have already been in the city for almost seven days (see 20:6), Luke reports: "On the first day of the week, when we met to break bread, Paul was holding a discussion with [the local believers]; since he intended to leave the next day, he continued speaking until midnight... after he had broken bread and eaten, he continued to converse with them until dawn." Here is an evening ritual at table — a Saturday/Sunday event if we follow the usual Jewish reckoning of time in which sundown marks the beginning of the day.[6] The meal is presided over by a visiting dignitary and framed by theological commentary. Given its occurrence on a Saturday evening (possibly an extended Sabbath), the meal was almost certainly thought by Luke to have involved a commemoration of Jesus' death and resurrection. So the two terms, "breaking of bread" and "Lord's Supper," must have overlapped for certain groups of believers by no later than the mid-first century. But we should be cautious about pushing this conflation all the way back to the earliest days in Jerusalem since Acts 2:46 shows that the phrase "breaking of bread" also designated *daily* meals.

As for the well-known phrase, "holy communion," it is never found as such in the New Testament. Nor does the word *koinonia* by itself, as used in the New Testament, refer specifically to a meal.[7] On the other hand, *koinonia* is applied to communal gatherings, some of which surely involved ritual meals (Acts 2:42); and Paul uses the word to describe a deep participation in Christ's body and blood that believers experience during the Lord's Supper, as well as their spiritual uniting into one body of worshipers (1 Cor. 10:16f.). Moreover, early in 1 Corinthians the apostle mentions "a *koinonia* of [or with] God's Son, Jesus Christ our Lord" into which believers are called (1:9). Given Paul's belief that such *koinonia* represents a bonding between the individual believer and Christ that excludes all comparable relationships with other deities and expresses itself physically at the table of the Lord (1 Cor. 10:18–22), we can understand how the phrase "holy communion" evolved into a favorite name for the chief ritual meal of the church.[8] Even so, it is not the most helpful designation for the meals associated with Jesus' presence as these developed in the church of the 40s and 50s.

Some scholars have proposed the Greek word *agape* ("love" in the sense of "love feast") as the best summary term available to us. *Agape* does turn up once in the New Testament, in Jude 12, as a ritual meal designation

("These [sins] defile your love-feasts"). Unfortunately, we cannot tell exactly what is being described there. A possible hint as to the meaning of the practice occurs in John's narration of Jesus' last supper with his disciples. According to this account, Jesus not only washes the feet of his followers "during supper" (13:2ff.) but also states that they should do the same to one another (13:14f.). Then, as part of an extended discourse following his action, we find the words: "I give you a new commandment, that you love one another. Just as I have loved you (*kathos egapesa hymas*), you also should love one another" (13:34). In context, this command probably refers back to the footwashing. Such humble service would embody the manner in which Jesus loves his followers and in which they are to love one another. By the time the Fourth Gospel was composed (about 90 C.E.), footwashing might well have comprised part of an *agape* feast that the Johannine churches associated with Jesus' last supper. Ignatius, the martyr-bishop of Antioch who lived and wrote about 115 C.E., makes one clear reference to an *agape* that is connected with, if not precisely equivalent to, the church's major liturgical meal (see Smyrnaeans 7:1–2, where the term "eucharist" is used to denote the meal as a whole; see also Romans 7:3 in which the word "love" might refer to table worship). Clearly, all the extant passages alluding to an *agape* feast are relatively late as witnesses to the first-century church's table worship. Consequently, for ritual meals prior to 60, we would do well to avoid this term.

There is, however, one expression that serves nicely as a comprehensive description of the church's communal eating and drinking from 34–60. This phrase, "eucharistic meal," is never found as such in the New Testament, but it can be derived from a solid cross section of passages in which variants or synonyms of the Greek verb *eucharisteo* ("to give thanks") occur. In each of these passages outpourings of gratitude appear as notable elements of a communal meal. Moreover, all texts presuppose a memorable act or presence of Jesus. If we combine this biblical data with the widely accepted view that the noun *eucharistia* came into common usage for the church's most prominent liturgical feast by about the turn of the first century (Didache; Ignatius), we find additional support for our chosen phrase.

Here are the New Testament witnesses that best help us to elaborate upon the character and meaning of that phrase:

1. Day by day [the believers] broke bread at home and ate their food with glad and generous hearts (*en agalliasei kai apheloteti kardias*), praising God and having the goodwill of all the people. And day by day the Lord [Jesus] added to their number those who were being saved (Acts 2:46f.).

2. [T]he Lord Jesus on the night when he was betrayed took a loaf of bread, and when he had given thanks (*eucharistesas*), he broke it and said, "This is my body that is for you. Do this in remembrance of me." In the same manner he took the cup also, after supper . . . (1 Cor. 11:23–25).

3. While they were eating [Jesus] took a loaf of bread, and after blessing it, he broke it, gave it to them, and said "Take; this is my body." Then he took the

cup, and after giving thanks (*eucharistesas*) he gave it to them... (Mark 14:22f.; see also Matt. 26:26f., which reproduces the substance of the Marcan reference).

4. Then [Jesus] took a cup, and after giving thanks (*eucharistesas*) he said, "Take this and divide it among yourselves...." Then he took a loaf of bread, and when he had given thanks (*eucharistesas*) he broke it and gave it to them.... And he did the same with the cup after supper... (Luke 22:17–20).

5. Then Jesus took the loaves, and when he had given thanks (*eucharistesas*), he distributed them to those who were seated; so also the fish, as much as they wanted (John 6:11).... Then some boats from Tiberias came near the place where they had eaten the bread after the Lord had given thanks (*eucharistesantos;* John 6:23).

6. Some judge one day to be better than another, while others judge all days to be alike. Let all be fully convinced in their own minds. Those who observe the day, observe it in honor of the Lord. Also those who eat, eat in honor of the Lord, since they give thanks (*eucharistei*) to God; while those who abstain, abstain in honor of the Lord and give thanks (*eucharistei*) to God (Rom. 14:5f.).

7. "...I [Paul] urge you to take some food, for it will help you survive; for none of you will lose a hair from your heads." After he had said this, he took bread; and giving thanks (*eucharistesen*) to God in

> the presence of all, he broke it and began to eat. Then all of them were encouraged and took food for themselves (Acts 27:34–36; cf. Luke 9:16f.).

In the interpretive section that follows, we shall attempt to show how this group of texts constitutes a surprisingly uniform witness to the development of ritual meals in the church's first thirty years.

Passage 1, from Acts, was probably composed by Luke sometime in the 80s, but as we have shown in chapter 2, it nevertheless gives us a reliable picture of the Jerusalem community's daily meals shortly after Pentecost. All of these were distinguished by a joy that expressed itself in praise. The verb *eucharistein* is not used, but the giving of thanks may be assumed as a regular element within the church's doxology. Furthermore, verse 47 appears to be making a connection between the missionary action of the risen Jesus and the reception of new believers at table.

In passage 2 we find Jesus' words and actions at the last supper in the form that Paul received them—no later than his first trip to Jerusalem as a believer. What makes this tradition especially noteworthy for our discussion is that the apostle, writing in the mid-50s, understands Jesus to have offered thanks over both the bread and the cup (see "in the same way"; v. 25). This is striking because what we currently know about Jewish practice in the first century indicates that it was customary to sanctify food and drink not with a thanksgiving per se but with a three-part formula initiated by some form of the Hebrew word "blessing" (*berakah*). This prayer came to be known as the *birkat ha-mazon* or "grace after meals." One pre-Christian form of the prayer (Jubilees 22:5–9) contains a thanksgiving as its second element; but the point is that this articulation of gratitude falls within the broader category of blessing, and not vice versa. Paul's nonuse of the term *berakah* (Greek: *eulogia*) in his institutional narrative suggests that a distinctive practice is emerging among believers in Jesus.[9]

Passage 3, from Mark's gospel, seems to reproduce the Jewish order of prayers at table more faithfully, since Jesus first blesses the bread and then gives thanks over the cup. But even here the act of thanksgiving assumes a finality that is not characteristic of what we know from the earliest Jewish texts that relate to meals.[10] Paul himself provides a clearer witness to typical Jewish practice when he writes, concerning the Lord's Supper, about "the cup of blessing which we bless" (1 Cor. 10:16). This obviously means that in commemorations of the last supper known to him, *berakoth* did constitute a part of the liturgy, along with thanksgivings. But when we look back to passage 2, we must hold to the likelihood that Pauline churches were more prone to understand their acts of worship at table as thanksgivings. This preference becomes evident also in 1 Cor. 14:16–17, where the word *eulogia* is interpreted and then displaced by *eucharista* or *eucharistein.*

Comparing passage 4 with passage 2, we note that Luke agrees with Paul in using eucharistein for all of Jesus' prayers at table during the last supper. This dual tradition may reflect a knowledge on the part of both writers that by the time of Paul's first visit to Peter the Jerusalem community had already begun to envision the whole range of its table rituals primarily as thanksgivings for the new work of God in Jesus and the Spirit. If so, we should probably conclude that the Marcan and Matthean supper narratives both show us attempts by the evangelists to conform their accounts more precisely to the Passover seders of their day, where blessing rather than thanksgiving took precedence. Luke also wanted to portray the last supper as a Passover seder, but he apparently deferred to what he knew of very early commemoration practices, and so he restricted the prayers of Jesus in his account to thanksgivings.

Passage 5 has been excerpted from the Fourth Evangelist's account of the feeding of the five thousand and was probably composed near the end of the first century. In contrast to the three synoptic versions of this event, where Jesus blesses the bread and fish, John's parallel story uses only the word *eucharistein* and emphasizes this action by citing it again in 6:23. Since the Fourth Evangelist's sixth chapter proceeds to develop the feeding miracle into a discourse by Jesus on why eternal life comes only to those who consume his very body and blood (6:33–58), we should conclude that the evangelist saw this miracle as a precursor of the bread and wine liturgies celebrated by his readers, in which eucharistic union with the risen Christ played a central role. The evangelist wished to show how already in the course of Jesus' Galilean ministry, the master was accustomed to giving thanks over symbolic elements *instead of blessing them.* Here we can detect a liturgical force at work in the forming of the gospel tradition. Prayers of thanksgiving, having established their prominence in the meals of the church, were now reaching backward to reshape the narrative accounts of Jesus' life and work.

Passage 6, from Paul's letter to Rome, was written late in the 50s just before the apostle set out on his final trip to Jerusalem (15:25ff.). The verses surrounding passage 6 show that it is part of an extended admonition by Paul urging his Roman readers to transcend calendrical disputes and disagreements about the purity of foods that might threaten their unity as believers (14:1–15:13). Clearly, the settings in which ruptures of this type would manifest themselves most painfully were meals for which the whole community was expected to gather. Rom. 14:5f. may not refer exclusively to the Lord's Supper. Probably the apostle has in mind all table rites that were open to dispute by his readers. The Pauline solution to such conflicts envisions all members of the community meeting together for worship.[11] Those who choose to eat and drink on such occasions are bidden to do so "in honor of the Lord [Jesus]" — literally "to the Lord" — as they give thanks. Simultaneously, the other group, the believers who feel conscience-bound to abstain, are to do that "to the Lord," along with prayers of thanksgiving. What governs the whole event and unites believers in their worship at table is thanksgiving to God in the presence of Jesus (see 15:7ff.).[12] Paul believes that this common thanksgiving should occur despite the fact that only some of those present actually partake of the meal.

Finally, in passage 7, we have an episode from Paul's voyage to Rome as a prisoner. The incident as narrated would have taken place about 60 C.E. Because these verses occur in one of the "we passages" from Acts, they might be based on an eyewitness account. In any event, they have to do with Paul's bold act of eating on the deck of a storm-tossed ship, even as other passengers and the crew have begun to despair of their lives. Indeed, they have ceased taking nourishment, probably because of fear and/or seasickness. In public view, the apostle begins his personal meal of bread not with a standard Jewish blessing but with a thanksgiving. For Luke, the apostle's prayer clearly hearkens back to Jesus' blessing and breaking of the bread prior to the feeding of the five thousand (Luke 9:16). It may also recall the Lord's thanksgiving over bread and wine at the last supper (Luke 22:17–20). Paul's act of faith induces his desperate shipmates to accept his prophecy that none of them will perish (Acts 27:34); immediately they "repent" of their hopelessness and join him in what is obviously a eucharistic meal. Here one might speak of a ritual eating that prepares the way for gospel proclamation.

The passages examined above represent a variety of historical periods, literary genres, and authorial intentions. Nevertheless, as a group, they confirm the emerging prominence of thanksgiving in the church's meals. Indeed, they do so incidentally, in a nonargumentative fashion. Furthermore, the writers of our passages all assume some presence or memory of Jesus in the events narrated. We may conclude, then, that we have more than ample justification for choosing the term "eucharistic meal" as our comprehensive term for the diverse kinds of eating and drinking "to the Lord" that took place during the church's most formative years. From the beginning, what believers practiced most consistently at their ritual meals was the offering up of thanks.[13] Here we may detect a primal pressure toward missionary behavior, for the church's regular expression of gratitude clearly put it into an expansive frame of mind characterized by a strong desire to share its gospel treasure.

Boundaries Expanding

But if meal liturgies of the church during this early period typically issued in joyful expressions of thanksgiving, they also served as occasions for conflict. We have already noted one example of this, in Paul's letter to the Romans (14:1ff.). It can also be argued that complaints in the Jerusalem church about inequitable distributions of money or food to Hellenistic widows surfaced mainly at eucharistic meals (Acts 6:1–6).[14] Conflicts over who should be welcomed at meals of the church, and under what circumstances, must have proved especially sharp. We may detect a lingering anger about the exclusion of Gentile believers from these rituals in Paul's letter to the Galatians, which was probably written not long after the Jerusalem conference of 50 C.E. The apostle writes:

> But when Cephas came to Antioch [a mixed Jewish-Gentile congregation], I opposed him to his face, because he stood self-condemned; for until certain people came from James, he used to eat with the Gentiles. But after they came, he drew back and kept himself separate for fear of the circumcision faction.

> And the other Jews joined him in this hypocrisy, so that even Barnabas was led astray. (Gal. 2:11–13)

This narrative seems to presuppose that at the time of the incident Paul was serving as one member of a leadership team in Antioch, along with Barnabas (Acts 13:1f.) and that Peter had regularly engaged in companionship at table with Gentiles (see Acts 10–11). But on the occasion to which Paul refers, Peter was apparently swayed by emissaries from James of Jerusalem—with or without whose blessing, we do not know—to change his usual practice. In Paul's eyes Peter's about-face was tantamount to reneging upon the agreement reached at the Jerusalem conference and had the effect of demoting Gentiles once again to the status of second-class citizens in the church. The meals referred to in Galatians ought not be restricted to celebrations of the Lord's Supper. But it is highly probable that these were uppermost in Paul's mind when he confronted Peter.[15]

Paul himself dealt with at least one situation in which, according to his lights, a believer had to be excluded from the church's table fellowship altogether—at least temporarily. The incident involved a Corinthian man who was openly conducting a sexual affair with his father's wife. From Paul's Jewish perspective, such behavior was equivalent to incest and therefore sinful in and of itself. Indeed (the apostle protests), such immortality was "of a kind...not found even among pagans" (1 Cor. 5:1), which meant of course that it provided ammunition to those who opposed the church and simultaneously created an unnecessary barrier for those who might have some interest in converting.

Proceeding from his judgment upon this individual, Paul creates a list of those who must be shunned by church members because of their public deportment:

> I wrote to you in my [previous] letter not to associate with sexually immoral persons—not at all meaning the immoral of this world or the greedy and robbers, or idolaters, since you would then need to go out of the world. But now I am writing to you not to associate with anyone who bears the name of brother or sister who is sexually immoral or greedy, or is an idolater, reviler, drunkard, or robber. Do not even eat with such a one. (5:5–9)

Here the apostle has in mind behavior on the part of self-identified believers that is habitual, well documented in the community, and not admitted by its practitioners to be at odds with sanctification in Christ (6:9–11, 19–20). Today we might call such patterns of behavior "addictive." While the apostle is much exercised by the social sins that believers are committing against one another at the Lord's Supper (1 Corinthians 11), his more basic concern has to do with modes of life that disqualify individuals from any participation whatsoever in the common life of the church. Put another way, the Lord's Supper itself, as a communion of "holy ones" (*hagioi*) with their risen Lord, creates boundaries against certain kinds of behavior. Partaking of the meal means walking on sacred ground.[16] Believers who persist in entering this numinous zone, while at the same time rejecting the Spirit's promptings to glorify God in their bodies (6:10ff.) or acting as if standards for holiness did not exist, must eventually suffer the discipline of ostracism.

To summarize: Paul believes that certain patterns of life by professed believers dishonor both God and neighbor and discourage potential converts from entering into Christ's redemptive work, which for him is always communal. The apostle assumes that nonbelievers regularly visit the worship gatherings of the church, and he foresees that on some occasions they will feel so convicted in their hearts by the prophesying of church members, one to another, that they must acknowledge God's real presence in the ecclesial assembly (1 Cor. 14:24f.). Presumably these visitors will then request baptism. But if individuals with a positive interest in the church are put off by hypocritical behavior on the part of its members, they will not be disposed to visit its services of worship at all.

The apostle's passion for an integral connection between behavior and worship also shapes his discourse in chapter 10 of 1 Corinthians. There he insists that believers, who are joined to Christ and one another in their eucharistic meals, dare not partake of table ceremonies in temples that honor pagan deities. Wayne Meeks offers this helpful overview of the apostle's argument:

> Paul uses traditional language from the Supper ritual [of the church], which speaks of the bread as "communion of the body of Christ" and the "cup of blessing" as "communion of the blood of Christ" [10:16], to warn that any participation in pagan

> cult meals would be idolatry. . . . Just as in 6:12–20 Paul argues that union with the body of Christ excludes union with a prostitute, so here he insists that the unity presented in the Supper is exclusive. "You cannot drink the cup of the Lord and the cup of demons. You cannot share the table of the Lord and the table of demons" (10:21). . . . Thus, Paul uses the symbolism of the Supper ritual not only to enhance the internal coherence, unity, and equality of the Christian group, but *also* to protect its boundaries vis-à-vis other kinds of cultic associations.[17]

In this context Meeks notes that pagans, who typically held that one could worship many gods at the same time or one god with many names, found the church's boundaries quite odd.[18] Yet elsewhere Meeks suggests that it was precisely the finality of the boundary claims made by believers concerning Christ and his presence in their communal life that proved most attractive to potential converts.[19] Paul, who seems to have understood this paradox, therefore lays great stress on the holiness of the church's table rituals.

In fact, for the apostle and his associates, eucharistic meals of the church were nothing less than apocalyptic events. In celebrating them, believers came face to face with "the ends of the ages" (1 Cor. 10:11), a phrase that denotes the meeting point between this present evil era and the final coming of God's righteous rule, namely, the kingdom. When Paul speaks of believers' lives as a locus for the juncture of the ages, he does not mean to limit the scope of his statement to meal settings (see 10:8–10).

Nevertheless, most of the material surrounding his bold assertion clearly alludes to the Lord's Supper (see 10:1–7; 14–22), so he must be thinking especially of this ritual in his use of apocalyptic language. To invest one's community meals with such cosmic meaning inevitably results in rendering judgments against contrary worldviews and the behaviors associated with them.

A similar concern for boundaries that are both apocalyptic and missionary lies behind Paul's discourse on the correcting of what he understands to be flagrant abuses in the Corinthian celebration of the Lord's Supper (11:20–34). This admonition is the longest treatment of a eucharistic meal found anywhere in the New Testament and contains what is probably the earliest extant version of Jesus' bread and cup words at the last supper (vv. 23–26). To gain an accurate perspective on the cosmic dimensions of the supper as Paul expounds them, we need to look at a summary of recent scholarship on this passage. In working through the consensus statements listed below, readers will find it useful to keep their Bibles open to 1 Corinthians 11.

1. As celebrated by the Corinthians, the supper (*deipnon;* v. 20) was an evening meal to which the whole church in Corinth was invited (vv. 18, 22) and was probably held at the home of one of its well-to-do members (Rom. 16:23). The ritual elements of the meal were somehow incorporated into an extended period of regular eating and drinking.[20]

2. What most troubles Paul about the practice of the Corinthians is that some of them regard the meal (or at least its initial stages) as a semiprivate affair for their own

households or favorite table companions. Thus they "go ahead" with their eating and drinking before all of their brothers and sisters in Christ have arrived; or they fail to share their provisions with other believers in attendance who have brought little or no food with them (11:21).[21]

3. A strong case can be made that those who engage in this self-aggrandizing behavior are among the wealthier members of the congregation, plus their dependents, who can exercise a significant degree of control over their time and are able to supply their own food. Those who arrive later (11:33) are probably slaves, women married to nonbelievers, and others who cannot make independent decisions about their personal schedules.

4. From Paul's point of view, the chief offense being committed at the Corinthian supper is that of publicly devaluing one's less privileged brothers or sisters, which in turn devalues the congregation as a whole. "Do you show contempt for the church of God and humiliate those who have nothing?" asks the apostle in 11:22. Far from structuring their eucharistic meals in a way that manifests unity and equality in Christ (10:16f.), some Corinthians are doing just the opposite. For the apostle, this abuse is far more than social indiscretion. It is, in fact, a hostile stance against God's world-redeeming activity.

5. Consequently, Paul stresses the judgmental quality of Christ's presence in the Corinthian supper (11:27–32), noting that weakness, illness, and even death have resulted from the insensitivity and pride of some church members. Unfortunately, countless misinterpretations of this passage have inflicted great injury upon sensitive consciences over the centuries. Fearing that they will not

discern the body of Christ well enough (through lack of faith) and will therefore "eat and drink judgment against themselves" (11:29), many Christians have refrained from partaking of the supper at all. But Paul addresses just the opposite situation. In his view, confident and casual believers, oblivious to the claims of their less privileged neighbors, are those who will suffer judgment (see 10:12 and 11:22).

6. Most contemporary interpreters now agree that "discerning the body" at the Lord's Supper (11:29) means primarily, though not exclusively, a reverent focusing upon Christ's presence in all those assembled, as well as oneself. This is the ecclesial body of Christ. At its most elementary level, the discernment Paul calls for translates into honoring both the needs and gifts brought by one's brother or sister believer during the ritual meal.[22]

7. The reason for Paul's citation of Jesus' bread and cup words at the last supper right in the middle of his admonition (11:23–26) is not immediately apparent, although he obviously thinks that the institutional tradition strengthens his argument. Hence he employs the causal conjunction *gar* in 11:23 ("*For* I received from the Lord what I also handed on to you, that the Lord Jesus, on the night when he was betrayed took bread, and when he had given thanks, he broke it and said . . . "). Were the Corinthians failing to cite these words or to remember them? Did some believers perhaps intone the words as a magical formula that was thought to create spiritual food and drink for their own private upbuilding (10:1–5)? We simply do not know. One plausible hypothesis is that since Paul understands the church's weekly eucharis-

tic supper to be a unique disclosure of and participation in the ongoing reality of Christ's death (11:26), he quotes the institutional words to urge that this same kind of self-offering might characterize the attitudes and actions of participants toward one another. Especially at the supper that commemorates Jesus' redemptive sacrifice, believers are called to behave as he did, giving up their advantage to their neighbors.

8. The frankly physical connection in the supper between church members and Christ's vicarious death is thought by Paul to signal — and produce — revolutionary changes in their social relationships. The Corinthians would know about some of these from earlier sections of Paul's letter to them. Already in what we now call chapter 1 the apostle asserts that Christ crucified has become the supreme sign of God's choosing what is foolish and weak and low and despised in the world to overturn the oppressive forces of this present age (1:18–28). Since the Corinthian believers themselves belonged largely to social groupings that the world looked down upon (1:26), but were nevertheless "being saved" (1:18), they were also being called to take up their mission as God's special agents in the work of redemption (1:30; see also 15:58). It is fair to deduce from Paul's assertions in chapter 1 that he considered the Lord's Supper a unique opportunity for the exercising of his readers' mission. In this deep communion with their Lord at table, they could begin to show forth the new order of his broadening rule over the cosmic forces of evil (15:25). As a first step, they were to honor their sister and brother believers as coworkers within Christ's redeeming body.

9. That is why Paul urges his readers to examine themselves (11:28) and judge themselves so that they will not be judged or condemned with the world (11:31). The word translated "examine" is *dokimazo* in Greek, which literally means "test out in practice." And in 11:31 the verb for judgment is *diakrino,* the same word that is rendered as "discern" in the decisive phrase "discerning the body" (11:29). Thus Paul's accent here lies not so much upon finding something wrong with oneself as on discovering anew how much one's personal identity and calling as a believer are knit together with the faith and life of one's brothers and sisters in Christ.[23]

In urging the Corinthians to reform their celebration of the Lord's Supper, Paul expresses his concern for the respecting of apocalyptic boundaries. These are enforced by Christ himself (1 Cor. 5:3–5; 11:27–32) and, paradoxically, are designed to empower the church's outreach. Christ's goal at his table, Paul believes, is not to exclude people from the communal salvation he has inaugurated but to draw them into it more deeply through the attractive force of the love and honor that believers show to one another (1 Cor. 13; 14:24f.).

Taking a sociologist's point of view, Wayne Meeks observes that the local Pauline church must be understood as "intimate and exclusive [with] strong boundaries. At the same time, its members interact routinely with the larger urban society, and both the local group and the leadership collective are vigorously expansive."[24] In other words, the church's borders, which display "the ends of the ages," are thought to be promoting its world-embracing mission. These boundaries move outward. Our study of the

Lord's Supper suggests that Meeks' assessment holds true not only for the church's general positioning within its environment but also, and most especially, for its distinctive meal practices. If Paul's censure of the Corinthians' behavior at the Lord's Supper seems heavy-handed, we need to recognize that his chief reason for pronouncing it is to help his readers experience the fuller blessings and growth in their missionary vocation that can be mediated to them through a more faithful celebration of the ritual meal. These positive dimensions of worship at table become more explicit in Paul's discourse on the manifesting of spiritual gifts and ministries (1 Corinthians 12–14).

Gifts Abounding

We will probably never know exactly what Paul meant by concluding his pointed admonitions to the Corinthians on the Lord's Supper with the sentence: "About the other things I will give instructions when I come" (1 Cor. 11:34). For our purposes, a more important question has to do with whether a major shift in the apostle's train of thought occurs when he asserts, in the very next sentence, "Now concerning spiritual gifts I do not want you to be ignorant" (12:1). Does Paul move at this point from the setting of the Lord's Supper to a very different event or series of events? The best answer, we shall see, turns out to be negative. In fact, we can make a strong case that the whole discussion of spiritual gifts, stretching over chapters 12–14, actually presupposes a single time of worship that involved (a) ritual words and acts relating to bread and wine; (b) a real communal meal; and (c) a sharing of Spirit-led revelations and ministries.

How does the data support this hypothesis? Nearly all interpreters agree that throughout chapters 11–14, Paul's central focus is upon problems that have emerged in the corporate worship of the believers in Corinth. So we are wise to inquire at the very outset about whether the apostle, in voicing his various concerns about worship, envisions two (or more) separate and distinct meetings of the church, say, a service of word and prayer on one occasion and a service of the table on another. Most probably he does not, for the following reasons.

First of all, whatever the transition from 11:34 to 12:1 means, it gives no clear indication that more than one time of coming together for worship is envisioned. On the contrary, everything we know about Jewish ritual meals and Greco-Roman symposium dinners of this period leads us to imagine that, like these two, church suppers would be relatively long affairs characterized by a good deal of interchange among the participants. Jewish table rites especially often included prayers, teachings, exhortations, and sometimes hymns (as in Mark 14:26/Matt. 26:30) — just the sort of activity that Paul places into the category of spiritual gifts in chapters 12–14.[25] If we assume that the gospel accounts of the last supper reflect to some degree the actual meal practices of the churches their authors knew best, then the verbal exchanges at table between Jesus and his disciples portrayed by Luke (22:24–38) and John (chapters 13–17) provide additional evidence for interpreting 1 Corinthians 11–14 as a single event.

Second, Paul's entire critique of the Corinthian Lord's

Supper celebration presupposes that it does not last long enough to include latecomers ("when you come together to eat, wait for one another"; 11:33) and that even when these believers do arrive, they find themselves humiliated by brothers and sisters who have already devoured the best food and drink ("If you are hungry, eat at home, so that when you come together, it will not be for your condemnation"; 11:34a in the light of 11:21–22). Paul's words here could well mean that he is taking a stand against a diminished time period for the sharing of spiritual gifts, a sharing that ought to begin during a time of equal access to food and drink.

Third, several pieces of linguistic evidence push us toward viewing the diverse activities sketched out in 11:20–34 and chapters 12–14 as a single event rather than two sharply divided times of worship. For example, the verb *synerchomai* ("come together") occurs five times in chapter 11 (vv. 17, 18, 20, 33, 34) and twice in chapter 14 (vv. 23, 26) as a description of communal worship. In two of these instances (11:18 and 14:23), the word *ekklesia* ("church") is used alongside *synerchomai* to indicate that the entire congregation of believers in Corinth is expected to be present, that is, the sum total of whatever small groups and household gatherings existed in the city (see Rom. 16:23). If, as we have argued in chapter 2, assemblies of local churches for communal meals tended to take place once a week, on a Saturday night,[26] and if this was the practice in Corinth (as 1 Cor. 16:2 suggests), then we must judge it improbable that an altogether different plenary meeting of the church, of the character and length described in chapters 12–14, took place on a different day. With a diverse membership that included slaves and spouses of unbelievers, many of whom exercised no independent control over their personal schedules, it would have been difficult to gather each and every believer to any single meeting.[27] We must imagine that the typical full assembly of the church combined the Lord's Supper with a sharing of spiritual gifts.[28]

A fourth piece of evidence for this view turns up in Paul's use of the word *soma* ("body") to describe both the crucified and risen person of Jesus and the corporate unity of believers in church assemblies.[29] This double meaning is found not only in 11:24–29 and 12:12–27, thereby joining these two sections conceptually, but also in 10:16ff. ("The bread that we break, is it not a sharing in the body of Christ? Because there is one bread, we who are many are one body, for we all partake of the one bread"). Indeed, 10:16ff. amounts to a kind of summary title for chapters 11 and 12 together, for in it Paul previews the communal meal as a feast of sharing that discloses and promotes unity. Readers of 1 Corinthians 10 would have recognized that Paul was assuming, and arguing from, the practice of combining the Lord's Supper with an exchange of spiritual gifts.

Finally, a probable connection between the communal meal and the sharing of gifts can be seen in Paul's employment of the word *pneumatikos* ("spiritual"). In 10:3–4 it functions adjectivally ("spiritual food and drink") to describe Israel's nourishment by God in the wilderness as a prototype of the Lord's Supper. By contrast, throughout chapters 12–14, the word *pneumatikon* usually appears as a neuter noun denoting "spiritual gift." But are these two usages really so different? Commenting on 1 Corinthians 10, Gordon Fee writes that Paul's emphasis "falls on the Spirit as present at the [Lord's] Table, freshly appropriating the benefits of Christ to the believers' lives."[30] This, however, is exactly what happens when the Spirit activates charismatic gifts among individual believers for purposes of building up the body (12:7–11).

Taken together, our data provides strong evidence for reading 11:18–14:40 as a composite reference to an extended Lord's Supper. Some manifestations of the Spirit for the common good (12:7) would have occurred during the eating and drinking itself, for when Paul urges each participant to engage in self-testing and discernment of the body — activities guided by the Holy Spirit and inherently connected with the evaluation of charismatic gifts (2:11–16) — he assumes a ritual eating and drinking in progress (11:27–29). Other *charismata* probably came into view after the meal proper was concluded but while people were still gathered around the table. Our evidence does not allow us to posit a rigid distinction between a supper, which was largely nonreligious in character, and an ensuing "symposium" specifically reserved for the manifestation of the gifts described in chapters 12–14.[31] In his popular book, *Going to Church in the First Century,* Robert Banks helps us to imagine how songs, readings, and spiritual discourses could occur during the supper or at interludes between courses.[32] I would add that other charismatic activities, like healings and prophecies, may well have taken place at such times.

This interpretation of 1 Corinthians 11–14 as a single event is consistent with the Johannine last supper narrative in which Jesus is portrayed as washing the disciples' feet "during supper" (13:2) and then moving immediately into a prophetic discourse on the eschatological life of the community that stresses the role of the Holy Spirit and culminates in the high-priestly prayer (chapters 14–17). As in 1 Corinthians 11–14, we find no indication that anything other than a continuous meal is presupposed.[33] Still we cannot be certain about exactly what the Corinthian practice was, and Paul lays down no hard-and-fast rules about sequence. His chief goal is that his readers will be able to combine the sharing of the meal with an exchange of gifts in such a way that the whole body of Christ is honored and built up. Some of these gifts could have been material, consisting of money, food, and clothing.

The comprehensive sharing urged by Paul is to happen through a diverse array of activities taking place within the allotted time of worship. With regard to the eating and drinking itself, we should probably think of small portions — some of them directly linked with liturgical words — that allowed for interludes of speaking, singing, or moving around the room so that believers could make personal contact with their sisters and brothers. The greeting of one another "with a holy kiss" (16:20) would have required such freedom of movement. So would the practice of healing (12:9) if it involved a laying on of hands (James 5:14). Yet there was no doubt in Paul's mind about the difference between this dynamic meal worship and a raucous Hellenistic symposium. His warning against any consumption of the communal food and drink that smacked of gluttony or unfair distribution (11:20–22) makes this clear. Instead, the Corinthians' supper was to display a just and abundant nurturing of the entire body through the interaction of its individual members.

Prophecy, which Paul considers to be the greatest of spiritual gifts and the one to which all believers should aspire (14:3) because it brings God's word to bear directly upon the human heart in language that everyone can understand (14:3–5, 24f.), would have occurred with some frequency.[34] But a number of other *charismata* probably came into play during the communal meal as well. Hence the apostle refers to words of wisdom and knowledge (12:8); *glossolalia* (12:10; 14:13–19); testimonies about the suffering of members or their honoring in the eyes of others (12:26); praying (11:5; 14:13–17); singing (14:15,26); and the most primal confession of the early church: *Kyrios Jesous* (12:3; literally "Lord Jesus"), which should be taken in this meal context as a greeting and welcome, an acknowledging of Christ's presence in the assembly (note the use of "Lord Jesus" just a few verses earlier in the institutional narrative of 11:23ff.). For Paul, every believer was a potential speaker or singer during the communal worship (14:26).[35]

Three other gifts are mentioned in the apostle's discussion of Spirit-led activities within the setting of worship: faith, healing (12:9), and the working of miracles (12:10). The first of these could refer to stories about exemplary deeds of faith or the regular manifestation of faithfulness — the Greek word *pistis* means both. The term "gifts of healing" denotes primarily healings received[36] and may presuppose a laying on of hands. Miracles or *dynameis* (literally "powers") is a general term in Paul's writings that includes a range of extraordinary phenomena that are most often linked to a proclamation of the gospel (1 Cor. 2:4–5; 2 Cor. 12:12; Rom. 15:19). Such disclosures of divine power would not have to be limited to events that occurred during the meal worship as such. In fact, it is worth considering the thesis that all three of these "action" gifts are mentioned by the apostle in the context of worship not because they were unusually prevalent there but because stories about them typically emerged in the table talk of believers. Personal testimonies of this kind could well have blended with prophecies and revelations and teachings to encourage all those present. Whether or not we choose this interpretation, however, the fact remains that Paul envisions a great deal of verbal and tactile interaction among the Corinthians at their congregational meal. This is the chief meaning of his pronouncement: "To each is given the manifestation of the Spirit for the common good" (12:7).

But along with the frequent speaking and singing assumed in Paul's observation came also an obligation to listen, to ponder, to evaluate, and to interpret. So we must imagine some periods of silence and inner reflection on the part of all worshipers. Throughout the time of the assembly, even during exuberant outbursts of praise, an underlying attitude of humility and forbearance toward one's neighbors was to prevail. We see evidence for this in Paul's urging of believers to examine themselves and discern the Lord's body in one another as they share in the consecrated food and drink (11:28–29). Self-examination and discernment are not really two separate actions but a profound seeing of oneself as blessedly connected with all the worshipers present. Instead of shaming others by their thoughtless meal practices (11:20–22), all members of the church are to cultivate a perception of their brothers and sisters that will honor them for the gifts and ministries that they bring. No gift and no bearer of a gift is less than essential in God's sight for the proper functioning of Christ's body. Indeed, Paul believes that it is God who distributes and activates the various gifts and configures each church assembly in its diversity according to the divine plan of redemption (12:7, 11, 24). Therefore no one can yield either to pride or to despair in assessing his or her value in the ministry of the whole church (12:14–26). All members are to welcome one another with a joyful expectation that mutual needs and ministries will converge during the eucharistic meal in such a way that everyone will be "built up."

This is not an easy mind-set for selfish and impatient humans to adopt, even those baptized into Christ's body. That is why Paul inserts his now famous hymn to love into his discussion of worship. If we understand the following words primarily as instructions on how to treat one's neighbor in an exchange of spiritual gifts and ministries at table, they take on a new specificity:

> Love is patient; love is kind; love is not envious or boastful or arrogant or rude. It does not insist on its own way; it is not irritable or resentful; it does not rejoice in wrongdoing but rejoices in the truth. It bears all things, believes all things, hopes all things, endures all things. Love never ends. But as for prophecies, they will come to an end; as for tongues they will cease; as for knowledge it will come to an

> end. For we know only in part, and we prophesy only in part.(13:4–9)

Here we find Paul's exposition of the Lord's Supper as a love feast. The clear implication of his message is that not only during the prescribed time of worship but also in daily life, a deep respect for neighbors that honors their value, contrary to any negative feelings one may have toward them, must become the community's norm. For Paul, growth in such love is most effectively stimulated during the celebration of the holy meal. Here, in the "table manners" of the assembly, love becomes most visible — or most tragically absent. Once again we catch sight of the apocalyptic and missionary dimensions of the Lord's Supper in Paul's understanding. For him, each meal setting presents itself as a decisive moment in the progress of salvation;[37] it is either a time of joyful upbuilding or a painful judgment upon believers by the risen Christ (11:29–32).

To summarize: we may conclude that the worship at table sketched out in 1 Corinthians 11–14 was assumed to be extraordinarily rich and energetic. On the one hand, believers received an abundance of blessings, not only through sharing in the consecrated food and drink but also (and here is where Paul's emphasis lies) through receiving God's empowerment in the spiritual gifts of sister and brother worshipers. Such gifts overflowed so that everyone present could experience love, honor, upbuilding, encouragement, and instruction. On the other hand, every believer was also to be present in the mode of giving. Each person could expect ministries of the Spirit to take unique shape through his or her own giftedness. All believers had to be ready for self-offerings in the assembly, for the exercise of their personal gifts at just the right time. A physical sharing in the body and blood of their sacrificial Lord helped to nurture a mind-set for such offerings and to stimulate their actual occurrence.

This service of the people to one another before God was no onerous task. Suffusing the whole flow of the meal worship was a buoyant sense of thanksgiving. God was felt to be present as endlessly generative Trinity (12:4–6), and that divine self-giving could only call forth praise. When Paul chides the tongue-speakers in Corinth for not praying in the vernacular, the chief act of devotion he has in mind, the one which best characterizes worship at the Lord's table and proves most efficacious for the whole community's upbuilding, is *eucharistia:*

> What should I do then? I will pray with the spirit [i.e., the inner self with which God's Spirit communicates], but I will pray with the mind also. I will sing praise with the spirit, but I will sing praise with the mind also. Otherwise, if you say a blessing with the spirit, how can anyone in the position of an outsider say the "Amen" to your thanksgiving, since the outsider does not know what you are saying? For you may give thanks well enough, but the other person is not built up. (14:15–17)

Here we find yet another confirmation for the descriptive phrase "eucharistic meal." This was exactly what Paul wished the Corinthian Lord's Supper to be.

The Eucharistic Shaping of Mission

At the end of Matthew's Gospel, a work that is largely structured around missionary concerns, the risen Jesus speaks these ringing words to his eleven disciples:

> All authority in heaven and on earth has been given to me. Go therefore and make disciples of all nations, baptizing them in the name of the Father and of the Son and of the Holy Spirit, and teaching them to obey everything that I have commanded you. And remember, I am with you always, to the end of the age. (28:18–20)

We find nothing quite so direct as this Great Commission in texts depicting the ritual meals of the church from about 34–60 C.E. On the other hand, as we have seen, the persistent outreach of the church to its neighbors during this period was never far removed from its table practices.[38] In fact, from Paul's point of view, one can formulate the connection between these two in fairly simple terms: to the degree that eucharistic suppers find their center in experiences of God's self-giving through Christ, in a rich sharing of Spirit-led gifts and ministries, and in frequent voicings of gratitude for all of this, they generate tremendous power for proclamations of the gospel both within and beyond the confines of the worshiping community.

The apostle believes that in Corinth the power for congregational outreach has become blocked. Insofar as the church there is not being optimally "built up" through its worship at table, neither its communal life nor its extra-ecclesial proclamation can serve as an effective enticement to the world. In Corinth, Paul holds, the church is disregarding the boundaries between this age and the age to come that emerge in its meals. Through a variety of bad table manners it has dishonored a significant number of its members. Hence, this church, with its aberrant practice, cannot be so "vigorously expansive" (Meeks) in its missionary enterprise as it ought to be. Paul's lengthy critique of the Corinthian Lord's Supper and his careful discussion of spiritual gifts within the context of the supper are designed to address this deficiency.

Paul seems optimistic about the outcome of his counsel. His tone is not one of desperation but of confidence that his readers, who "are not lacking in any spiritual gift" (1:7), will actually grow in their exercise of discernment and acts of self-offering so that maximum upbuilding can take place during their worship and spill out into the whole city. Indeed, this outreach begins already within the congregation's liturgy, as indicated by Paul's story about what will happen to an unbeliever when he or she visits a eucharistic meal and is "called to account" through the prophesying of believers one to another. The amazing result is that "that person will bow down before God and worship him, declaring 'God is really among you' " (14:25). Paul's hope for the conversion of visitors arises from his conviction that it is none other than the trinitarian God who directs the course of the Corinthians' table worship. Indeed, 1 Corinthians 10–14 contains the greatest concentration anywhere in the New Testament of references to divine presence and activity in the assemblies of the church. Christ is particularly close in the sharing of bread and wine (10:16f., 21; 11:25–32), while God, Christ, and Holy Spirit together manifest themselves in exchanges of gifts and ministries (12:4–11). God "arranges" the members of the christological body in such a way that mutual care and upbuilding are enhanced (12:18, 24).

The decency and order in table worship that Paul urges upon his readers (14:40) reflect the very character of the divine presence ("God is a God not of disorder but of peace"; 14:25). Without suppressing energy and spontaneity, the divine protocol serves to focus them for the larger task of winning new believers. With mission in mind, the apostle moves immediately from a discourse on table worship to an exposition in chapter 15 of gospel fundamentals, especially their rootedness in Christ's death and resurrection. This great chapter has mostly to do with how one links the paschal mystery, the very content of the gospel, to the world's full redemption at "the end" (15:24). Paul writes both to misguided believers (especially those who still fail to comprehend the apocalyptic features of the gospel message) and to more mature members of the congregation who may need help in speaking the good news forcefully to their pagan neighbors. Finally, the apostle enjoins all believers residing in Corinth, whom he addresses collectively as "beloved," to become "steadfast, immovable, always abounding in the work of the Lord, knowing that in the Lord your labor is not in vain" (15:58; RSV).

What, precisely, is this work of the Lord to which believers must join their efforts "in the Lord"? It clearly denotes the mutual upbuilding empowered by the risen Jesus during congregational worship at table (12:4); but it must also include the specifically gospel-oriented activities of speaking the good news cogently and serving with Christ in his redemptive subjection of "every ruler and every authority and power" (15:24).[39] Each believer's share in the Lord's work grows out of a *koinonia* with Christ (1:9) that is most pointedly displayed in and renewed by the thankful partaking of his body and blood (10:16).

It can be fairly asked whether the Pauline vision of the Lord's Supper as a catalyst for missionary energy actually prevailed in churches of the apostle's network during the 50s and 60s. And we may wonder about the extent to which such a vision shaped the congregations of this era that had no connections with Paul. The answer to these questions is that we cannot know for certain. In our next two chapters, however, we shall uncover a broad stream of evidence indicating that both the eucharistic understanding of mission advocated by Paul and the regular celebration of eucharistic meals in the first-century church as a whole are far better attested in our New Testament writings than we have previously thought.

CHAPTER FOUR

A HOST OF WITNESSES: THE PAULINE AND GENERAL EPISTLES

OUR OBJECTIVE in this chapter and the next is a double one. First, we want to demonstrate that the New Testament contains a good many references to ritual meals of thanksgiving, some of which may not have been noticed before. Second, we wish to show that in most of these passages concerns about the church's missionary vocation are expressed or implied. The task of establishing that eucharistic meals were central to the worship life and mission of New Testament believers should not have to depend upon an argument from silence (sometimes put forward by high sacramentalists) according to which table liturgies occurred so regularly and frequently that the New Testament writers hardly needed to mention them! This approach seems desperate and not at all necessary if we adopt the kind of lens for viewing the New Testament meal practices that we have fashioned in chapters 2 and 3.

What exactly is this lens? We may understand it as a threefold criterion for determining which of the numerous eating and drinking events chronicled in our New

Testament documents should be properly tagged as references to eucharistic rituals. The first and most obvious feature of meals qualifying for this category would be that they serve as occasions on which praise and thanksgiving are articulated. Here we need not insist upon the use of *eucharisteo/eucharistia* per se; instead, the appearance of close synonyms for these key words will suffice (see, for example, Acts 2:42). Second, the potential references we examine will have to be christological in character, which means that some indication of the Crucified and Risen One's presence at table is essential. We will not necessarily expect to find this presence directly linked to the blessing and/or consumption of bread and wine, for experiences of Jesus in eucharistic meals may well have been expressed in forms other than those of institutional narrative (Mark 14:17–25 and parallels), liturgical instruction (Didache 9–10), and critical assessments of practice (1 Cor. 11:23ff.). If a special devotion to Christ can be identified in the meals we examine, if he is remembered or anticipated in the near future or extolled in confessional statements, that will be enough to satisfy the second part of our criterion. Third, we must expect that authentic references to eucharistic meals will typically be marked by charismatic activity among the worshipers. Here we may look for special manifestations of the Holy Spirit, exchanges of spiritual gifts for mutual upbuilding, and inspired acts of discernment and self-offering by the participants. Clearly, we can make our best case for references to eucharistic meals when all three elements of our criterion are in evidence. Sometimes, however, we will argue that probable references exist when a passage under consideration exhibits only two of the three criteria. A number of the passages to be examined do not contain direct evidence of meals being celebrated. In these cases, we shall attempt to show that table worship is nevertheless the most likely context.

Our criteria for identifying references to eucharistic meals will change somewhat in chapter 5, when we examine the Gospels, Acts, and the Apocalypse. In this literature (apart from the institutional narratives recorded by Matthew, Mark, and Luke, plus a few stories in Acts), we will come upon references that are typically allusive and analogical rather than descriptive of actual church practice. A prime example is the story of the feeding of the five thousand, found in all four of our canonical Gospels. We can imagine first-century readers responding to these accounts with thoughts something like the following: "Yes, this story foreshadows the last supper, and in some ways it resembles our own eucharistic practice. It reveals to us yet again the harmony and consistency of God's redemptive plan." We might consider the eucharistic references contained in these feeding stories to be rather indirect. But indirect references still count, and because they tend to be subtle or even incidental to the narratives in which they appear, they could be said to count even more heavily in establishing our thesis that eucharistic meals belonged to the warp and woof of the church's common life throughout the New Testament period. In summary, we are arguing that, based on evidence presented in this chapter and the next, the New Testament presents us with a "host of witnesses" to ritual meals of thanksgiving through which participants are drawn ever more deeply into the mission of God in Christ.

Paul and His Literary Successors

We have argued that 1 Corinthians 11–14, along with some portions of chapter 10, should be understood as an extended commentary on the meaning and practice of the Lord's Supper. We have also agreed with a number of other interpreters that the communal eating and drinking at Antioch mentioned in Gal. 2:11–14 must have included celebrations of a ritual like the Lord's Supper. Furthermore, we took the position that Rom. 14:6 ("the one who eats, eats to the Lord [Jesus], for he/she gives thanks to God; and the one who does not eat, to the Lord does not eat and [at the same time] gives thanks to God"; my literal translation) refers to a ritual meal of thanksgiving. This, too, was probably envisioned by Paul as some form of the Lord's Supper. As such, it was meant to include all the believers in Rome, even if some felt conscience-bound not to partake of the food and drink because they considered the menu unclean (14:14) or understood the days on which celebrations were being held as times of fasting (14:5).

Here we want to take a closer look at the ritual meal presupposed in Romans 14 and show that it is central to Paul's concerns throughout the section bounded by chapters 12 and 15. We may begin by taking note of an unexpectedly grand confession that occurs midway through chapter 14: "For the kingdom of God is not food or drink but righteousness, peace, and joy in the Holy Spirit" (v. 17). James D. G. Dunn rightly rejects the view that Paul is here downplaying the importance of meals.[1] Actually, he makes just the opposite point, namely, that the church's common meal should normally be an occasion for the presence of the kingdom in the power of the Spirit. What obscures or prevents this realization of the kingdom is divisive argumentation about the supper menu and whether or not all parties in attendance must necessarily eat and drink together (14:2–6).

Many have pointed out that Paul rarely hints at the presence of God's kingdom here and now — 1 Cor. 4:20 may be the only other direct reference — and so Rom. 14:17 takes on unusual importance. Dunn offers these observations on the background and meaning of the confession:

> For both Jesus and Paul the Spirit is the presence of the kingdom, still future in its complete fulfillment. ... For both Jesus and Paul the character and power of the still future rule of God can provide inspiration and enabling for the present.... The implications of Paul's teaching here for the theology and administration of the Eucharist are rarely noted, but should not be ignored.[2]

As far as I can tell, Dunn does not press his last observation to its logical conclusion, which would be that the worship at table alluded to in Romans 14 is itself a eucharistic meal on the order of the Lord's Supper. Here, in Rome, is a meal of thanksgiving to God (v. 6). One either eats or abstains "to the Lord [Jesus]" (v. 6), while manifesting the fruit of the Spirit (v. 17). As in 1 Corinthians 11–14, this table worship must facilitate the "mutual upbuilding" of believers (v. 19). Indeed, Paul considers the meal he describes to be no less than a disclosure of God's kingdom—a vision reminiscent of Jesus' final vow at the last supper (Mark 14:25).

Operating with this eucharistic hypothesis, we can examine the material surrounding Romans 14 to determine whether other references to such a meal show up. I think they do. Prominent among them is a section of chapter 15 (vv. 7–13) where Christ is depicted as present in the midst of the congregation to welcome and lead believers—Jews and Gentiles together—in the praise of Israel's God (see esp. vv. 9–11).[3] An impressionistic sketch of this worship published some years ago in my *New Testament Hospitality* may help us to sharpen our focus on Paul's message for his readers:

> Both groups at Rome [Jews and Gentiles] are to praise God "among" or "with" the other [15:9–10]; for it is God's will, unfolding on earth in the progress of the gospel, that all nations join together in worshipping their Creator.... Paul's argument functions to convince his Roman readers that their meal practices, displayed before the world in the imperial capital, should serve as windows into God's cosmic plan. Everyday welcomings of the "other," especially at table, are really acts of worship "for the glory of God" (15:7). Indeed, Paul seems to be hinting that these little breaches in the walls that isolate various

> members of the human family from one another will actually speed the final coming of God's kingdom (see the unexpected shift from language about praise in 15:11 to a prophecy about Jesus' return in 15:12, which suggests that Paul linked the two in a causal relationship).[4]

To supplement this assessment, I would now emphasize the high probability that Paul understood the special uniting of Jews and Gentiles in eschatological praise (15:9–12) to be happening at ritual meals of thanksgiving like those referred to in chapter 14. The literary *inclusio*[5] formed by the kingdom confession of 14:17 and the benediction of 15:13 ("May the God of hope fill you with all joy and peace and believing so that you may abound in hope by the power of the Holy Spirit") provides additional evidence that Paul envisions a single event throughout this discourse, namely, a service of worship at table. Here, as in 1 Corinthians 11–14, eucharist becomes mission.

But there is another passage, prior to Romans 14, which should almost certainly be taken as a reference to the community's eucharistic meals. I refer to Rom. 12:1–8:

> [1]I appeal to you therefore, brothers and sisters, by the mercies of God, to present your bodies as a living sacrifice, holy and acceptable to God, which is your spiritual worship. [2]Do not be conformed to this world but be transformed by the renewing of your minds, so that you may discern what is the will of

> God — what is good and acceptable and perfect. [3]For by the grace given to me I say to everyone among you not to think of yourself more highly than you ought to think, but to think with sober judgment, each according to the measure of faith that God has assigned. [4]For as in one body we have many members, and not all the members have the same function, [5]so we, who are many, are one body in Christ, and individually we are members one of another. [6]We have gifts (*charismata*) that differ according to the grace given to us: prophecy, in proportion to faith; [7]ministry, in ministering; the teacher, in teaching; [8]the exhorter, in exhortation; the giver, in generosity; the leader, in diligence; the compassionate, in cheerfulness.

It must be admitted at the outset that we find no clear indication of a meal constituting the primary setting for these verses. Nevertheless, 12:1–8 provides a set of parallels with 1 Corinthians 11–14 that is little short of astonishing. Here, as in the passage from 1 Corinthians, the key thought is one of thankful and humble self-offering within a community of worshipers (see esp. 12:1 and 3). In 1 Cor. 11:28 the verb *dokimazein* refers to a self-examination that is urged upon each participant at the Lord's Supper so that he or she will be able to "discern the body," while at the same time entering into it more deeply through loving exchanges of charismatic gifts (1 Corinthians 12–14). In Rom. 12:2, *dokimazein* is translated as "discern" and has as its object the will of God. But verses 3–8 show that the will of God here means quite specifically the proper use of one's charismatic endowments in service to brother and sister members of Christ's body. And that is just the kind of mutual ministry Paul associates with table worship in 1 Corinthians 12–14.

The language used in Rom. 12:1–8 may have evolved from Paul's commentary on eucharistic practice in Corinth. Indeed, since the apostle mentions an exchange of spiritual gifts that will take place between himself and the Romans early on in his epistle, without elaborating upon what this means (see 1:11f.), we may conclude that some such practice was already known to believers in the capital city. 1 Corinthians 11–14 gives us grounds for positing that from Paul's side at least the most natural occasion for this exchange would be a eucharistic meal. Although the list of *charismata* in Romans does not coincide exactly with the one provided to Paul's Corinthian readers, a high degree of correlation exists. In both epistles the gifts highlighted are prophecy, teaching, and *paraklesis* (1 Cor. 14:3, 31; Rom. 12:8). Additionally, both Romans 12 and 1 Corinthians 12–14 show the trinitarian presence and work of God coming to the foreground.

As in 1 Cor. 12:24, 28, so also in Rom. 12:3, God determines the parameters of giftedness in the community; Christ ensures interdependence among believers through their common membership in his body (12:4; compare 1 Cor. 12:12, 27); and the Spirit, not explicitly mentioned in verses 1–8 but already associated with the *charismata* in 1:11f. (see also 12:11), acts to distribute and energize the gifts (12:6–8; see 1 Cor. 12:7, 11). In both Pauline letters an awareness that one's worship takes place at the boundary of the ages is assumed. Here we note the eschatological usages of the Greek word *aion* in 1 Cor. 10:11 ("the ends of the ages") and Rom. 12:2 ("this world") Finally, in both epistles love provides the guiding principle for mutual ministry (compare 1 Corinthians 13 with Rom. 12:9, a pivotal verse in which *agape* functions as a touchstone for virtually everything that precedes and follows).

Yet the question persists: Is not Paul in Romans 12 simply offering a general set of exhortations that apply equally to all times and places? Does the apostle really have in mind particular assemblies of Roman believers during which meals of thanksgiving take place? Three concluding observations tip the balance in favor of the second alternative.

1. It is hard to believe that Paul's heavy use of cultic language in 12:1–2 is not meant, first and foremost, to describe actual gatherings for corporate worship. How else, on a regular basis, could all the believers in Rome (addressed as "you" plural in v. 1) effectively offer their physical selves to God and one another so that their action results in a corporate "living sacrifice" (v. 2)?

2. It seems legitimate, and even necessary, to read the setting for Romans 14–15 back into chapter 12. In 12, Paul presents a broad appeal, based on the charismatic endowments of his readers, for a mutual upbuilding of all in the context of worship. The apostle's Roman readers, aware that their divisions are being played out chiefly in terms of conflicting meal practices, would almost certainly have these in mind as they consider the argument of chapter 12.

3. There is one piece of data in Romans 12 that sug-

gests that Paul is in fact thinking about a meal as the ideal setting for his appeal to "present your bodies." It is a quotation, near the end of the chapter, from Prov. 25:21f.; and it is couched in a way that recalls the distinctive teaching of Jesus to love one's enemies. Paul writes: "Beloved, never avenge yourselves.... No, 'if your enemies are hungry, feed them; if they are thirsty, give them something to drink; for by doing this you will heap burning coals on their heads.' Do not be overcome by evil, but overcome evil with good" (12:19–21). We cannot argue that the meals with enemies commended here are necessarily to be taking place within the eucharistic assemblies of believers. However, given the literary unity of chapters 12–15,[6] we must observe that 12:19–21 prefigures just the sort of reconciliation advocated by the apostle in 14:10–19. For Paul, it is precisely at meals, and especially at eucharistic meals (see 14:6ff. and 1 Cor. 11:17–34), that the walls separating believers from one another are to be leveled.

If the evidence just presented does not compel us to see an intentional reference to eucharistic meals in Romans 12, it nevertheless points strongly toward such a view.

Entertaining this hypothesis also allows us to expand upon Ernst Käsemann's classic assessment of Romans 12:

> It is true that no system of Christian "ethics" is being propounded here; but for the first time in the history of the Church the total activity of the community and its members is being looked at from a unified perspective. It is theologically defined as the response of faith in the everyday life of the world to the call of

> the grace by which that world is being grasped and held.[7]

What if this "unified perspective" and this "response of faith in the everyday life of the world" are thought by Paul to emerge most forcefully in regular gatherings of the church for eucharistic meals? Clearly, this ritual would present a major opportunity for believers in a particular locale to discern, receive, and exchange with their neighbors the peculiar forms of grace that constitute their own "measure of faith" (12:3). From such worship at table the church's mission to the world would find its inspiration and take its shape (see 12:9–21).[8]

The famous Christ hymn of Philippians 2 may also give us a glimpse into eucharistic worship as practiced by the Pauline churches. The text, printed in the NRSV by strophes to indicate its poetic structure, goes as follows:

> 6 [Christ] who, though he was in the form of God,
> did not regard equality with God
> as something to be exploited,
> 7 but emptied himself,
> taking the form of a slave,
> being born in human likeness.
> And being found in human form,
> 8 he humbled himself,
> and became obedient to the point of death—
> even death on a cross.
> 9 Therefore God also highly exalted him,
> and gave him the name
> that is above every name,
> 10 So that at the name of Jesus
> every knee should bend,
> in heaven and on earth and under the earth,

11 and every tongue should confess (*exomologesetai*)
that Jesus Christ is Lord (*Kyrios Jesous Christos*)
to the glory of God the Father.

The verses preceding the hymn refer to a "sharing in the Spirit" (*koinonia pneumatos* in 2:1) and contain exhortations reminiscent of Rom. 12:3–13 ("be of the same mind, having the same love... in humility regard others better than yourselves" in 2:2f.). This hint of charismatic sharing, with due respect for one's brothers and sisters in the faith, is just what we would expect to find in a Pauline eucharistic meal (1 Corinthians 11–14). So is the apostle's urging at the end of the hymn that his readers "work out" their salvation in community "with fear and trembling" (2:12), that is, with great reverence for God's work among them (2:13, see 1 Cor. 12:4–6).

But the hymn itself also suggests a eucharistic setting since it collapses the past, present, and future salvation history into what worshipers may experience as a single visionary moment.[9] Jesus' words at the last supper give evidence of such an experience on his part (see chapter 1), and Paul's exposition of the Lord's Supper in apocalyptic terms (see 1 Corinthians 10–11 and chapter 3 above) presupposes something akin to it. Furthermore, the Philippian hymn praises Jesus' self-offering, both in his incarnation generally and especially in his death (2:7f.). A similar liturgical accent turns up at the end of the last supper tradition cited in 1 Corinthians 11, where the apostle reminds his readers: "For as often as you eat this bread and drink this cup, you proclaim the Lord's death until he comes" (11:26). Could it be that the Philippian hymn itself, or something like it, formed part of this proclamation? N. A. Dahl observes that all hymnic material in the New Testament evokes the memory of Christ and then goes on to hypothesize that such remembering would typically occur in table liturgies associated with the last supper (see 1 Cor. 11:24f. and Luke 22:19).[10] Finally, the confession *Kyrios Jesous Christos* in 2:11 looks very much like the acclamation/greeting *Kyrios Jesous* of 1 Cor. 12:3, which we have shown to be an utterance taking place in eucharistic worship. Also in Philippians, it appears, Paul envisions a congregational setting in which Jesus' presence calls forth a liturgical acknowledgment.

We can hardly argue that the Philippian hymn (or any other spiritual song referred to in the New Testament) necessarily accompanied the celebration of table rituals. But we know that songs of this type did sometimes occur in eucharistic worship (1 Cor. 14:26; see below on Col. 3:16; Eph. 5:19). On the whole, we should entertain the strong possibility that Phil. 2:5–11, understood within its context, offers us yet another witness to a Lord's Supper liturgy. In any case, we can discern a missionary thrust within this hymn, since those who chant or recite it look forward to every knee bowing at the name of Jesus . . . to the glory of God the Father (2:10f.).

Besides 1 Corinthians, Romans, and Philippians, three other letters in the Pauline corpus contain possible indicators of eucharistic worship. The first of these occurs in 2 Corinthians 8–9 where 8:1–5 and 9:11–15 form, respectively, the opening and closing of an appeal to Paul's readers to complete the collection of funds they have been assembling for poor believers in Jerusalem (see 1 Cor. 16:1–4).[11] Urging the Corinthians to imitate their sister and brother believers in Macedonia, the apostle writes:

> [1]We want you to know, brothers and sisters, about the grace (*charis*) of God that has been granted to the churches of Macedonia; [2]for during a severe ordeal of affliction, their abundant joy and their extreme poverty have overflowed in a wealth of generosity on their part. [3]For, as I can testify, they voluntarily gave according to their means, and even beyond their means, [4]begging us earnestly for the privilege of sharing in this ministry (*ten charin kai ten koinonian tes diakonias*) to the saints [5]and this, not merely as we expected: they gave themselves first to the Lord and, by the will of God, to us . . . (chapter 8)

> [11]You [Corinthians] will be enriched in every way for your great generosity, which will produce thanksgivings to God (*eucharistian to theo*) through us; [12]for the rendering of this ministry (*he diakonia tes leitourgias tautes*) not only supplies the needs of the saints but also overflows with many thanksgivings to God (*pollon eucharistion to theo*). [13]Through the testing of this ministry (*dokimes tes diakonias tautes*) you glorify God by your obedience to the confession of the gospel of Christ and by the generosity of your sharing (*koinonias*) with them [i.e., believers in Jerusalem] and with all others, [14]while they long for you and pray for you because of the surpassing grace of God (*charin tou theou*) that he has

> given you. [15]Thanks be to God (*charis to theo*) for his indescribable gift! (conclusion of chapter 9)

In seeking to determine whether these two passages contain references to eucharistic meals, we need to answer a pair of questions. First, does the apostle envision actual periods of worship during which (a) the Macedonians gave themselves to the Lord, electing as a congregation to contribute generously to the fund for Jerusalem (8:5); and (b) the believers in Jerusalem, upon receiving the gift of money from Paul's largely Gentile churches (including Macedonia and Corinth), will meet to thank God for this act of generosity (8:1; 9:14) and intercede for their benefactors? Second, if worship events like this are presupposed in 2 Corinthians 8–9, do Paul and his Corinthian readers associate them specifically with ritual meals, on the model of the Lord's Supper? Several pieces of evidence support a positive answer to our questions.

First, as we noted in chapter 2, the entire process of gathering and delivering the collection for Jerusalem was understood by Paul to be both charismatic and cultic. The very names given by him to this corporate gift demonstrate as much. In 2 Corinthians 8–9, the apostle refers to the fund variously as a grace (*charis;* see 8:4, 6, 7, 19, with v. 7 clearly implying that *charis* is equivalent to *charisma*); a blessing (*eulogia;* see 9:5–6); a ministry (*diakonia;* see 8:4; 9:1, 12, 13); and a ritual service (*leitourgia;* see 9:12 and *leitourgesai* in Rom. 15:27). The collection is also called a self-giving "by the will of God" (8:5) and a "testing" (*dokime;* see 9:13), language that parallels the apostle's urging of his Roman readers to present their bodies at a eucharistic meal so that they may discern or test out (*dokimazein*) the will of God (12:1–2). Throughout 2 Corinthians 8–9, activities associated with completing the gift for Jerusalem are placed by the apostle into just the charismatic categories we have found in 1 Corinthians 11–14 and Romans 12–15.

Second, Paul refrains from calling the collection itself a thanksgiving. Instead, it is a *charis* bestowed and enacted, with the result that *eucharistia* to God will abound (2 Cor. 9:11f.). Paul's word play suggests that *eucharistia* is already becoming something of a technical term for cultic activities; hence, it does not function here as a figure of speech for good works. Indeed, whenever the apostle elsewhere calls attention to believers giving thanks to God in groups, he always links these acts of devotion with a meal (1 Cor. 10:30; 11:24f.; 14:16–7; Rom. 14:6).

Third, a focus by believers on the presence of Christ is assumed by Paul both in his description of the Macedonian self-offering ("they gave themselves to the Lord"; 8:5) and in the predicted thanksgiving at Jerusalem for "obedience to the confession of the gospel of Christ" (9:13). Paul evidently hopes that Jerusalem believers will interpret the Corinthians' gift as an act of participation in Christ's sacrifice — see the confessional expression of this in 8:9, "You know the generous act (*charis*) of our Lord Jesus Christ, that, though he was rich, yet for your sakes he became poor, so that by his poverty you might become rich."[12] The apostle predicts that a new manifestation of the Lord's *charis,* in the gift of the Corinthians, will be celebrated by the Jerusalem church in a ritual of *eucharistia* (9:12–13).

Fourth, as Paul wrote 2 Corinthians 8–9, he was almost certainly recalling 1 Cor. 16:1–4, where he had urged a weekly assembling of the collection at eucharistic worship. His readers would also make this connection (see chapter 3 above). Supporting our interpretation is a parallel usage of the verb *perisseuein* ("excel" or "abound") in 1 Cor. 15:58–16:1 and 2 Cor. 8:7, where both occurrences of the verb relate to the completion of the collection.

Finally, some insights into 2 Cor. 9:12–15 from Hans Dieter Betz push us decisively toward the conclusion that Paul and his Corinthian readers saw the gathering and delivery of the collection against the background of eucharistic meals. Betz proceeds from the hypothesis, accepted by a large number of modern interpreters, that verses 12–15 constitute the end of a Pauline letter to Corinth that a later editor combined with chapters 10–13. Betz observes that, rhetorically speaking, these final verses resemble the conclusions of other Pauline letters, where blessings or admonitions in liturgical language often occur. The particular element of liturgy that comes to prominence here, however, is the prayer of thanksgiving. Jerusalem believers will offer this *eucharistia* in response to the money granted them.[13]

At this point Betz takes a creative leap, for he posits that specific prayers of thanksgiving, with wordings based on the Jewish *Birhat-ha-Mazon* ("grace after meals"), would have been well known among the believers of Paul's day, both Jew or Gentile.[14] An early Christian version of this prayer appears in the postsupper thanksgiving of Didache 10, the elements of which are said by Betz to "closely resemble Paul's ideas in 2 Cor. 9:13–14."[15] What the apostle is doing in 9:15, Betz thinks, is literally quoting the first line of a thanksgiving prayer in the expectation that the Corinthians, while reading his epistle out loud during their church assembly, will recite the rest of the prayer themselves. Indeed, by speaking it together, they will be drawn more deeply into partnership with worshipers in Jerusalem (see *koinonia* in 9:13, mistranslated as "ministry" in the NRSV), who in turn will offer the same kind of prayer themselves when they receive the gift from Corinth.[16] Betz summarizes his conclusion as follows:

> Thus the first line of the prayer turns the [Corinthian] worshipers into active participants. By reciting the first line of the prayer, Paul assumed the role of liturgist leading the congregational prayer, which they were encouraged to continue on their own. . . . Thus the letter set in motion a thanksgiving service in the Achaian churches.[17]

Exegetically, this all makes good sense. Yet we can take one further step. What the evidence from Jewish prayer forms and Didache 10 most strongly suggests is that the "thanksgiving service" in Corinth (and, by implication, in Macedonia and Jerusalem as well) would be understood by Paul and his readers alike to be a eucharistic eating and drinking, probably along the lines of the Lord's Supper. All things considered, we may reasonably conclude that 2 Cor. 8:1–5 and 9:11–15 contain intentional references to ritual meals of thanksgiving. Paul believes that the multiplication of praise and thanksgiving to God occurring at such meals will only further the divine plan of redemption (see 2 Cor. 4:15).

Many interpreters have noted similarities between Col. 3:15–17 and Eph. 5:17–20. The majority view among scholars today is that Pauline disciples, not Paul himself, wrote the letters in which these passages occur, although the writers might be using memories of the apostle's own words.[18] It will be useful to examine our passages in parallel columns as a first step toward determining whether or not they assume a eucharistic meal as their primary setting. Almost everyone agrees that the authors of both these passages point to occasions of congregational worship at which charismatic gifts come into play for

Colossians 3	*Ephesians 5*
15Let the peace of Christ rule in your hearts, to which indeed you were called in the one body. And be thankful (*eucharistoi*). 16Let the word of Christ dwell in you richly; teach and admonish one another in all wisdom; and with gratitude (*en te chariti*) in your hearts, singing psalms, hymns, and spiritual songs to God. 17And whatever you do, in word or deed, do everything in the name of the Lord Jesus, giving thanks (*eucharistountes*) to God the Father through him.	17So do not be foolish, but understand what the will of the Lord is. 18Do not get drunk with wine, for that is debauchery; but be filled with the Spirit, 19as you sing psalms and hymns and spiritual songs among yourselves, singing and making melody to the Lord in your hearts, 20giving thanks (*eucharistountes*) to God the Father at all times and for everything in the name of our Lord Jesus Christ.

devotion to God or Jesus and for the mutual upbuilding of the community. Moreover, in both passages believers are counseled to interpret such infillings by the Spirit as power for an ongoing *eucharistia* that will permeate every moment of their lives. The author of Colossians makes explicit reference to *agape* as the chief force for harmonizing the gatherings of believers (3:14). He also mentions their unity "in the one body," which almost certainly means Christ's ecclesial body (see 1:18); and he calls attention to Christ's presence at worship both in the peace he grants (v. 15) and in his word (v. 16). A sharpened consciousness of the Lord's presence is also assumed in Ephesians 5:17, 19; and specific teachings about Christ's body, the church, along with the importance of love for mutual upbuilding, occur throughout the letter (see 1:22; 2:13–22; 3:19; 4:2, 14–16; 5:2, 23). Finally, if we conclude with Gordon Fee that the adjective *pneumatikais* in Col. 3:16 has as its referent the work of the Holy Spirit,[19] we can characterize both passages as trinitarian, exactly the dynamic view of God we have come to expect in Pauline descriptions of eucharistic meals.

Clearly, what we do not find is direct evidence that the congregations addressed here are engaged in eating and drinking. However, one could argue that because infilling by the Spirit (Eph. 5:18) is contrasted with drunkenness from wine, some kind of worship at table is presupposed. In addition, when we place the texts from Colossians and Ephesians next to 1 Corinthians 11–14 and Romans 12–15, we have to give due weight to the obvious parallels. Rudolf Schnackenburg offers the following assessment of Eph. 5:17–20: "Even if [the passage] does not say so in words, from the context it is possible that the author has in his mind's eye a celebration connected with the Eucharist.... The praise given to the Lord (v. 19) becomes an inclusive thanksgiving to God the Father in view of and in reference to the work of Jesus."[20] On balance, we may conclude (but just barely) that Colossians and Ephesians also count as witnesses to a type of Lord's Supper.[21]

Hebrews, 1 Peter, and Jude

None of these three writings, which are variously dated from about 60 to 100 C.E., contains a direct reference to what we have termed eucharistic meals.[22] Nevertheless, the author of each book offers one or more descriptions of a congregational assembly for worship. Furthermore, contained within these short descriptions we find just enough evidence of the activities or teachings associated with the Pauline meals to warrant an inquiry into whether here, too, table rituals might be taking place.

It is notoriously difficult to determine the extent to which the cultic language employed in Hebrews, which occurs in virtually every section of this writing, describes actual liturgical practices. Still, a worship assembly of some kind is clearly presupposed in 10:24–25: "And let us consider how to provoke one another to love and good deeds, not neglecting to meet together (*ten episynagogen heauton*), as is the habit of some, but encouraging one another (*parakalountes*), and all the more as you see the day approaching." This passage recalls Pauline references to eucharistic assemblies in which believers are expected to build one another up in love through gifts of the Spirit, especially prophetic admonitions and encouragements (1 Cor. 11–14; Rom. 12:4–10; note the prominent use of *parakalo* and *paraklesis* in these texts). Moreover, the congregational gatherings enjoined by both Paul and the author of Hebrews are to be marked by lively expectations of Christ's coming (1 Cor. 11:26; Heb. 10:25).

The verses just preceding Heb. 10:24f. may give us more detailed information about what was thought to be happening in these assemblies:

> [19]Therefore, my friends, since we have confidence to enter the sanctuary (*eis ten eisodon ton hagion*) by the blood of Jesus (*en to haimati Jesou*), [20]by the new and living way that he opened to us (*enekainisen hemin*) through the curtain, that is, through his flesh, [21]and since we have a great priest over the house of God, [22]let us approach (*proserchometha*) with a true heart in full assurance of faith, with our hearts sprinkled clean from an evil conscience and our bodies washed with pure water. [23]Let us hold fast to the confession of our hope (*ten homologian tes elpidos*) without wavering, for he who has promised is faithful.

One of the first things we notice about this passage is how the author weaves together Jewish temple imagery (especially as it pertains to the Day of Atonement on which the high priest enters the Holy of Holies to sprinkle blood on the ark) and the worship of those who base their hope on Jesus' sacrificial death. Clearly, such believers are to be engaging in some activity that gives them access to the divine presence. They are to "enter the sanctuary" (19) and "approach with a true heart" (22), just as they were earlier bidden to "approach the throne of grace with boldness" (4:16). The question then becomes: Are these prescribed movements thought to be communal acts of worship at specified times and places? And if so, which acts are envisioned?

Specifically, could the naming of Jesus' blood and flesh in this context constitute a reference by the author to worship at table? Such a position is at least possible in view of the clear allusion to baptism in verse 23 as an already accomplished cleansing that grants believers the confidence (19) and assurance (22) they need in order to "approach." By analogy, the approach being urged would also be a concrete liturgical act. Furthermore, the use of the hortatory subjunctive *proserchometha* ("let us approach") suggests that, unlike baptism, this act is thought to be repeatable. Eucharistic meals inevitably come to mind as prime candidates for such events.[23]

In fact, a eucharistic hypothesis helps to clarify verses 19–25 as a whole. The term "sanctuary" (19) is a multivalent image in Hebrews, but here it almost certainly stands for the blessings of the new covenant—Jer. 31:33f. is quoted verbatim in verses 16–18 — as these become available in Jesus' blood. If that is an accurate reading of the author's focus, one can hardly avoid comparing verse 19 with Paul's version of Jesus' institutional words: "This cup is the new covenant in my blood" (1 Cor. 11:25). According to Hebrews, believers have already entered into the new covenant by baptism; but that covenant is also a "way" that must be followed or observed by repeated actions. This new and living way has been inaugurated or opened by Jesus[24] through the "curtain" (*katapetasma*) of his flesh. The "curtain" refers first of all to the temple veil and could be thought of as an obstacle to communion with God (see Mark 14:38). But Harold Attridge is probably right in concluding that for the author of Hebrews this covering is the "point of entry to God's presence."[25] Thus Jesus' flesh becomes a passageway through which believers come, again and again, to the throne of grace. We can still hold to the majority view among commentators that the references to Jesus' blood and flesh in verses 19–20 designate his once and for all sacrifice, eternally valid and unrepeatable. But the emphasis here upon human activity in a congregational assembly seems to require that we also identify a pointing on the author's part to some form of the Lord's Supper where believers can renew their participation in Christ's sacrifice.

A parallel reference to Jesus as the one who establishes and sustains the new covenant through his blood occurs in Heb. 12:22–24; and this passage too seems best understood as a description of communal worship:

> [22]But you have come to Mount Zion and to the city of the living God, the heavenly Jerusalem, and to innumerable angels in festal gathering, [23]and to the assembly of the firstborn who are enrolled in heaven, and to God the judge of all, and to the spirits of the righteous made perfect, [24]and to Jesus, the mediator

> of a new covenant, and to the sprinkled blood that speaks a better word than the blood of Abel.

What stands out immediately here is the perfect tense of the verb *proserchesthai* in verse 22 ("you have come"). This almost certainly denotes some experience of the age to come already now. Here we may compare 6:4–5, where the metaphor of tasting is used in this connection: "It is impossible to restore again to repentance those who have once been enlightened, and have tasted the heavenly gift, and have shared in the Holy Spirit, and have tasted the goodness of the word of God and the powers of the age to come." The scene in verses 22–24 is also reminiscent of the vision in Rev. 14:1–5, where the prophet-author joins in heavenly worship. It is hard to believe that the author of Hebrews, who has already used the verb *proserchesthai* in 10:22 to designate a liturgical "approach" to God "by the blood of Jesus" (10:19), does not refer here also to an eschatological ritual taking place at table. Once again, we may recall Jesus' visionary promise at the last supper recorded in Mark 14:25.

Yet another indicator of eucharistic meals has been found by some in Heb. 13:9–10. Here the author cautions:

> 9Do not be carried away by all kinds of strange teachings; for it is well for the heart to be strengthened by grace, not by regulations about food, which have not benefited those who observe them. 10We have an altar (*thusiasterion*) from which those who officiate in the tent have no right to eat.

Commentators have identified in the term "altar" a reference to cultic meals held by believers,[26] though not because the early church is thought to have already constructed a sacred table in its house assemblies for the honoring or reenacting of Christ's sacrifice. Instead, this eucharistic interpretation rests on an analogy between Heb. 13:10 and Paul's exposition of the Lord's Supper in terms of Israel's temple cult in 1 Cor. 10:17f. ("Because there is one bread, we who are many are one body, for we all partake of the one bread. Consider the people of Israel; are not those who eat the sacrifices partners in the altar?"). Attridge holds that the warning of verse 9 has to do with "cultic dining of some sort" and that the activity counseled against probably had Jewish roots but "was being presented as a Christian practice."[27] On the whole, it seems probable that Heb. 13:9–10, like 10:19–23 and 12:22–24, contains an assumption by the author that eucharistic meals are taking place with some regularity in the congregational assemblies of his readers.[28]

Building upon insights published by Ernst Lohmeyer in 1937,[29] E. G. Selwyn finds a eucharistic meaning in 1 Pet. 2:2–5:

> [2]Like newborn infants, long for the pure spiritual milk, so that by it you may grow into salvation — [3]if indeed you have tasted that the Lord is good. [4]Come to him (*proserchomenoi*), a living stone . . . and [5]like living stones, let yourselves be built into a spiritual house, to be a holy priesthood, to offer spiritual sacrifices (*pneumatikas thusias*) acceptable to God through Jesus Christ.

Selwyn focuses upon the term *pneumatikas thusias*, noting that it echoes (or prefigures) the phrase "pure offering" in Didache 14:1–2, which clearly refers to the eucharist.[30] Since we have previously concluded that the "living sacrifice" of bodies mentioned in Rom. 12:1 has a eucharistic meal as its background (and noting also the phrase "spiritual worship" in 12:1), we may accept Selwyn's proposal as a working hypothesis.

Selwyn next calls attention to the parallel use of *thusia* ("sacrifice") in Heb. 13:15–16, where the author writes: "Through him [Christ], let us continually offer a sacrifice of praise to God, that is, the fruit of lips that confess his name. Do not neglect to do good and share what you have, for such sacrifices are pleasing to God."[31] The context for this passage is probably one of congregational worship (see 13:1); and indeed we have found strong eucharistic overtones in the metaphorical use of the word "altar" (13:10; see above). When we combine this "altar" terminology with the double occurrence of the word "sacrifice" in 13:15–16, we come up with a picture of the community's self-offering to God through Christ that interweaves verbal expressions of praise (v. 15) and generous sharing with those in need (v. 16). Here we seem to have uncovered one of the early church's common worship traditions, for we observed similar combinations in 1 Cor. 16:1–2; 2 Cor. 8–9; and Rom. 12:1–8, all of which were identified as eucharistic passages.

1 Pet. 2:2–5 contains key elements of this common tradition. The self-sacrifice of the congregation is "spiritual," an adjective that calls to mind the charismatic gift exchanges detailed in 1 Corinthians 11–14 and Rom.

12:1–8. Members of the community addressed by our Petrine author are to come to Christ repeatedly (*proserchomenoi* is present tense and recalls the liturgical use of this same verb in Heb. 10:22; 12:22) as those who have already tasted the goodness of the Lord (2:3). Moreover, they are to be "built up" (see 1 Cor. 14:3, 12; Rom. 14:19) into a "spiritual house," probably a synonym for the Body of Christ. Selwyn may well be right that for the author of 1 Peter the spiritual sacrifices of verse 5 denote first of all the proclaiming of God's mighty acts (2:9).[32] If so, we can see a parallel to Paul's observation in 1 Cor. 11:26 that by eating and drinking at the Lord's Table, the Corinthians are proclaiming his death until he comes.

But Selwyn then goes on to amplify his initial interpretation of the spiritual sacrifices by noting an extended ethical discourse that follows close upon verse 9 (see 2:11–3:22): "The Eucharistic sacrifice consists in the Eucharist *as a whole;* the entire Eucharistic service, with its prayers and praises, its almsgiving and social brotherhood no less than its strictly sacramental features is included in the term."[33] Selwyn's conclusions make good sense. Moreover, when we link his holistic view of 1 Pet. 2:2–5 to passages like 2:9, 12 and 3:1, 15, all of which encourage behavior on the part of the congregation that is designed to facilitate the conversion of unbelievers, we discover yet another instance of the vital connection between eucharist and missionary outreach.

Selwyn's work on 1 Pet. 2:2–5 pushes us toward considering the possibility of a eucharistic reference also in 4:7–11. It is generally acknowledged by commentators that in this passage the author wishes to depict congregational gatherings:

> [7]The end of all things is near; therefore be serious and discipline yourselves for the sake of your prayers. [8]Above all, maintain constant love for one another, for love covers a multitude of sins. [9]Be hospitable (*philoxenoi*) to one another without complaining. [10]Like good stewards of the manifold grace of God, serve one another with whatever gift each of you has received (*hekastos kathos elaben charisma eis heautous auto diakonountes hos kaloi oikonomoi*). [11]Whoever speaks must do so as one speaking the very words of God; whoever serves (*diakonei*) must do so with the strength that God supplies, so that God may be glorified in all things [or among all people] through Jesus Christ. To him belong the glory and the power forever and ever. Amen.

Here we have an abbreviated description of something much like the charismatic activities documented in 1 Corinthians 11–14 and Romans 12. In fact, apart from Paul and our Petrine author, no one in the New Testament employs the actual term *charisma*. The regnant idea, as in Paul's letters, is that each worshiper has a special gift for ministry to bring to the assembly.

But can we find any indication that the mutual ministry encouraged by the writer takes place within the context of a meal? Two hints of a positive answer appear. First, the hospitality required for the emergence of spiritual gifts would plausibly involve a sharing of food and drink as well as physical space. Second, the metaphor of good household stewards "serving up" their gifts as if they were edible provisions—*auto diakonountes* in verse 10 means something close to this—points to a table setting. Parallel lines of thinking occur in two sayings of Jesus recorded by the evangelist Luke:

> Who then is the faithful and prudent manager (*oikonomos*) whom his master will put in charge of his slaves to give them their allowance of food at the proper time? (12:42) For who is greater, the one who is at table or the one who serves (*ho diakonon*)? Is it not the one at the table? But I am among you as one who serves. (22:27)

While we cannot claim this data as proof positive for a reference by the author of 1 Peter to cultic meals, we have to take the possibility seriously, especially given the substantive argument of Selwyn for a eucharistic meaning in 2:2–5.

This possibility edges toward probability when we give attention to other similarities between 4:7–11 and the Pauline passages that describe eucharistic meals. These include:

1. An accent on the imminent return of Christ (4:7; see 5:4 and 1 Cor. 11:26; 15:51f.)

2. The highlighting of *agape* toward one another in the assemblies (4:8; see 1 Cor. 13 and Rom. 12:9f.)

3. A focus upon the ultimate goal of welcoming and serving one another with gifts, namely, the glorification of God through Jesus Christ (4:11; see Rom. 15:5–7)

All things considered, our study of 4:7–11 yields a fairly clear indication that both the author and first readers of this passage would have seen it against the background of eucharistic meals.

Jude 11–12 presents us with even firmer grounds for positing a reference to table worship in the assemblies of believers:

> 11Woe to them! For they go the way of Cain and abandon themselves to Balaam's error for the sake of gain, and perish in Korah's rebellion. 12These [people] are blemishes on your love-feasts (*en tais agapais hymon*), while they feast with you without fear, feeding themselves.

We do not know exactly who these unsavory individuals were or what sins they were alleged to have committed; but the people in question seem to be participating in church meals as if they were members in good standing, and the author finds this offensive.

Jude 12 is the only verse in the New Testament in which the word *agape* can be construed as a term denoting a ritual meal.[34] "Love-feast" is probably a good translation since Ignatius, the bishop of Antioch in about 115 C.E., knows of an *agape* ritual that is roughly on a par with baptism as a liturgical act and appears to be synonymous with or closely related to the church's eucharist: "Let that be a valid eucharist (*bebaia eucharistia*) which is celebrated by the bishop, or by one whom he appoints. . . . It is not lawful either to baptize or to hold an *agape* (*agapen poiein*) without the bishop" (*Ignatius to the Smyrneans,* VIII, 1–2).

Jude is one of the latest New Testament writings, probably originating close to the turn of the first century, so we may posit that its author and Ignatius would be using approximately the same terminology for church rituals. As a consequence, it seems likely that Jude 12 does point to some form of eucharistic meal, a liturgical event that, like baptism, requires official sanctioning for its validity. It is true that no specifically christological interest is evident in Jude 12, and the writer's urging of prayer "in the Holy Spirit" (v. 20) may or may not be a feature of the meal to which he earlier refers. On the other hand, Ignatius understands the eucharist, and perhaps the *agape* as well, to be conveying the flesh and blood of Christ (*To the Philadelphians,* IV), so this belief may be implicit in Jude. In any case, Jude closely resembles the compiler of Didache in his concern to maintain the integrity of the church's table worship (Didache 9:5; 10:6). Both authors seem to be telling their readers: "Many are watching as your community deals with Holy Things! Think of the witness you give at your ritual meals."

Joining with Jesus in Mission

Not all of the passages in this chapter that we have identified as references to eucharistic meals disclose a conviction on the part of their authors that the resurrected Jesus will be present among those worshiping at table. But the great majority of our references carry precisely this expectation. Paul, for example, believes that his readers in Rome will eat and drink (or abstain from food and drink) "to the Lord" while giving thanks to God (Rom. 14:6). Similarly, the apostle's exhorting of the Romans to "welcome one another [at table], just as Christ has welcomed you" (15:7) assumes a memory among his readers that Christ has actually extended this welcome, probably at baptism and some form of "first communion." Again, Paul's sketch of Christ's prayer in the midst of the congregation, during which the Lord urges Gentile believers to praise God with him and the people of Israel (15:10f.), presupposes the table setting described in the preceding verses and is therefore best construed as an image for devotion during this liturgy (see 1 Cor. 7:35). In Romans 12, the apostle gives only one clear indication that Christ will be present in the worship setting he is interpreting ("be ardent in the Spirit, serve the Lord"; 12:11), although it could be argued that the assertion "we are . . . one body in Christ" (12:15) also focuses the consciousness of the Romans on the present reality of Jesus. In any event, there are good reasons for understanding chapter 12 eucharistically (see above), which means that we can read the christological emphases of 14 and 15 back into it.[35]

When we turn to the passages in 2 Corinthians, Philippians, Colossians, and Ephesians that we believe to be eucharistic, we find similar indicators of Jesus' presence with worshipers:

> [T]hey gave themselves to the Lord and, by the will of God, to us [as participants in the collection for Jerusalem] (2 Cor. 8:5); For you know [i.e., call to mind repeatedly] the grace of our Lord Jesus Christ, that though he was rich, yet for your sakes he became poor (2 Cor. 8:9); Let the same mind be in you that was in Christ Jesus. . . . Therefore God also highly exalted him . . . so that at the name of Jesus every knee should bend (Phil. 2:5–10); Let the word of Christ dwell in you richly . . . sing psalms, hymns, and spiritual songs to God . . . in word or deed, do everything in the name of the Lord Jesus, giving thanks to God the Father through him (Col. 3:16f.); . . . be filled with the Spirit as you sing psalms and hymns and spiritual songs among yourselves, singing and making melody to the Lord in your hearts . . . giving thanks to God the Father . . . in the name of our Lord Jesus Christ (Eph. 5:19f.).

In most of these texts, Jesus' presence is realized through acts of remembrance or confession or thanksgiving, which is just what we would expect in celebrations of a Pauline Lord's Supper.

Two of the three passages in Hebrews that we have taken to be eucharistic presuppose an approach to God in worship through the mediation of Jesus (10:19–25; 12:22–24), while the third passage implies Christ's presence by the use of the word "altar" (13:10) and then affirms it more clearly in the exhortation that believers are to offer a sacrifice of praise to God "through him" (13:15). The author of 1 Peter also makes use of approach and mediation language when he admonishes his readers to "come to [Christ] a living stone... and like living stones let yourselves be built into a spiritual house, to be a holy priesthood to offer spiritual sacrifices acceptable to God through Jesus Christ" (2:2–5). Later, having recommended to his readers an exchange of charismatic gifts (probably at a table liturgy), the author concludes with this doxology: "so that God may be glorified in all things through Jesus Christ" (4:11). As in Hebrews, the central figure in the worship of God is Jesus.

Can we be more specific about what Jesus does at the eucharistic meals detailed in our epistolary passages? I think we can. The chief image that emerges from these references is that of the reigning Messiah, already "sitting" at the right hand of God but nevertheless active among his people and drawing them further into his cosmic mission. Thus Jesus receives believers (Rom. 15:7; 1 Pet. 2:2) or accepts their self-offerings (Rom. 12:1; 2 Cor. 8:5) or mediates their entrance into God's heavenly sanctuary already during their earthly worship (Heb. 10:19–25; 12:18–24). All of this he does for the purpose of joining them more firmly to his work of redemption, which will culminate in the glorification of God by every creature "in heaven and on earth and under the earth" (Phil. 2:10f.; see also 1 Cor. 15:24–28). In a way that is hard for twenty-first-century people to understand, the increasing glorification of God by humans, which can also be termed praise and thanksgiving (2 Cor. 4:15, 9:11–15; Col. 3:17; Eph. 5:20; Heb. 13:15), is expected to contribute fundamentally to cosmic redemption.[36] Especially at eucharistic meals Jesus stirs up this praise among believers (Rom. 15:9–12) or incorporates them more profoundly into himself as "living stones" so that they can offer spiritual sacrifices to God through him (1 Pet. 2:4f.; Heb. 13:15).

It is important to note that no New Testament writer we have surveyed conceives of these eucharistic sacrifices apart from practical good works that will themselves witness to the gospel and attract those who do not yet believe. The Macedonians offer themselves to Christ in order to help Paul complete the collection for Jerusalem (2 Cor. 8:5). The Romans who present their bodies as a living sacrifice to God (12:1) are bidden to live sacrificially, not only among their believing neighbors, but also among those outside the church (12:14–13:10), thus overcoming evil with good in all circumstances (12:21). The readers of 1 Peter, by offering their Spirit-led sacrifices, simultaneously proclaim the mighty acts of God (2:9)[37] and must then live in such an exemplary manner that their proclamation will prove winsome, causing also their pagan neighbors to glorify God (2:12; see also 2:13–3:1). Although the we can hardly describe the Letter to the Hebrews as a missionary document per se, the "love and good deeds" that are expected by the author to emerge from eucharistic worship (10:24f.) almost certainly extend to outsiders (see 12:14; 13:1–3). This means that when the author stretches the meaning of eucharistic praise to include righteous actions (especially sharing with others; see the use of *koinonia* in 13:16), he probably has an outreach vocation in mind.

In summary, we can say that the eucharistic Christ in the passages examined above works energetically to enlist those at table ever more fully in his messianic work. He does this chiefly through encouraging the self-offering of believers "by the mercies of God" (Rom. 12:1) as these are displayed in the re-presentation of his cross and resurrection and in the gifts of the Holy Spirit. We do well to remember that just this sort of enlistment was already taking shape when Jesus gathered his disciples for a last supper to share his vision and promise with them. Eucharistically speaking, the historical Jesus and the risen Christ are of one missionary mind.

CHAPTER FIVE

A HOST OF WITNESSES: THE GOSPELS, ACTS, AND REVELATION

IN THIS CHAPTER we continue with our program of demonstrating that eucharistic meals not only constituted a major element in the common life of the New Testament churches but also served at a basic level to fashion and fuel the missionary vocation of believers. Instead of functioning as secret rites for a sect wishing to isolate itself from the world, these meals had the effect of enhancing the public roles played by believers in Christ's ongoing redemption of all creation. The New Testament literature examined below consists largely of stories about Jesus and sayings by him (the Gospels), narratives about the growth of the early churches (Acts), and a visionary prophecy issuing from a late-first-century disciple named John (the Apocalypse). In previous chapters we have already identified a number of stories in the Gospels and Acts that point to the church's practice of eucharistic meals. We found such vignettes in the last supper narratives recorded by Matthew, Mark, and Luke, the postresurrection meals described by Luke and John (as well as the author of Mark 16:9–20), and the sketches of congregational meals in

Acts (2:42, 46; 20:7–11). But we have yet to consider as potential indicators of the church's table worship the numerous allusions to meals occurring in the records of Jesus' ministry before his passion, not to mention the multitude of stories about eating and drinking in Acts that are not directly related to congregational worship.

As we prepare to study these passages, we do well to heed the counsel of Eugene LaVerdiere on the meaning of the term "eucharistic reference." He writes that "a story can refer to the eucharist in different ways: historically, or literally and symbolically. A meal that was not eucharistic historically can be presented symbolically as eucharistic as part of a story."[1] One example of a symbolic reference cited by LaVerdiere is Luke's narrative of the release from prison in Philippi of Paul and Silas when an earthquake providentially levels the building confining them (Acts 16:25–34). Instead of fleeing, the two missionaries remain in place to deal with the anguish of their jailer, who cries out: "What must I do to be saved?" "Believe in the Lord Jesus Christ" is their instantaneous response; and the jailer does just that. Then, after tending to the wounds of his former prisoners, he confirms his conversion by submitting to baptism, with his whole household, and invites the two evangelists into his home where he prepares a meal of celebration for everyone present. LaVerdiere argues, persuasively I think, that by describing this chain of events in a "sacramental" manner, Luke means to guide his readers toward reflecting on their own baptisms and congregational meals of thanksgiving. The same assessment can be made of Luke's stories about Paul's conversion (especially Acts 9:17–19) and that of the centurion Cornelius (10:1–11:18), both of which describe guest-meals preceded by baptisms. We need not posit that Luke conceived of these meals as congregational eucharists per se; but given the prominence of such worship in the churches of the first century, it seems likely that he intended to create resonances with contemporary table liturgies, perhaps in order to stress their inherent connection with the missionary vocation of his readers.

Symbolic references to eucharistic meals of a different sort will be found in the Fourth Gospel and the Apocalypse. For example, Jesus' sudden and provocative announcement in the Johannine version of the feeding of the five thousand that only those who eat his flesh and drink his blood will enjoy eternal life (6:53–55) alerts readers to the strong possibility that eucharistic allusions will turn up elsewhere in the gospel. And indeed, when one allows 6:53–55 to work both forward and backward through the gospel as a whole, it is hard *not* to hear overtones of what Paul calls the Lord's Supper in the Baptist's introduction of Jesus as "the Lamb of God" (1:36), in the miracle of the water becoming wine at Cana, where Jesus acts as the True Bridegroom (2:1–11), and in the Johannine last supper, with its footwashing ritual and lengthy farewell discourse on the nature of Jesus' presence in and with believers (chapters 13–17). Detailed studies of these passages will follow, but even on the basis of this short overview we must suspect that table liturgies known to John played a significant role in his narration of Jesus' ministry.

Two structural features of the Apocalypse predispose us toward finding in this strange document at least allusory references to eucharistic meals. First, the visions granted to John the Seer, which form the basis for his book, are said to have occurred on the Lord's Day (1:10).[2] This is almost certainly Sunday (or Saturday after sundown by Jewish reckoning), the day on which the church's table liturgies typically took place. Second, most of John's visions have to do with scenes of worship in the heavenly sanctuary. Numerous hymns are sung (a phenomenon otherwise unattested in the apocalyptic literature known to us), and full homage is paid not only to God the Creator but also to the Lamb enthroned. We need not argue that John's visions took place within an actual eucharistic service of the church. He was after all in exile on the island of Patmos and may have been alone on the Sunday in question. Nevertheless, passages like the following strongly suggest that eucharistic liturgies on earth formed a basic part of John's consciousness and that of his readers:

> Listen! I [Jesus] am standing at the door knocking; if anyone hears my voice and opens the door, I will come into that person and have dinner (*deipneso*) with him/her and he/she with me (3:20; my literal translation). And the angel said to me, "Write this: Blessed are those who are invited to the marriage supper (*deipnon*) of the Lamb" (19:9). Amen, come Lord Jesus! (22:20; cf. "Maranatha" in 1 Cor. 16:22 and Didache 10:6).

A fuller treatment of these and other passages from the Apocalypse will be presented below, along with a proposal that John's work as a whole serves to encourage his readers in their vocation of faithful witnessing, an activity shaped and strengthened by participation in the eucharistic assemblies of their churches. But first we shall look for evidence of such liturgies in the gospels and Acts.

Mark and Matthew

In the discussion that follows we can examine Mark and Matthew together since they frequently transmit the same information about food, drink, and meal settings in the ministry of Jesus. Nevertheless, several variations in the two gospel accounts will be noted and treated. With the majority of interpreters today, we shall assume that Mark was the earliest of our four canonical gospels and that Matthew and Luke both had access to some form of Mark. The two-volume work Luke-Acts requires separate treatment. Although Luke presents a good deal of material that overlaps with that found in Mark and Matthew, he also introduces many stories and sayings found nowhere else in the New Testament, and these often have to do with meals. In fact, Luke-Acts as a whole gives unusual prominence to the table talk and ministry of Jesus and subsequently to the role of hospitality in the missionary expansion of the first-century church.[3]

In looking at Mark and Matthew, we shall take the cautious view that only material that gives some evidence of being shaped by the church's meal practices or concerns about them *as we have already come to know these* needs to be considered. Consequently, many references in Jesus' pronouncements and parables to food and drink (e.g., the sower, the mustard seed, the fish caught in a net, the good tree producing good fruit, the fig tree, the bad tenants of the vineyard, and the disciples' eating from the grainfields on the Sabbath) will be dropped from our purview because nothing in these texts indicates that either writer or readers would have understood them to be specifically eucharistic. Our goal is to identify analogues and allusions to eucharistic meals that were intended by Mark and Matthew (or the pregospel traditions transmitted in their writings) and would have been taken as such by most original readers. We shall err on the conservative side of things, eliminating some passages from consideration where interpreters of previous generations have found clear references. Nevertheless, when we build on the results of chapter 4, which support a widespread practice of eucharistic meals in the Pauline churches and those associated with the authors of Hebrews and 1 Peter, we can posit that the first readers of the Gospels, too, regularly celebrated such meals and as a matter of course tended to read previews and foretellings and symbols of their liturgical practice back into narratives about Jesus. Inspired by the activity of prophets in their worship, particularly worship at table (1 Corinthians 14; Didache 10:7), they expected to learn of extraordinary continuities and connections between themselves and the years of salvation history immediately preceding their own time.[4]

We begin our study of the Gospels by looking at four blocks of tradition that both Mark and Matthew transmit. One of Mark's sketches of a "day in the life of Jesus" commences at 2:13 and continues to the end of the chapter. Standing first in this collection of vignettes and pronouncements is the call of Levi the tax collector to be Jesus' disciple (vv. 13–14). Immediately afterward comes a scene inside a house (probably Levi's) where Jesus celebrates at table with his new follower and receives criticism from scribal officials, who complain about his eating "with tax collectors and sinners" (vv. 15–17). Jesus responds by alluding to himself as a physician who has come to call not the righteous but sinners (v. 17). Then the story line shifts to a controversy about fasting, which Jesus' disciples, unlike those of John the Baptist, do not practice. Jesus defends his followers by calling them "wedding guests" who must feast in the bridegroom's presence (vv. 18–20). Clearly, he means this as a self-reference. Jesus goes on to compare his ministry with "new wine" that will burst out of old wineskins (v. 22), presumably old sets of rules and prejudices that cannot comprehend the advent of God's messiah. Matthew's variations on this block of material include changing the tax collector's name to Matthew (9:9), adding a quotation from Hos. 6:6 to Jesus' defense against the scribal complaint ("I desire mercy and not sacrifice"), and appending a line to the pronouncement about new wine to ensure that the Lord meant to preserve old wine and old wineskins (9:17). This last change dovetails with Matthew's concern to portray Jesus as fulfiller, not destroyer, of Torah (Matt. 5:17).

There are good reasons for believing that something like the call of Levi/Matthew actually took place in Jesus' ministry and that certain of his contemporaries did express their indignation at Jesus' feasting with the wrong kinds of people.[5] For our purposes, however, it is important to focus upon how this story and the sayings connected with it were heard in the churches to which Mark and Matthew wrote. When we take this approach, keeping in mind the results of chapter 4, we can hardly avoid the conclusion that both evangelists intended to teach their readers, by Jesus' example, that "outsiders" must be welcomed to their eucharistic meals.[6] The messianic Bridegroom wishes to dine with all who accept his invitation in this season of new wine. Already now, the great feast of the kingdom impinges (Mark 14:25). The most likely candidates for the position of outsider in the middle of the first century, when this pre-Marcan tradition was forming, would be Gentiles. LaVerdiere correctly identifies the story about Levi/Matthew as a "eucharistic teaching on mission."[7]

This narrative finds an echo in the Marcan/Matthean account of a Syrophoenician/Canaanite woman, who protests against Jesus' announcement that he has come only for Jews by quipping that even the dogs (Gentiles like herself) eat crumbs from their master's table. Jesus, delighted by the woman's verbal jousting and perhaps learning something new about the breadth of his mission, grants her request that her daughter be healed (Mark 7:24–30; Matt. 15:21–28). This story probably addresses not only the issue of Gentiles' admission to the church's ritual meals but also their participation in the healing ministry of believers, which would regularly surface in eucharistic contexts (1 Cor. 12:9, 28; note also the christological title of "physician" in the story of Levi/Matthew's feast). Here we can see how Mark and Matthew have adopted the Pauline and Lucan view that the church's table practice is to function as a kind of magnet. All four writers believe that Jesus himself will be present with all those who respond to his call, or to his reputation as a healer.

The theme of "open admission" to the church's meals[8] comes through even more forcefully in Mark's second telling of a miraculous multiplication of loaves and fish by Jesus (8:1–10). In contrast to the feeding of the five thousand (Mark 6:30–44), this event takes place in the region of the Decapolis, across the Jordan from Galilee, in Gentile territory. The crowd following Jesus on this occasion seems mostly interested in his healing power (see 7:31–37), and Mark gives no indication that the Lord will ask any of them to become his disciple. Yet Jesus has intentionally ventured into their country (7:31), and as in the previous story of feeding he elects to provide sustenance for the crowd out of compassion for them (6:34; 8:2). What we have, then, is an aggressive mission on Jesus' part that combines healing and feeding. Mark alone tells this story as an outreach to Gentiles (contrast Matt. 15:32–39), and because he shows special interest in the healing vocation of believers during the Neronian terror of the 60s,[9] it may well be that 7:31–8:10 reflects eucharistic practices of the first-century Roman church in which gifts of the Spirit for healing came to the foreground for everyone present, including those who were not baptized.

In all gospel versions of the feeding of the five thousand only Jews participate. They are the first to receive the benefits of Jesus' mission (Matt. 10:23). Here the accent of the gospel tradition seems to lie on Jesus' role as the messianic shepherd who provides an abundance of food, even in the wilderness. Parallels with Moses and the desert wanderings of Israel are surely intentional, especially in Matthew's version of the story. What this narrative teaches the readers of Mark and Matthew is that in their eucharistic meals God recapitulates, confirms, and fulfills the ancient covenant with Israel (see the institutional words in both Mark 14:24 and Matt. 26:28: "This is my blood of the covenant" — not *new* covenant). Yet only through the agency of Jesus' disciples (Mark 6:37; 8:6; Matt. 14:16–19) does God's bounty for Israel appear. Here we may be catching sight of a foundational connection between the early Jewish church's table liturgies and its generous almsgiving. According to Luke in Acts, this almsgiving stimulates much goodwill on the part of the people of Jerusalem toward the church, and a steady growth in the number of new disciples results (2:42–47).

One more Marcan/Matthean allusion to eucharistic practice may be cited at this point. It occurs in a saying by Jesus spoken after the two sons of Zebedee (or their mother, according to Matt. 20:20) have proposed that they be given places of honor by Jesus "in your glory" (Mark 10:37)/"in your kingdom" (Matt. 20:21). This kind of imagery suggests place settings at the messianic feast and would have been recognized as such by many first-century readers (see Luke 22:28–30). The table symbolism is sharpened when Jesus asks the petitioners: "Are you able to drink the cup that I drink, or be baptized with the baptism that I am baptized with?" (Mark 10:38) It becomes sharper still when Jesus turns to his other disciples, who have not asked for special treatment, and instructs them that

> whoever wishes to be great among you must be your servant (*diakonos*), and whoever wishes to be first among you must be slave of all. For the Son of man came not to be served but to serve and to give his life a ransom for many. (10:43–45; the Matthean parallel in 23:11 omits most of this material, reading simply: "The greatest among you will be your servant.")

Martin Hengel has noted that the Marcan version of this story functions within the structure of his gospel as a final summary of Jesus' teaching about the necessity of servanthood and sacrifice just before he leads his disciples up to Jerusalem, the scene of his atoning death.[10] The words "give . . . for many" (v. 45) are unique to Mark and clearly find their origin in Isaiah's description of the suffering servant (Is. 53:10–12). We find one and only one echo of these words later in the gospel, in Jesus' saying over the cup at the last supper: "This is my blood of the covenant, which is poured out for many" (14:24). In this pair of passages, more clearly than anywhere else, we discover what the evangelist means by God's redemption of the world through Christ.[11]

However we may regard the historicity of 10:43–45, we should probably see it *in the light of* 14:24, which we believe to be close to Jesus' actual words. Most likely Mark's last supper tradition allows us a glimpse of the table worship in his church at Rome. As a regular congregational practice, this worship exerts force on the composition of his gospel by reaching backward and helping to shape his earlier narration of Jesus' ministry. Many interpreters have noted that the First Evangelist's work looks like a passion story with a long introduction; and this is nowhere more evident than in his use of the last supper. Here, according to Mark, is the most regular opportunity in the church's common life for disciples to unite themselves with the sacrifice of Jesus, benefiting from his "ransom" but also presenting themselves for the renewal of their vocation as bearers of the cross (see 8:34–35). In the Roman church of Mark's day, still reeling from persecution under Nero, eucharistic meals would provide just the right preparation for witnessing before hostile rulers and officials, even to the death (13:9–13). By omitting much of Mark 10:43–45, Matthew deemphasizes the role that eucharistic meals play in the equipping of martyrs. He reproduces Mark 14:24 verbatim in his own last supper account but then adds to it the words "for the forgiveness of sins" (26:28), thus accenting the benefits to all participants in the table liturgy. Nevertheless, as we shall see, Matthew too is concerned about eucharistic mission.

One last observation on Mark's understanding of eucharistic meals is in order here. The First Evangelist's highlighting of the word "many" in 10:45 and 14:24 by itself gives his last supper narrative a missionary thrust.[12] And that forward movement into the world gets heightened in the cryptic ending of his gospel. The risen Christ never appears to anyone in Mark. Instead, an angel instructs the frightened women at the empty tomb to "tell his disciples and Peter that he is going ahead of you to Galilee; there you will see him, just as he told you" (16:7; cf. Jesus' prediction in 14:28). For Mark, the word "Galilee" is a symbol for crossing over into new territory, just as it had been in Jesus' ministry (see especially 8:27ff. and 9:30–32). In effect, Mark tells his readers that the risen Christ will encounter them as One who stands on the frontiers of Gentile lands and moves boldly into them. Whoever wrote the longer ending of Mark picked up on this hint when he or she pictured Jesus' first post-resurrection reunion with the eleven disciples as a meal at which the Lord commands them to "Go into all the world and proclaim the good news to the whole creation" (16:14–15). At first implicitly, and then explicitly in the longer ending, Mark's last supper narrative reaches forward in the gospel to inspire his church's missionary vocation.

Matthew transmits a good deal of material about the final messianic banquet that is not found in Mark. This includes Jesus' sayings about the many who will come from east and west to eat in the kingdom (8:11), as well as the parables of the wedding banquet (22:1–14), the wise and foolish bridesmaids (25:1–13), and (probably) the entrusting of the talents, where the two faithful servants are bidden to "enter into the joy [i.e., feast] of your master" (25:21, 23). Along with Luke, Matthew also records a Q saying about the celebratory eating and drinking with sinners that characterizes Jesus' ministry (11:18f.; Luke 7:33f.). This data already suggests a lively practice of meal liturgies in the church to which Matthew wrote; and that hypothesis is strengthened when we add the large amount of eucharistic material Matthew takes over from Mark. Matthew's pictures of the final banquet indicate that his church probably experienced its ritual meals as previews of the kingdom's completion at Jesus' return. Such an interpretation fits with the evangelist's version of Jesus' saying about new wine at the last supper: "I will never again drink of this fruit of the vine until that day when I drink it new with you in my Father's kingdom" (26:29). Here the Matthean addition "with you" serves to excite hopes for full reunion with Jesus.

But even now the Matthean congregation knows Jesus' presence in its common life (18:20; 28:20). Do these passages about presence reflect eucharistic practice in the evangelist's church? At first reading they give no such indication. Matt. 18:20 comes at the end of a section on church discipline (18:15–19). When members meet to facilitate reconciliation among themselves — or to impose a ban upon those who refuse to attempt reconciliation — they can be assured that their decisions will be ratified in heaven, "for where two or three are gathered in my name, I am there among them." This assurance would seem to apply to many different situations. In Matt. 28:20, the last words of the gospel, the risen Jesus delivers his great commission to "make disciples of all nations" (v. 19), encouraging his followers with the promise: "Remember (*Idou*), I am with you always [literally: "all the days"] to the end of the age." This passage is most easily understood as an open-ended promise that is not specific to ritual celebrations. Nevertheless, a closer look at these passages encourages us to posit that here too Matthew wants his readers to reflect on experiences that would typically come to them in the context of table worship.

We begin by noting that 18:15–20 sketches out a process culminating in an actual meeting of the whole church as *ekklesia* (18:17). Prior to this meeting, Jesus is present with only two or three as they try to bring about mutual forgiveness (18:20). But will he not be present all the more when the whole church assembles to struggle toward institutional decisions about the status of its members? (See 1 Cor. 5:3–5, where a disciplinary ban is to be imposed upon an unrepentant sinner at a congregational gathering "in the name" and "in the power of the Lord Jesus.") Is the Matthean Jesus present then specifically at table? The evangelist's addition to the cup saying at the last supper ("for the forgiveness of sins"; 26:28) supports an affirmative answer since it confirms that for him table rites conveyed forgiveness to already baptized members.[13] So does the fact that the rabbinic text m. Aboth 3:2f., which is often cited as a parallel to 18:20 (. . . two who are sitting, and words of Torah . . . pass between them — the Presence [*Shekinah*] is with them. . . . Three who eat at a single table and . . . talk about the teachings of Torah while at that table are as if they ate at the table of the Omnipresent"), envisions a meal setting.[14] Whereas the pharisaic sages described here study Torah together in their meal fellowships (*haburoth*) and thus enjoy a visitation from the Holy One of Israel, Matthew wants his readers, in their table rites, to rehearse Jesus' extensive Torah on forgiveness[15] and receive that forgiveness directly from him in their sharing of the eucharistic cup. A similar linkage between the meal and forgiveness may be found in Matthew's warning to his readers not to attend a messianic (eucharistic?) banquet without a wedding garment, perhaps a symbol of baptism (22:11f.).

As for 28:20, we hardly want to argue that it contains a univocal reference to Christ's presence in the eucharistic liturgies of Matthew's church since no meals are evident in the context. On the other hand, baptism in the name of the Father, Son, and Holy Spirit is confirmed as a church practice. Indeed, the risen Christ "institutes" it here as a ritual for making disciples, who are then to be taught, probably over a period of time, "everything I have commanded you" (28:19). This last clause must mean the higher righteousness that Matthew's Jesus has expounded throughout the gospel. But we have seen that one important key to the living of this righteousness is the forgiveness of one's own sins, mediated through the eucharistic cup (26:28). Aware of these resonances in the gospel text, should we not ask ourselves how likely it is that Matthew and his readers simply forgot about their meal rituals in attempting to fulfill the Great Commission? More probable, I think, is the thesis that Matthew's missionary vision included both of the dominical "sacraments." For him, Jesus' presence was expected to manifest itself especially in the baptism and teaching accomplished by his disciples. But both of these activities must have occurred with some regularity just prior to, or even within, a form of eucharistic liturgy. It is just possible that 11:28f., where Jesus the meek king invites those reading Matthew's gospel to approach him so that they can find refreshment for their souls and take his yoke of discipleship upon them, formed one element of such a liturgy. Like 18:20 and 28:20, this passage affirms Jesus' special presence in what appears to be a ritualaction ("Come to me . . . ")[16]

Luke and Acts

In the Third Gospel and Acts, which together account for more than one-quarter of the New Testament, accounts of eating and drinking take center stage and even become something of an organizing principle for Luke.[17] From the very outset, then, we are justified in looking for intentional references to eucharistic liturgies. And we have plenty of help. In two substantial monographs (*Dining in the Kingdom of God: The Origins of the Eucharist According to Luke* and *The Breaking of the Bread: The Development of the Eucharist According to the Acts of the Apostles*) Eugene LaVerdiere has blazed the trail for this search.[18] According to LaVerdiere, Luke, in his gospel, sets forth the origins of the eucharist in a series of meals with Jesus. The last supper forms the climax in this chain, but for Luke the eucharist per se cannot be understood apart from the seven meal stories that precede the last supper and the two postresurrection appearances of Jesus at table that follow it. None of these meal stories exactly reproduces the table liturgies in use among the churches Luke knew, "but they all have something to say about the eucharist. Each meal symbolizes the [church's] eucharist, preparing for it or pointing back to it in some way."[19]

LaVerdiere identifies as Luke's ten meals with Jesus: the banquet at Levi's house (5:27–39); dinner at the house of Simon the Pharisee (7:36–50); the breaking of the bread at Bethsaida; the feeding of the five thousand (9:10–17); hospitality at the home of Martha (10:38–42); a noon meal at the home of a Pharisee (11:37–54); a Sabbath dinner at the home of a Pharisee (14:1–24); hospitality at the house of Zaccheus (19:1–10); the last supper (22:7–38); the breaking of the bread at Emmaus (24:13–35); and an appearance at table with the community in Jerusalem (24:36–53). Apart from 5:27–39, 9:10–17, and the last supper, these narratives are unique to Luke. Moreover, six of the ten — not counting the last supper — occur while Jesus is in transit to or from Jerusalem, a fact suggesting that Luke understands them to be vital features of the Lord's itinerant mission. This view is confirmed in the very last meal story when the risen Jesus announces to his followers in Jerusalem: "Thus it is written, that the Messiah is to suffer and to rise from the dead on the third day, and that repentance and forgiveness of sins is to be proclaimed in his name to all nations, beginning from Jerusalem. You are witnesses of these things" (24:46–48). In Luke's gospel only here, at table, is such a missionary charge delivered.

We should raise a few caveats about LaVerdiere's approach. He may be insufficiently critical when he treats all the Lucan stories of meals with Jesus as "origins of the eucharist" — neither of these two terms is clearly defined — and he does not investigate the potentially eucharistic allusions taken over from Mark or Q (e.g., Jesus' saying on the bridegroom's presence and new wine in Mark 2:18–22 and the eating and drinking of the Son of man in Matt. 11:18f./Luke 7:34) or the discourses on meals by Jesus that are unique to Luke but do not occur within actual dining scenes (e.g., 12:35–38; 15:1–32; 16:19–31; 17:7–10). These, too, may be eucharistic references. Moreover, the title of LaVerdiere's work on Luke's gospel appears not to summarize his results accurately, since none of the meal stories studied by him portrays an example of dining *in the kingdom of God.* Nevertheless, we owe LaVerdiere a great debt of gratitude, for at the very least he has demonstrated that Luke, who resembles the other evangelists in shaping his gospel outline to address the needs of his readers, considers meals with Jesus to be a constitutive feature of the church's unfolding missionary vocation. Luke's second volume, which offers us many guest and host stories about missionaries, broadens this perspective.

We can build on one of LaVerdiere's major insights, modifying it slightly so as to reveal, even more clearly than he does, the missionary contours of Luke's eucharistic references. While LaVerdiere identifies the last supper as the climactic moment in a chain of ten stories, he also recognizes that the supper becomes the first in a new series of three meals that are explicitly messianic (22:30; 24:26, 46). Thus it seems best to treat these three stories together as the climax of Luke's teaching about eucharistic meals. Forming a unit bound together by the cross and resurrection, they reach backward into the narrative of Jesus' life and forward into the church's mission. Already at the last supper itself this missionary impulse begins to emerge, for in Luke's version of the supper, in a symposium discourse unique to his gospel, Jesus announces: "You are those who have stood by me in my trials; and I confer on you, just as my Father has conferred on me, a kingdom, so that you may eat and drink at my table in my kingdom, and you will sit on thrones judging the twelve tribes of Israel" (22:28–30). This passage resembles Matt. 19:28

and may be part of the Q tradition, but we note three important differences between the two gospel pronouncements. First, Matthew's version is not located within a last supper narrative. Second, it contains no words about "my table in my kingdom." Third, it must be understood as a prophecy about the final establishment of God's kingdom ("at the renewal of all things"), whereas Luke 22:28–30 could be taken as a picture of the church's life during the reign of Jesus but prior to his return in glory (see 1 Cor. 15:24).

In fact, Jacob Jervell has shown that a pre-Parousia reading of the Lucan saying fits nicely with the overall program of the gospel and Acts. Jervell argues that for Luke, what Jesus promises here at the last supper is at least partly fulfilled in the earliest days of the Jerusalem church. The twelve apostles — Judas has now been replaced by Matthias (Acts 1:15–26)—do not simply evangelize the people of Israel after Pentecost. They also function as the nation's eschatological regents and prophets. In God's eyes, they take over the positions of the Jerusalem leaders who bore responsibility for Jesus' crucifixion by winning respect from the people (Acts 2:47; 5:12–16). In the power of the Spirit, they speak prophetically, calling upon all Jews in the holy city to repent (Acts 2–5). For Luke, Jervell maintains, the apostles are the vanguard of Israel's original tribes, now regrouping in the last days. They become the heart of Israel as it is being renewed by Jesus' resurrection and exaltation to messianic kingship. Already now they share in his rule as Viceroy over God's kingdom.[20]

On one issue that is critical for our study Jervell maintains a curious silence: he offers no analysis of the phrase "at my table" (22:30). If he is right that the twelve are sharing Jesus' messianic kingdom already through their activity in the church — and this seems likely — then they must also be playing a special role in Jesus' ongoing table ministry (previewed for them in Luke 22:24–27). Luke supports this interpretation when he includes within Peter's evangelistic speech to Cornelius a proviso that the risen Jesus appeared not "to all the people but to witnesses chosen by God, to us, namely, those who ate and drank with him after he rose from the dead" (Acts 10:41; my translation).[21] Here we find a direct link between Jesus' discourse at the last supper, table sharing with the Risen One, and the church's proclamation. We may think of the Lord's words in 22:30 as a prophecy of the church's eucharistic mission, with Emmaus as the first phase of its fulfillment. At the meals following this story (Luke 24:36–48 and Acts 1:4), it becomes even clearer that all those who eat and drink with the risen Lord are his special witnesses. We will see, in studying Acts, that Luke does not simply equate this messianic table fellowship with commemorations of the last supper on the first day of the week. He includes these in his understanding of ritual meals (see Acts 20:7–12) but also seems to believe that the Lord's resurrected presence (or influence) sanctifies many other events of eating and drinking, particularly in missionary contexts. That, at any rate, is the thesis we will test as we shift our search for eucharistic references more directly into Acts.

As we do this, we can call once again on LaVerdiere for a panoramic view of what Luke means by eucharistic meals. In the title of his volume on Acts, LaVerdiere properly highlights the phrase "breaking of the bread." We have already noted in chapter 3 that this must have been one of the earliest terms for the church's meal liturgies (see 1 Cor. 10:16; Acts 2:42). As far as Luke's gospel is concerned, the term occurs in the story of the feeding of the five thousand, in the last supper narrative, and (decisively) in the Emmaus account, where the two disciples involved explain to their Jerusalem friends "how [Jesus] had been made known to them in the breaking of the bread" (24:35). The same phrase (or close equivalent) turns up not only in Acts 2:42 but also in 20:7–12 and 27:33–38. LaVerdiere believes that all three of these passages "treat directly of the eucharist." In addition, he finds two stories in Acts, the choosing of the seven to serve tables (6:1–6) and the meal celebrated by Paul and Silas with their jailer in Philippi (16:25–34), "that have indirect bearing on the eucharist." Finally, LaVerdiere examines four passages that "may not be eucharistic, whether directly or indirectly, but have important implications for the nature of the eucharist and its assembly." These are Jesus' repeated sharing of salt with the apostles after his resurrection (Acts 1:4); the echo of this in Peter's speech to Cornelius (10:41); the first story of Saul's conversion, which ends with a postbaptismal meal (9:17–19); and the apostolic council in Jerusalem (15:1–35), which "shows how Gentiles are integrated at the one table of the Lord."[22]

The three categories LaVerdiere has devised for classifying eucharistic references seem overprecise, and it is not clear that they prove ultimately useful for interpreting the meal scenes in Acts. Based on our previous study, we can agree with LaVerdiere that Acts 2:42 and 20:7–12 "treat directly" of eucharistic meals. But 27:33–38, in which we see Paul breaking bread on the deck of a storm-tossed ship, gives no indication that the believers who have accompanied him on this voyage are joining in his prayer of thanksgiving. We shall offer our own interpretation of the passage below. As for the other passages in Acts that relate to meals, it is probably best to treat them as eucharistic references or allusions only when we can show that Luke and his readers would have understood them as such.

That would almost certainly be the case with the "sacramental" meal involving Paul, Silas, and their Philippian jailer's household, and with the nourishment taken by Paul in Luke's first story of the apostle's conversion. Both of these events portray a coming to faith in Christ, a baptism, and a celebratory meal at which one or more believers "preside" as welcomers to the church even if they are not, technically speaking, the hosts. The same can be said of the guest-meals in which Peter, his companion-disciples, and the newly baptized members of Cornelius' household join in the home of the centurion (10:34–11:3). Luke's readers would not necessarily identify these meals with their own eucharistic rituals, but they would probably tend to see their practices in the light of such meals. Above all, they would catch Luke's point that these exchanges at table in Acts are missionary events and might therefore shape their own liturgies accordingly.[23]

The rather obscure reference to Jesus' sharing salt with the apostles — a practice that Luke apparently understands to have been a regular feature of his post-resurrection appearances with them "during forty days" (1:3–4) — may symbolize a kind of covenant renewal ceremony, if not a meal as such.[24] At any rate, Luke's narration of one such sharing contains a directive from the Risen One that his followers are not to leave Jerusalem but to wait for baptism by the Holy Spirit. This "promise of the Father" recalls a similar phrase in the missionary command that Jesus utters at table in the closing verses of Luke's gospel (24:49) and should probably be taken as an extension of it. Luke's readers, already acquainted with the Spirit through baptism and aware of its special power for mission, are here encouraged to accept the Spirit's guidance on such matters within their own table rituals (cf. 1 Corinthians 12–14).

Acts 6:1–6 centers upon problems connected with a "daily distribution" (*diakonia*), probably of food to the needy, that has become a regular feature of the Jerusalem church's common life. We cannot tell whether the distribution is thought to be happening within the context of a community meal, but this is a distinct possibility. The seven believers chosen by the Hellenists to ensure that their widows will be equitably served are held to be "of good standing, full of the Spirit and of wisdom" (6:3). Their implied task is to "serve tables" (6:2), and this they undoubtedly do. But when we see two of them (Stephen and Philip) in action, they actually function as Spirit-led prophets and missionaries (Acts 7–8). In other words, they resemble the twelve in their primary tasks. Luke makes two major points with this story. First, he wishes to convince his readers that since the earliest church provided daily distributions for the needy, they ought to do the same, at least weekly, when they meet for eucharistic meals (see Acts 20:7–12). Second, Luke wants his readers to conclude that their table rituals should ideally be led by those charismatically endowed for prophecy and mission, like the seven (see Acts 20:7–12, where Paul's leadership at table is implied, and Didache 10:7; 11:3–12; 15:1).

As for Luke's account of the apostolic council (15:6–35), we can agree with LaVerdiere that it tells us a good deal about the church's eucharistic table fellowship, whether or not the council itself involved such worship. Like Paul in Gal. 2:1–14, Luke wants to argue that full access to the Lord's table must be granted to Gentile converts without their males having to undergo circumcision. There is much debate among contemporary scholars about whether the rules of purity imposed upon Gentile members of the church (15:19–21) were actually spelled out at this conference. Paul in his letters admits to no knowledge of them. But the chief point remains: the Jewish church in Jerusalem has accepted the radical position that God wants Gentile believers to feel altogether welcome at all table rituals of the church, wherever they take place. In fact, however, that issue may not have been fully resolved on a practical basis even toward the end of the first century, when Luke writes. Luke wants his mostly Gentile readers to know that this major decision in their favor was made early, by consensus, at the initiative of James, the brother of Jesus, and with the guidance of the Holy Spirit. Consequently, Luke also wishes to show how the decision at Jerusalem clears the way for his readers' unfettered use of eucharistic meals in their missionary outreach.

A possible advocacy of this practice occurs in Paul's prayer of thanksgiving and breaking of bread on shipboard near the end of Acts. Because Luke describes Paul's prayer with the verb *eucharistein,* we must suspect that this story focuses on something other than standard Jewish piety at meals.[25] A close look at the details of the story reveals an alternative hypothesis. Tossed about by a storm for many days, Paul's fellow passengers have lost hope of survival and have ceased eating. They appear not to believe an earlier prophecy by the apostle, whom they know as a prisoner charged with preaching a subversive new religion, that no one on board will be lost (27:21–25). But now, in the midst of their despair, Paul speaks for the second time as a prophet:

> Just before daybreak, Paul urged all of them to take some food (*metalabein trophes*), saying, "Today is the fourteenth day that you have been in suspense and remaining without food, having eaten nothing. Therefore I urge you to take some food (*metalabein trophes*), for it will help you survive (*pros tes hymeteras soterias hyparchei*). . . . " And after he had said this, he took bread; and giving thanks to God in the presence of all, he broke it (*labon arton eucharistesan to theo . . . kai klasas . . .*) and began to eat. Then all of them were encouraged and took food (*trophes*) for themselves. (27:33–36)

Clearly, Luke intends no portrayal of a community meal shared by believers. Yet a table fellowship of sorts has been created, among pagans, by the combination of Paul's encouraging words and his ritual act. Luke's readers would almost certainly associate this event with one or more of the meal scenes already transmitted to them in the Third Gospel and Acts. For example, in the Lucan last supper narrative, when Jesus takes bread, gives thanks, and breaks it (22:19), the wording used (*labon arton eucharistesas eklasen*) seems to preview that of Acts 27:35. Unlike Jesus, Paul does not distribute the bread he breaks, but the distinct impression given in the story from Acts is that the apostle's shipmates begin to take their nourishment from the loaf sanctified by his thanksgiving (*metalabein* literally means not simply "take" but "receive one's share in").

In fact, the clause *metalabein trophes* would surely spark another kind of recognition on the part of Luke's readers, for just this expression occurs in Acts 2:46f., where the worship practice of the earliest Jerusalem church is described as follows:

> Day by day, as [the believers] spent much time together in the temple, they broke bread at home and ate their food (*metelambanon trophes*) with glad and generous hearts, praising God and having the good will of all the people. And day by day the Lord added to their number those who were being saved (*tous sozomenous*).

As in these early days, so also on a storm-tossed ship in the Mediterranean, those who witness a breaking of bread with gratitude toward God find themselves drawn into the divine plan of salvation. The readers of Acts could hardly fail to make a three-way connection between these two accounts of bread breaking and their own table practices.

Luke's missionary message to his readers is reinforced by Paul's use of the word *soteria* (27:34). Literally, the word means "salvation," and of course it refers in the first instance to the saving of physical lives. But Luke must have meant it to signify also a joining together with God's saving activity in Jesus (see 2:47 above and 4:12). Here, in the story of Paul's shipboard meal, Luke's readers would see that everyone present enters into the orbit of the graced apostle, whom God has marked for survival so that he can witness even to the emperor (27:24; note especially *kecharistai soi ho theos pantas... meta sou*). Initially, God's saving grace manifests itself when Paul breaks bread and his shipmates find courage. Shortly thereafter, grace takes the form of their physical deliverance as the ship runs aground and breaks apart. But who knows (Luke seems to be asking his readers) how the *soteria* of these passengers will unfold after that? Perhaps some of them will even become disciples!

If this reading of the final meal story in Acts comes close to Luke's intent, our narrative turns out to be nothing less than a portrait of the Lord's missionary table in his expanding kingdom (Luke 22:30). While this table manifests itself most clearly and consistently in the meal liturgies of the church, it also exists in the world, appearing wherever Christ's missionaries seek to fulfill their vocation (Luke 10:1–9). Every breaking of bread with thanksgiving by believers "in the presence of all" helps to make Jesus known (Luke 24:35). Acts 27:33–36 does not depict a church meal as such. And yet it is a eucharistic meal that contributes to the upbuilding of Christ's kingdom. Here Luke's readers probably recognized his counsel to discern their own missionary opportunities in meals with nonbelievers. Perhaps we could even title this story "A Proto-Lord's Supper."

The Fourth Gospel and Revelation

Far more than our synoptic records of Jesus' life, the Fourth Gospel has provoked strenuous debate among scholars about whether or to what extent its author witnesses to sacramental rites of the first-century church. At one end of the spectrum is Rudolf Bultmann's view that John's gospel must be considered antisacramental because those sections of it that point to baptism and the eucharist were added to the original writing by a later "ecclesiastical redactor." But Bultmann's position has not won wide acceptance. As our new century commences and the dust of debate begins to settle, a broad scholarly consensus is emerging that in at least one passage the original author of the Fourth Gospel, not a later redactor, provides us with an unambiguous (and positive) reference to something like the Lord's Supper.[26] This text occurs in a disputation between Jesus and some Jewish critics that takes place in the synagogue at Capernaum just prior to Passover and just after Jesus has fed the five thousand with loaves and fishes. The argument takes many turns — it has a midrashic character — and includes such pronouncements by Jesus as "the bread of God . . . comes down from heaven and gives life to the world. . . . I am the bread of life. . . . Whoever comes to me will never be hungry, and whoever believes in me will never be thirsty" (6:33–35). But the particular verses that nearly everyone now takes as a reference to a eucharistic meal come toward the end of the exchange between Jesus and his critics, in 6:51c–58:

> ". . . and the bread that I [Jesus] will give for the life of the world is my flesh." The Jews then disputed among themselves, saying, "How can this man give us his flesh to eat?" So Jesus said to them, "Very truly, I tell you, unless you eat the flesh of the Son of Man and drink his blood, you have no life in you. Those who eat my flesh and drink my blood have eternal life, and I will raise them up on the last day; for my flesh is true food and my blood is true drink. Those who eat my flesh and drink my blood abide in me, and I in them. Just as the living Father sent me, and I live because of the Father, so whoever eats me will live because of me. This is the bread that came down from heaven, not like that which your ancestors ate, and they died. But the one who eats this bread will live forever."

If we understand this passage redactionally, we have to posit that it discloses some very high claims by the Johannine community for its table liturgy. The "sacramental theology" evidenced here may well have provided the basis for Bishop Ignatius's understanding of the church's eucharist as "the medicine of immortality" (*To the Eph.* 20:3). We are justified in calling the Johannine rite "eucharistic" because the verb *eucharistein,* with Jesus as the subject (he "gives thanks" rather than "blesses"), occurs twice in John's narration of the feeding of the five thousand (6:11, 23) just prior to the synagogue discourse.

Two problematic issues relating to 6:51c–58 have generated much scholarly discussion over the past two centuries. First, commentators have asked why this overt reference to church practice comes so early in John's outline of Jesus' life. Second, students of the Fourth Gospel have puzzled over why John's last supper, stretching all the way from chapter 13 through chapter 17, contains no words at all by Jesus over bread and wine. Many solutions to these two anomalies have been proposed; but David Rensberger, drawing on the work of Wilhelm Wilkens, offers what may be the most comprehensive and satisfying hypothesis. For Wilkens and Rensberger, the key to understanding what appears to be a misplaced "founding" of the eucharist lies in recognizing that John's entire gospel is a passion story.[27] Already in the first chapter John the Baptist identifies Jesus as "the lamb of God who takes away the sins of the world" (1:29). From his very entry into human history, Jesus is the Passover lamb whose death will redeem not only the Jewish people but everyone on earth (see 12:32). Consequently, John can locate another crucial event in Jesus' passion, his "cleansing" of the temple, "too early" in the narrative — indeed, very close to the beginning of Jesus' public ministry (2:13–25). Already on this occasion Jesus predicts his death and resurrection, with the latter being understood ecclesiastically in the Johannine community as the raising up of "the temple of his body" (2:21). Similarly, in chapter 3, in a conversation with Nicodemus, Jesus introduces the new birth of water and the Holy Spirit that John's readers would surely recognize as the initiatory rite of baptism (3:3–10; contrast Mark 16:16; and Matt. 28:19, where this practice originates in a command of the risen Christ).

Rensberger is almost certainly correct that these "displacements" of events would not have troubled the first readers of the gospel. No doubt they already knew the conventional chronology of Jesus' life transmitted in the synoptic tradition. But they also knew that the document growing out of their own community's history had to be constructed along different lines so as to guide them in their worship and mission after their painful separation from a local synagogue.[28] Such a guidebook gospel did not need to be rigidly diachronic. Its order and logic were determined by the unique experiences of the community and therefore came to consist largely of discourses by Jesus on his identity ("I am . . . "), each addressing some critical issue in the congregation's faith and life. In fact, Barnabas Lindars has advanced the view that many of these gospel discourses developed from homilies based on short sayings of Jesus and preached to worship assemblies of the Johannine church.[29] This thesis remains viable and deserves our consideration as we turn our attention now to John's last supper, asking in particular about its eucharistic qualities, if any, despite the author's silence about bread and wine.

The Johannine last supper, better known as the Farewell Discourse, begins with a pre-Passover meal during which Jesus washes his disciples' feet (13:1–11). Beyond chapter 13, the actual eating and drinking of Jesus with his disciples receives no attention. Jesus assumes the role of an after-dinner speaker at a symposium, delivering his "last words" on a variety of topics. The major themes addressed in these speeches include Jesus' departure and return, his glorification, and his new commandment to love as he has loved. The final section of the discourse (chapter 17) is not so much a speech as an intercessory prayer by Jesus on behalf of his disciples. Running through this material are two red threads: (1) the abiding presence of Jesus and his Father with the disciples; and (2) the disciples' vocation in light of this holy communion.

We need to say more about these interlacing threads. Every chapter of the Farewell Discourse contains some variant on Jesus' promise to be with or in or among the disciples, whether or not they see him in his physical form (13:8, 13; 14:1–6, 16–28; 15:1–11, 26; 16:7, 12–16; 17:20–26). In several of these promises the Holy Spirit figures prominently as the Divine Force who effects the memory or presence of Jesus. The chief consequence of Jesus' abiding with his disciples is that they will bear much fruit (15:5). Indeed, Jesus prophesies that his followers will do even greater works than he has done when he goes to the Father (14:12). We can understand the nature of these works along two lines. First, the disciples are to love one another, humbly (13:1–17) and radically, even to the point of dying for their brothers and sisters (15:12ff.). But second, while they are doing this and sometimes even by means of doing this, they are to reach beyond their own circle of "friends" to proclaim Jesus' preeminence abroad in the world (13:16, 20; 15:26f.; 17:20–23).[30]

Because a number of commentators have taken the last reference cited above as the climax of the entire Farewell

Discourse, we should look at the passage with some care. Nearing the end of his high-priestly prayer, Jesus speaks these words:

> [20]I ask not only on behalf of these [the disciples present at the last supper] but also on behalf of those who will believe in me through their word, [21]that they may by one. As you, Father, are in me and I am in you, may they also be in us, so that the world may believe that you have sent me (*apesteilas*). [22]The glory that you have given me I have given them, so that they may be one, as we are one, [23]I in them and you in me, that they may be completely one, so that the world may know that you have sent me (*apesteilas*) and have loved them even as you have loved me.

We must stand in awe at the richness and complexity of this text. In many ways it defies interpretation. Nevertheless, we can draw three relatively simple conclusions from it. First, the saying combines, like no other in the gospel, Jesus' mutual indwelling of believers (including John's readers) with their missionary vocation. Second, the primary goal of the missionary activity mentioned here has to do with the world's coming to believe in the authenticity of *Jesus'* mission, which means acknowledging that it is really the living God of Israel who has sent him as the Divine Word made flesh. Third, Jesus ends his prayer, just as he presides over the dinner forum, in the role of prophet and missionary. He lays out the world's future, and this future hangs on the fulfillment of his work as it is continued in the work of his disciples.

What shall we make of all this data as we attempt now to determine the degree to which John's last supper was intended to be and understood by the first readers of the gospel to be "eucharistic"? Against the use of this key adjective stand the obvious facts that no reference is made to Jesus' flesh and blood and no use of the *eucharistein* word group can be found in chapters 13–17. On the other hand, the heavy concentration of Trinitarian language in the Farewell Discourse reminds us of the Pauline Lord's Supper material (1 Corinthians 11–14). So do Jesus' frequent prophecies and his references to the charismatic activity that will take place in the Johannine community after his departure, especially teaching and prophecy inspired by the Holy Spirit (14:25f.; 15:26; 16:7ff.; 16:13f.) and quite possibly healing as well.[31] Even more telling is the accent on mutual indwelling throughout the Farewell Discourse, which is exactly what we would expect to find in a eucharistic homily. Not surprisingly, we hear just this note, plus a reference to Jesus' mission from the Father, in 6:56f., which we have already identified as a eucharistic passage. There Jesus states: "Those who eat my flesh and drink my blood abide in me and I in them. Just as the living Father sent me, and I live because of the Father, so whoever eats me will live because of me." Though not an exact parallel, 6:56f. in some ways constitutes a preview of 17:20–23.

Noticing this phenomenon, Rensberger cites other marks of correspondence between 6:56f. and material in the Farewell Discourse (6:56 // 14:20 and 15:4–7; 6:57 //

14:19b and 15:9–10). He concludes–rightly, I think–that such data indicates an intention on the evangelist's part to present two complementary perspectives on the meal liturgy of his community. In other words, John has designed chapter 6 and chapters 13–17 to interpret each other.[32] When we add to this mix Lindars's thesis on the homiletical origins of Jesus' discourses, it becomes easy to imagine the Johannine last supper speeches as typical examples of what preachers in the community delivered to its eucharistic assemblies. Speaking prophetically in Jesus' name, these leaders would not necessarily intone words of the Lord over bread and wine. Their eucharistic prayers issued from the Spirit's guidance and varied from one occasion to the next ("... suffer the prophets to hold eucharist as they will"; Didache 10:7). Like their Lord, the Johannine leaders presided over church assemblies in the threefold role of prophet, teacher, and missionary. Readers of the gospel would know this protocol and automatically carry 6:51c–58 forward into their understanding of chapters 13–17.

It seems quite likely that John wishes to highlight the importance of his community's eucharistic assemblies in his telling of the Jesus story. Probably he had multiple reasons for doing so.[33] Insofar as our research is concerned, though, we may simply note the prominence among these reasons of John's desire to draw his readers more deeply into Jesus' redemptive mission from the Father. Nourished by his body and blood and renewed by the Holy Spirit that he and the Father have sent, Johannine believers will become, ever more effectively, his apostles in the world (13:16).

We have concentrated here on just two sections of the gospel, which together spell out John's vision of eucharistic mission. But we can detect much the same message in at least three other passages unique to the Fourth Gospel: the story of the wedding at Cana, where Jesus the true Bridegroom causes wine to flow in abundance so that his disciples come to faith in him (2:1–11); the post-resurrection appearance of Jesus to his disciples on Easter Sunday evening (possibly at a meal), when he grants them a rich measure of the Holy Spirit for their mission (20:19–23); and the epilogue to the gospel in which the risen Jesus hosts a breakfast for some of his disciples that quickly becomes a new missionary charge to the church leader Simon Peter (21:1–23). By means of these interlocking texts, each serving to elucidate the others, John encourages his readers in their eucharistic practice so that they will bear much fruit as they witness to Jesus as "the bread of God . . . which comes down from heaven and gives life to the world" (6:33).

The last book of our Christian Bible seems not to have emerged directly from the community that produced the Fourth Gospel. Although the author of Revelation employs titles and metaphors that are characteristic of those in the gospel (especially the christological titles "Word" and "Son of Man"; the noun "life" to denote authentic existence; and the self-designation "I am . . . " with Jesus as subject and a predicate nominative that is nonhuman), two significant differences between the writings stand out. First, the term "Lamb," prominent in both works as a title for Jesus, is designated by the Greek word *amnos* in the

Fourth Gospel, whereas only *arnion,* the Greek diminutive, serves this function in Revelation. Second, the Fourth Gospel typically presents a realized form of eschatology in which eternal life is understood as a present reality, while the author of Revelation tends to look forward to a future coming of Christ that alone will bring human life to its fulfillment. Still, these divergences do not prove that the two documents came into being under totally different circumstances. Many interpreters think that both writings emanate from a Johannine "school" that developed when the community of the Fourth Gospel migrated from Palestine or Syria to Asia Minor, where it became more diverse in its faith and practice.

On one issue close to the heart of our project the Fourth Gospel and Revelation have more in common than is generally supposed. This is the role of prophecy in congregational worship and mission. We have maintained, with Lindars and others, that many of the Fourth Gospel discourses attributed to Jesus have been shaped by prophetic homilies delivered to assemblies of the Johannine community. This process is suggested in the opening chapters of Revelation. Indeed, at the very beginning of his book, the author introduces himself as John, a servant of Christ and visionary who understands the report of his experience as "words of . . . prophecy" (1:1–3; see also 22:10). John is also careful to inform his readers that his visions came to him when he was "in the Spirit on the Lord's day" (1:10), that is, the day on which eucharistic assemblies typically took place during the New Testament era. Then, having related his initial encounter with the risen Christ (1:11–19), John writes prophetic messages to seven churches of Asia Minor couched in Christ's own words (chapters 2 and 3). Immediately afterward, the locus of John's prophecy shifts from earth to a heavenly sanctuary. Transported there, the author sees present and future events blending together within a paean of praise to God and the Lamb that issues from heavenly creatures and human disciples who have met their death as faithful witnesses (chapters 4ff.). Only at the end of Revelation does this scene shift, for then the heavenly Jerusalem descends to earth and the ultimate redemption of God's creation takes place (chapters 21–22). But even at this end point, worship remains the primary activity.

Why does John's prophecy take such a distinctive form, unique among the books of the New Testament? Perhaps no contemporary scholar has given a more satisfactory answer to this question than Richard Bauckham. Bauckham takes the position that for John worship on earth must play the key role because through it believers are most fully incorporated into God's redemptive activity and strengthened for their vocations as faithful witnesses of Jesus Christ to the nations and hostile powers. We find Bauckham's views pungently expressed in a small book titled *The Theology of the Book of Revelation.*[34] Several formulations of his thesis are worth quoting at some length:

> Since Christian prophets normally prophesied in the context of Christian worship meetings, we must assume that this is what John usually did. The reading of this written prophecy [that is, the Book of Revelation itself] in the worship service (1:3) was therefore

> a substitute for John's more usual presence and prophesying in person. . . . Especially prominent in the vision [of chapter 4] is the continuous worship by the four living creatures and the twenty-four elders. It is a scene of worship into which the reader who shares John's faith is almost inevitably drawn. We are thereby reminded that true knowledge of who God is, is inseparable from worship of God. . . . [In the worship visions of chapters 5 and 15 we see that] redemption of a special people from all the peoples is not an end in itself, but has a further purpose: to bring all the peoples to acknowledge and worship God. In the first stage of his work, the Lamb's bloody sacrifice redeemed a people for God. In the second stage, this people's participation in his sacrifice, through martyrdom, wins all the peoples for God. This is how God's universal kingdom comes. . . . Worship, which is so prominent in the theocentric vision of Revelation, has nothing to do with pietistic retreat from the public world. It is the source of resistance to the idolatries of the public world. . . . The truth of God is known in genuine worship of God. To resist idolatry in the world by faithful witness to the truth, the church must continuously purify its own perception of the truth by the vision of the utterly Holy One, the sovereign Creator, who shares his throne with the slaughtered Lamb. (pp. 3, 32, 101, 161, 162–163)

As far as I can tell, no one has seriously challenged these thoughts on the vital connection between worship and mission in John's visionary prophecy. Indeed, G. K. Beale's magisterial commentary on Revelation formulates this connection in ways that are altogether compatible with Bauckham's.[35]

For our purposes it is necessary to determine how, if at all, worship that is specifically eucharistic figures into John's prophecy. We can begin our discussion of this issue with another look at 1:10 ("I was in the Spirit on the Lord's day . . . "). We have already noted that the term *kyriake hemera* would have been read by many first-century believers as a reference to Saturday night or Sunday morning, when the church's most important worship—often eucharistic (1 Cor. 16:2; Acts 20:7–12; Did. 14:1)—took place. We may then go on to observe that for readers who knew Paul's traditions or writings, the phrase *kyriake hemera* would almost certainly resonate with the apostolic term *kyriakon deipnon* or "Lord's Supper" (1 Cor. 11:20; see also Did. 14:1, where *kyriaken de kyriou* is directly linked with the celebration of the eucharist). In addition, we ought to place some weight on the words immediately preceding 1:10, where our author commends himself to his readers as follows: "I John, your brother, who share with you in Jesus the persecution and the kingdom and the patient endurance (*synkoinonos en te thlipsei kai basileia kai hypomone en Jesou*), was on the island called Patmos . . . " (1:9) Both the expressions *synkoinonos* (a variant of koinonia) and *en Jesou* signal John's consciousness of a church-wide communion with Christ marked by severe affliction, participation in God's reign, and courageous behavior in the world, as if these were all parts of one reality.[36] If we were to posit a ritual event whereby these diverse experiences might be united in Jesus and prophetically interpreted on a regular basis, that would most likely be worship each Sunday at the Lord's table. Here we can pick up on a hint dropped by Beale, who points to the likelihood that even as John's book begins with a reference to the church's corporate worship (1:10), it also ends that way, with the solemn invocation: "Amen. Come Lord Jesus!" (22:20; *Amen, erchou kyrie Jesou*). But this prayer, as we have already seen, occurs in the Aramaic form *Maranatha* in 1 Cor. 16:22 and Didache 10:6, where the first text probably envisions eucharistic worship and the second one quite definitely does.

The weight of this evidence tilts in the direction of an expectation on John's part that his work would typically be read and heard in the course of worship at table. One commentator, Jürgen Roloff, has even concluded that with 22:20 John's book "moves directly into the liturgy of the eucharistic worship service."[37] This proposal seems overconfident, given the small amount of data available to us; but it is not impossible in the light of what we have discovered about 2 Cor. 9:15 as the beginning of a eucharistic prayer. Other investigators who see a eucharistic reference in 22:20 formulate their views more cautiously, but it is worth noting that this group of scholars is no small one and is not restricted to members of the more "catholic" denominations.[38]

Can we find other passages in Revelation that describe or allude to eucharistic meals? For many commentators, the most likely candidate is 3:20f., which occurs just at the end of Jesus' words to the seven churches of Asia Minor.

There the Lord announces, ostensibly to the church of Laodicea:

> [20]Listen (*Idou*)! I am standing (*hesteka*) at the door and knocking (*krouo*). If anyone hears my voice and opens the door, I will come into him/her (*eiseleusomai*) and have supper with him/her (*deipneso*) and that person with me. [21]The one who conquers, I will grant to him/her [to be] with me on my throne, as I myself have conquered and taken a seat with my Father on his throne. The one who has ears, let him/her hear what the Spirit is saying to the churches. [My translation.]

Although these words apply specifically to Laodicean believers, they seem also to provide a summary of Jesus' oracles to the other churches, for nowhere else in this letter section of Revelation (chapters 2 and 3) does the Lord extend a promise of intimate communion with himself or the sharing of his throne (the major symbol of divine honor in the worship visions that follow). These verses seem climactic and perhaps emblematic of how John understands worship.

Bauckham has made a plausible case that the prophetic invitation of verse 20 is based on a Jesus saying contained in Luke 12:35–38, where a master returns home from a wedding banquet late at night, knocks on the door of his house, and finds some of his servants ready to welcome him. These faithful servants are rewarded with a meal at which the master, atypically, serves them. Bauckham reasons that since the Lucan passage refers to the Parousia, and so, in all likelihood does Rev. 3:21, we must decide against a eucharistic reference in 3:20. For Bauckham, it too symbolizes Jesus' final coming.

But it is possible to accept a modified version of Bauckham's thesis about the provenance of 3:20 without assenting to his view that it looks forward only to the Parousia. Here a number of observations by Beale help to clarify the situation. While acknowledging a possible connection between Luke 12:35–38 and Rev. 3:20, Beale accents the more obvious dependence of 3:20 upon Song of Songs 5:2, where the bride-to-be speaks of her betrothed as follows: "the voice of my beloved, he knocks on the door. Open to me, my beloved." The scene depicted here fits so well with bridal imagery found elsewhere in Revelation (19:6–9) that we should consider Song of Songs the primary source for the invitation of Jesus in 3:20. And this conclusion, in turn, opens up the possibility that the passage refers to a communion with Jesus that can be realized in the current world order, immediately after one has repented (see 3:19). Strongly supporting such a view are the perfect tense *hesteka* and the present tense *krouo* ("I am standing... knocking"), which indicate durative action on Jesus' part. What the Lord desires is a response from the believer now that will issue in a communal supper. In Beale's words, "this is an invitation not for the readers to be converted but to renew themselves in a relationship with Christ that has already begun."[39]

Beale notes that a eucharistic meaning for 3:20 is also indicated by the use of the verb *deipneso* ("have supper with"). John's readers would probably recognize in this term the noun *deipnon,* which elsewhere in the New Testament describes the Lord's Supper (1 Cor. 11:20, 21, 25) or the last supper (Luke 22:20; John 13:2, 4; 21:20). In contrast to Bauckham, who thinks that the individualism of 3:20 ("If anyone [singular] hears my voice . . . ") counts against it as a eucharistic reference,[40] Beale asserts that the personalized appeal "accords best with a solution to the local problem [in Laodicea] and not with an expectation of the universal last coming."[41] Beale could have added that an individual reception of Christ's presence *in a communal setting* is exactly what Paul conceives of in his commentary on the Lord's Supper (1 Cor. 11:27–29). Moreover, in John 14:23, a passage from the last supper narrative of the Fourth Gospel, Jesus declares: "If anyone loves me, he/she will keep my word and my Father will love him/her and we will come and make a dwelling with him/her" (my translation). Here too, in a eucharistic tradition that the readers of Revelation could well have known, Jesus promises communion with an individual. To sum up: our evidence as a whole leads us toward the conclusion that Rev. 3:20 constitutes a direct reference to the table liturgies of first-century churches in Asia Minor.[42]

If that is so, we should consider two additional passages in Revelation as possible allusions to eucharistic meals. The first occurs in a hymn sung to God by the heavenly host: "Let us rejoice and exalt and give him the glory, for the marriage (*gamos*) of the Lamb has come, and his bride has made herself ready" (19:7). This is followed, just two verses later, by an angelic command to John: "Write this: Blessed are those who are invited to the marriage supper of the Lamb (*deipnon tou gamou*)" (19:9). Clearly, both passages point toward the final messianic banquet, yet each one also treats this future event as if it were somehow present. Those assembled in heaven for worship see that the marriage "has come" (*elthen*), and John informs his readers that they, as invited guests, are already blessed by that status. Given John's predisposition toward anticipating the future with his prophecy and his desire to draw his readers into a blending of the times through participation in heavenly worship, we must posit church gatherings on earth where such things could actually happen. The eucharistic framing of the book provided by 1:9–10 and 22:20, combined with the reference to eucharistic meals in 3:20, suggests that table liturgies would be assumed by John as the typical context for his readers' appropriation of his message. Consequently, it seems likely that these readers would have no difficulty recognizing 19:7, 9 as allusions to their experiences at the Lord's table.

We can now return to Bauckham's thesis on the central importance of worship for mission in John's Revelation. Bauckham tends to write generically of worship, without specifying its details — apart from stressing the prominence given to prophecy. Our study has led us toward the conclusion that it is particularly in the church's eucharistic liturgies, replete with prophecy and other charismatic phenomena, that John expected his readers to discern, accept, and grow up in their vocation as faithful witnesses. Through communing with Jesus at his supper, where they hear and see and touch him in a most personal way, they will enter ever more fully into his sacrificial mission to free the nations from their bondage to idolatry. Strengthened and purified by the blood of the Lamb, they will conquer Satan "by the word of their testimony" (12:11).[43]

Joining with Jesus in Mission

In this chapter we have surveyed a wide range of materials, most of them allusions to the practice of eucharistic meals rather than direct references. In the synoptic Gospels especially we found hints, previews, symbols, and echoes of meals related to the last supper. We also argued that the last supper accounts in Mark, Matthew, and Luke tend to radiate backward and forward in the gospel narratives to color each evangelist's work. First-century readers of the synoptics, themselves engaged in regular meal rituals, would have understood many of the sayings attributed to Jesus and stories about him eucharistically. Among the synoptic writers Luke appears to be most intentional about fashioning his life of Jesus with an eye toward the table liturgies of the church. He continues this approach in Acts, where he provides vignettes of meals that are not ecclesiastical in the strict sense but might be understood as proto-eucharists (see, e.g., 10:44–11:3; 16:25–34; 27:33–36).

In the Fourth Gospel we discovered a different phenomenon: an early "founding" of the eucharist (6:25–59) coupled with an extended last supper account (chapters 13–17). These two passages interpret each other to give a fuller picture of ritual meals than we are able to discern in any one of the synoptic traditions or any combination of them. We accepted as the most plausible theory for John's composition of his book Barnabas Lindars's hypothesis that many of the long dominical speeches in the gospel, as we now have them, represent layers of homilies on shorter sayings by Jesus or pronouncements in his name delivered by prophets during the congregation's worship assemblies. Given the prominence of chapters 13–17 in the gospel, we must guess that many of these assemblies involved table rituals. The Book of Revelation, which appears not to have originated with the author of the Fourth Gospel but nonetheless belongs to the Johannine tradition, can be read as a book of eucharistic prophecy. It begins with John's vision in the Spirit on the Lord's Day (1:10), when table liturgies would typically occur, and ends with the eucharistic prayer "Amen. Come, Lord Jesus!" (22:20). Moreover, the end of chapter 3, a summary of the risen Christ's counsel to the seven churches of Asia Minor, is best taken as an invitation to worship with the Lord at table (" . . . if you hear my voice and open the door, I will come in to you and eat with you . . . ").

As in the epistolary passages we have examined (see chapter 4), Jesus proves to be the dominant figure. Even when he is not visibly present at table — often the case in Acts — his activity is assumed. Indeed, Luke can organize his entire missionary narrative in Acts under the banner of a promise made by Jesus to his disciples at the last supper: "I confer on you, just as my Father has conferred on me, a kingdom, so that you may eat and drink at my table in my kingdom" (22:29f.). This kingdom, we have suggested (following Jacob Jervell), is the expanding reign of Christ through the spread of his church. With some frequency spiritual gifts issuing from the Messiah's reign are seen to be operative, or at least predicted, within the context of the meals we identified. These include healing (John 14:12; Acts 9:17–19; 20:9–11), inspired praise (Acts 2:46f.; 10:44–48), radical generosity (Acts 2:43–46; 6:1–6), sacrificial service (Mark 10:43–45; Luke 22:24–26; John 13:1–11), and, above all, prophecy (Luke 22:28–34; 24:27–49; John 13–17; Acts 27:33–36; Revelation as a whole). In fact, if we were to group the presiders at the meals we have examined into a single vocational category, we would have to choose the term "prophet." This title certainly applies to the author of Revelation, to Paul in Acts (see 13:1, 9; 27:34), to Jesus himself, and probably to many of the tradents of the synoptic gospel material. Here we do well to recall again Didache 10:7, where the author states: "But permit the prophets to hold eucharist as they will."

Finally, we must add that all of these prophetic figures show themselves to be also missionaries. Indeed, their chief goal as liturgical leaders is to welcome those at table (including those who do not yet believe) into an ever richer participation in God's redemption of the world through Jesus. With the Lord himself as primary Host their success is assured, whether the guests to be sent out require forgiveness and the ability to pass it on (Matthew), the courage to suffer as martyrs (Mark), the imagination to witness through their ordinary residential lives (Luke), the strength to love as Jesus did in the face of traumatic loss (John), or the steadfast endurance to testify faithfully in struggles against oppressive powers

(Revelation). Thus worship becomes the normal way to mission, especially worship at table, where the crucified and risen Messiah invites his followers most physically to join his self-offering for the life of the world (John 6:33, 51).

CHAPTER SIX

THE CALL TO EUCHARISTIC MISSION

We Christians have this meal. It is a meal from Jesus and about him, but above all with him in his mission as Messiah. Indeed, during the composition of the New Testament frequent celebrations of such meals with Jesus were considered basic to full participation by believers in God's ongoing redemption of the world. That, in short, is what we have presented throughout our study of eucharistic origins as its most consistent result. Can this finding offer significant help to the church today?

As we conclude our study, we shall attempt a restating of the individual conclusions that combine to produce our overall result. Our aim will be to formulate these component pieces in such a way that they enrich discussions between those trained primarily in biblical studies and those whose chief responsibility is the shaping of liturgical practice and missionary strategy in the church today. This conversation is no novelty. I suspect that various forms of it have been taking place from the earliest days of the church (for example, at the Apostolic Council described in Acts 15). In recent decades, however, the full set of partners in this Bible-liturgy-mission conversation has not come together all that often; and even when we have done so — mostly at large denominational or ecumenical conferences — we have tended to act as specialists intent upon protecting the boundaries of our disciplines. Consequently, we have not always spoken or listened with proper sensitivity toward our partners. On behalf of my own field I want to acknowledge considerable responsibility for these shortcomings. I am confident that we can all do better.

In this chapter I hope to present some biblical results that will prove useful to contemporary liturgists and missiologists — from whose responses, plus those of my biblical colleagues, I expect to learn a great deal. But before moving on with this summary I need to offer a proviso and an observation. The proviso is that if I make seemingly definitive statements about what I am calling eucharistic mission, I must trust readers to understand that I write primarily as a historian with an avid interest in the contemporary church's vocation. So, even if I am able to demonstrate that X was always and everywhere the case during the New Testament period (well, most of the time anyway!), my assertion should not necessarily be taken to mean that the prevalence of X in Christian churches of the twenty-first century will automatically produce more authentic proclamations of the gospel than we now enjoy. Only the Holy Spirit can lead us into such a future, though sometimes the Spirit's guidance takes the form of helping us remember what we have long forgotten (John 14:26). That is what I am banking on as I fashion the current chapter. As for the observation, I know that some documents on mission issuing from denominational and ecumenical study groups during the past thirty years or so appear already to be heading in directions that are supported by our study of the New Testament material.[1] In fact, I expect a few of my colleagues in other fields to report that what I offer here as exegetical discoveries became their own working hypotheses some years ago. If so, I am glad to be contributing to an emerging consensus. But unless I misjudge the current state of affairs, no combination of late-twentieth-century statements on liturgy and mission has so far managed to spark a broad-based movement in the church. If the readings of New Testament authors presented in our study hold up under close scrutiny, they may help to make key initiatives of the past few decades more accessible to everyday Christians and thus encourage a wider, richer practice of eucharistic mission.

Five Perspectives

How can we best enter into what this term, eucharistic mission, denotes? My suggestion is that we try five doorways, five different views of what eucharistic mission might signify for the church. Each of these (promise, presence, practice, abundance, and co-missioning for redemption) derives from our study as a whole; and each can be said, in its way, to summarize the biblical data we have examined that pertains to eucharistic origins. Moreover, all of the perspectives noted carry rich meanings already for the Christian life, and this is particularly so in the areas of liturgy and mission, where much has been written about them. My hope is that these doorway perspectives can function as meeting places where our three-way conversation will thrive. As we consider each of the five, I will try to move beyond my own specialty in biblical studies by introducing material from colleagues in other fields, along with a few personal testimonies about the eucharist that seem relevant.

Promise

Our study has highlighted Jesus' emphatic saying at the last supper that he will not drink of the fruit of the vine until he drinks it new in the kingdom of God (Mark 14:25). We treated this utterance not as a vow of abstinence but as a vision of the heavenly banquet at which Jesus expects soon to celebrate the fullness of his messianic rule. But Jesus also holds out this near future to his disciples as they share in the bread and wine that symbolize his ministry—especially his impending sacrifice. Most likely they did not understand much of what was happening on that night. If they caught any of Jesus' meaning, they would have experienced high hopes for an imminent completion of God's redemptive work (the final coming of the kingdom) and their own places in it. Jesus intends the stirring up of great expectations, not only at this last supper, but in all the subsequent meals where he appears as the Risen One or is honored by the church for his mighty acts and addressed in prayers and hymns even when he cannot be seen.

Throughout his ministry Jesus drew on the prophecy recorded in Is. 25:6ff., according to which "all peoples" will share in Israel's restoration on Mount Zion at a great feast. We have no reason to believe that after he was raised from the dead Jesus' longing and labor for the world's redemption in any way diminished. On the contrary, we see this mission intensifying in the church's eucharistic meals. What believers do by celebrating eucharistic meals is to join Christ's ministry for the life of the world (1 Cor. 15:24–28)—not apart from the church but through the agency of the church as Christ's body. This means that something of huge importance will always be taking place in our table liturgies, whether or not we feel personally edified on each occasion. The promise of the great feast opens itself up for the healing of the nations (Rev. 22:2), and we believers have the high privilege of sharing in the beginning of its fulfillment. Indeed, we may offer ourselves as living sacrifices to speed that fulfillment. Sections D and E of the World Council of Churches' *Baptism, Eucharist and Ministry* statement (1982) express well what I am trying to say here and are worth quoting at some length:

> [The eucharist] is a representative act of thanksgiving and offering on behalf of the whole world. The eucharistic celebration demands reconciliation and sharing among all those regarded as brothers and sisters in the one family of God and is a constant challenge in the search for appropriate relationships in social, economic, and political life. . . . As participants in the eucharist, therefore, we prove inconsistent if we are not actively participating in this ongoing restoration of the world's situation and the human condition. . . . The eucharist opens up the vision of the divine rule which has been promised as

> the final renewal of creation, and is a foretaste of it.... The very celebration of the eucharist is an instance of the Church's participation in God's mission to the world.... The eucharist is precious food for missionaries, bread and wine for pilgrims on their apostolic journey.[2]

Some readers may be tempted to dismiss the sentiments above as the overblown rhetoric of a committee. Yet our biblical study has found a basis for nearly all of these claims in the table liturgies of the first-century churches. Moreover, it has established that such liturgies, and the claims implicit in them, occupied a far more prominent place in the common life of New Testament believers than most of us have previously supposed.

The one accent we should add here is that the Crucified and Risen One presents himself at eucharistic meals with the special intention of helping us worship sacrificially. Answering the command to join Christ's mission becomes possible only when we can savor the eager and compassionate welcome that he extends to each of us personally (Matt. 11:28f.; Rom. 15:7ff.). No one has pictured this interchange more gracefully than George Herbert in his immortal poem "Love III." There Christ draws near with a smile to clasp the hand of a soul that shrinks from taking its place at the communion table because of the profound unworthiness it feels. Even when the soul is won over by Christ's welcome, it protests that only its service at the table can establish its personal worth. And then the poem simply ends, with a rhymed couplet that somehow resolves everything: "You must sit down, says Love, and taste my meat. So I did sit and eat." Jesus knows that we cannot truly offer ourselves to him until we have rested in his love and tasted fully of his loving service (John 13:1–11). It is this promise to each table participant that opens up God's promise to the world.

Both of these gospel visions, welcoming and self-offering, need to find their place in our eucharistic celebrations. Liturgically speaking, we have not put much emphasis on creating spaces for our responses to God's world-embracing promise. Perhaps we need to consider certain revisions of our rituals precisely here. In any event, it is vital that our orders of eucharistic worship (including sermons and other proclamations of the word) help to stimulate the high expectations that characterize Jesus' own participation in the meal. Throughout our worship we must grasp, as he does, that something momentous is happening for "all peoples." This means, I think, that we need to find opportunities within the worship itself and immediately afterward for committing ourselves to concrete sacrifices of praise and thanksgiving for the life of the world (Heb. 13:15f.).[3]

Presence

When we consider the notion of presence in eucharistic meals, we naturally think first of Jesus. But from the very beginning of the church's table tradition Christ's presence has been a complex one. In most liturgies taking place during the New Testament period he remained invisible to worshipers. Paul's writings on the Lord's Supper, for example, do not presuppose visionary experiences.

Still, some eucharistic visions of Jesus continued beyond the postresurrection meals of reunion with his disciples (Acts 10:41), especially, it seems, in Johannine circles.[4] For most worshipers, however, Jesus' presence was sensed through intentional acts of remembrance and through words spoken in his name by prophets of the congregation. This sharing at table in song, story, prayer, and oracular sayings called forth an imaginative participation by worshipers in the words and deeds of the Lord that occurred during his ministry. Such commemorations drew heavily on Sabbath and Passover practices but were also infused with great praise and thanksgiving to God for what had been recently accomplished through the Messiah and what was imminently to be completed.

In at least some of the New Testament churches liturgical references to what we now call the words of institution ("This is my body.... This is my blood") helped to surround the bread and wine served at eucharistic meals with a numinous aura. Already in Paul's congregations eucharistic food and drink were thought to be spiritual substances that automatically transmitted eternal life to those who consumed them (see 1 Cor. 10:1ff.). Paul discouraged extreme versions of this view, but he did not distance himself altogether from the conviction that Christ's sacrificial body and blood were uniquely combined with the ritual elements (1 Cor. 11:26f.). In the Fourth Gospel something close to an identification between body and bread and blood and wine occurs (John 6:51–56). Taking Jesus' atoning sacrifice into oneself through eating and drinking was a foundational experience for many New Testament believers, as it still is for worshipers today in the more catholic churches. But in neither Paul nor John does this consumption motif receive primary attention. Instead, it is Christ the royal president and host of the meal who comes to the foreground. This free and active messianic presence undercuts all theories that Christ is somehow confined to the food and drink and wishes to be worshiped in the ceremonial display of them.

In 1 Corinthians Paul plays up Christ's activity as judge, but only because the apostle believes that the contentious church to which he writes has distorted the meaning of the Lord's Supper and humiliated some of its members. If we excise the material relating to abuses from Paul's discourse on eucharistic meals in Corinth, we see Christ hosting his people primarily as a dispenser of charismatic gifts through the agency of the Spirit (chapters 12–14). This he does with the intention of calling believers ever more fully into his world-embracing body, thus enabling them to take up their vocations in his ongoing work of redemption (1 Cor. 15:24–28; 15:58–16:4). Later, in Romans, Paul adds to this picture by envisioning the eucharistic Christ also as leader of the congregation's praise to God and chief motivator of its evangelical outreach (Rom. 15:7ff.). In the Fourth Gospel the contours of Christ's presence at table become, if anything, richer still. Because the Jesus of the Farewell Discourse (chapters 13–17) is also the eucharistic Christ, we can posit that his activity during the worship of the community was experienced in a variety of ways. At table he is not only a humble servant and teacher of love by example but also a prophet who shows himself to be the Way, Truth, and Life, True Vine, sender of the Holy Spirit, and Intercessor par excellence. Through all these facets of his eucharistic identity the Johannine Christ helps to prepare his disciples for their apostolic vocation (John 13:16; 15:16; 17:18). In the strongest possible way Christ makes known to those who approach his table that he ardently desires their company, just as they are (John 14:18–23; 15:12; 17:2f.; 21:12; see also Luke 22:15; Rom. 15:7). He welcomes believers with compassion, refreshment, and forgiveness (Matt. 11:28ff.; 26:28). But then he also summons them to renewed discipleship (John 20:11–23; 21:9–22); for more than anything else the eucharistic Christ of the New Testament presents himself as a vigorous king, moving decisively toward the final appropriation of his rule over all creation.

Having said this, however, we need to add immediately that the Lord of the eucharistic table continues to bear the marks of the cross. He moves forward in his messianic vocation, not by transcending suffering and death, but by embracing them. In this way he receives all the pains and griefs we bring to the eucharist. None of us comes unworthily because of doubt or fear or anger or desolation of any sort. Jesus has been in all those places ("My God, my God, why have you forsaken me?"), and in a way he still is. He gathers up all the variants of our human condition into his table ministry and communes with us in their midst, blessing us through them and strengthening us for his mission. Typically that is not an experience of ecstasy or complete healing for us (although both of these can occur), but of renewed hope. Much has been written about Jesus' real presence at the eucharist. At the same time, however, we also need to take note of what

Donald Gray has called the "real absence" of the Lord.[5] In all honesty, we have to admit that we do not often feel altogether embraced by the Risen One at table. That is understandable because he himself does not yet enjoy that full communion. He knows how incomplete his presence with us now remains. God's kingdom has not come with finality. Much evil continues to exist. And so Jesus, on the other side of the resurrection, longs for our presence with him there (Matt. 26:29; John 17:24). This means that our remembrance, praise, and thanksgiving at table must usually be disciplined acts of faith, not spontaneous outbursts of joy. Every eucharistic celebration exposes the "not yet" of our lives in Christ, and this too must be incorporated into our rituals. One can easily imagine the groaning in the Spirit depicted in Rom. 8:18–27 as part of a eucharistic liturgy. Students of the Old Testament have taught us that the distance between lamentation and thanksgiving, especially in the Psalms, is not great.

Worshipers at table during the New Testament period did not limit themselves to language about Jesus when naming the presence of the divine in their liturgies. God, rather than Jesus, received most of their praises (e.g., 1 Cor. 14:25, 28; 2 Cor. 9:13–15; Phil. 2:11; Eph. 5:20; Col. 3:17; 1 Pet. 4:11). The eucharistic celebrations depicted in 1 Corinthians 11–14 and John 13–17 are full of what we can only call Trinitarian language; and our study has shown that the Holy Spirit in particular looms large in the consciousness of believers because of the charismatic gifts that surface so frequently at table rituals. We shall say more about these below. In addition, we should note that God's kingdom, while not fully present, is thought to be radiating its saving power toward worshipers in a special way. Jesus' own visionary words at the last supper call attention to the kingdom's nearness (Mark 14:25), and we find a strong affirmation of it in Paul's epigrammatic commentary on the conflicted meal practices in Rome: "For the kingdom of God is not food and drink but righteousness and peace and joy in the Holy Spirit" (Rom. 14:17). What the apostle seems to be telling his readers here is that whether or not they actually eat and drink when they sit down together at the Lord's table (given the legitimacy of differences among them about what food should be served, and when), they can all expect to receive the benefits of the kingdom through the Spirit that indwells their assemblies. Dovetailing with this view is Paul's exposition of the Lord's Supper as an apocalyptic event, where the age to come overlaps with this present age in a unique way (1 Cor. 10:11; compare also Rom. 12:1f.). Much the same outlook characterizes the petition of the Johannine Jesus in his high-priestly prayer at table on behalf of his disciples: "As you Father are in me and I am in you, may they also be in us so that the world may believe that you have sent me. The glory that you have given me I have given them, so that they may be one, as we are one, I in them and you in me . . ." (17:21–23). Clearly, Jesus expects an answer to his prayer in the present world order. The glory of God has already appeared (perhaps in the eucharistic assembly itself), and so the union of believers with himself and the Father can to some degree take shape on the stage of human history even now as an effective sign to the unbelieving world. Here we see realized eschatology writ large; and its form is distinctively eucharistic (see also Heb. 12:22–24).

Building on passages like these, some interpreters of the eucharist have pictured the ritual as a Grand Intersection of all times and places. This view has usually been associated with the Orthodox branches of Christianity, but it is not at all limited to that spectrum of believers. Roman Catholic exegete Bonnie Thurston cites three Protestant scholars (F. F. Bruce, Krister Stendahl, and Eduard Schweizer) to support her conclusion that for the Corinthians, "all of time was mystically present in the moment of time in which the bread was broken and shared and the wine poured and passed."[6] Anglican priest and physicist John Polkinghorne, commenting on 1 Cor. 11:26, writes that the eucharist "is both the commemoration of Calvary and the anticipation of the heavenly banquet in the kingdom of God." And then he goes on to state: "I would add my own testimony to the mysterious but undeniable experience of the sense of meeting past event and future hope in the present reality of the Eucharist."[7] Although we cannot possibly apprehend very much of this compressed presence in any one service of worship, we can catch glimpses of its breathtaking grandeur with the eyes of faith. In this meal God's grace works intensely — perhaps more so than in any other moment known to us — to restore and inhabit "all things" (1 Cor. 15:26–28). Polkinghorne stretches our imaginations even further when he posits that the new creation of which Paul writes (2 Cor. 5:17) is best understood as a redeemed form of matter that presents itself first of all in Christ's resurrected body and becomes uniquely available to believers at the eucharist.[8] The results of our inquiry suggest that Polkinghorne's speculation is no rash judgment and in fact runs with the grain of the New Testament eucharistic witnesses. We find rich food for thought here, especially as we ponder the ecological dimensions of the church's mission. How can we best incorporate concerns about the redemption of matter into our liturgical practice?

As we end our discussion of the perspective we are calling "presence," we do well to consider one more form of it in the eucharistic meals of the New Testament churches, and in our own eucharists. That is the presence of ourselves — to ourselves, to others, and especially to God, all of which can be extraordinary blessings in a chaotic culture like ours. We rightly complain that our daily lives are too frequently ruled by distractions. We often feel fogged in by too much data, obsessed with matters that seem hugely important but which, in our hearts, we know to be far from ultimate. But if our biblical witnesses are telling the truth, we have in the eucharist an opportunity to focus on who we are apart from the powers of this age, on our own "real presence." Entering into God's promise with our neighbors around the table can bring us home to ourselves, not in ways that feed our narcissism but in those that reveal to each of us our distinctive identity and purpose for living within God's redemptive plan.

Much has been written in recent years about the corporate nature of the eucharist. The church, we are told, does not lay on this feast to nurture our private pieties but to build up the whole congregation, the people of God as a group. That insight is true as far as it goes, and our study has confirmed it. At the same time, we have to honor the fact that each communicant eats and drinks and meets the eucharistic Lord in a particular manner. The consciousness of each person in corporate worship has its own integrity, its own gifts to offer, its own cries for help. Paul picks up on this feature of eucharistic participation when he counsels the Corinthians to "Let a person at worship continue to evaluate him- or herself (*dokimazeto . . . heauton*) and in that process eat of the bread and drink of the cup. For whoever eats and drinks without discerning the body (*diakrinon to soma*) eats and drinks judgment upon him- or herself "(1 Cor. 11:28f.; my translation).

Because this passage ends on a frightening note, interpreters have tended not to spell out the positive goal Paul has in mind here. What the apostle hopes for is that each Corinthian will develop the habit of self-evaluation at table, not (primarily) to discover some hidden sin but rather to see oneself more clearly as a vital and unique body part within the assembly of believers. Neither of the two prominent verbs used by Paul in these verses really means "to judge." Instead they both denote a deep perceiving, a probing of things in their essence. Earlier in 1 Corinthians Paul attributed the ability of believers to discern the ways of God to the activity of the Holy Spirit (2:6–16); and that conviction is surely present as well in his discussion of the Lord's Supper. Because of the Spirit's intensive presence at the eucharistic celebration, we are able — if open to that presence — to see ourselves with the loving eyes of God, and our neighbors as ourselves.[9]

As a result, we can then offer ourselves up for God's mission, along with our neighbors at the Lord's table, who are engaged in the same process of discernment. Paul elaborates on this sequence of events in Romans 12:

> I appeal to you, therefore, brothers and sisters, by the mercies of God, to present your bodies as a living sacrifice, holy and acceptable to God, which is your spiritual worship. Do not be conformed to this world but be transformed by the renewing of your minds, so that you may discern (*eis to dokimazein*) what is the will of God — what is good and acceptable and perfect. (1–2)

At the Pauline eucharistic meals, it seems, personal acts of discernment typically led to a corporate self-offering, which in turn led to corporate discernment.[10] All of this was empowered by the Spirit to the end of building up the body for its apostolic vocation (see the fuller discussion of 1 Corinthians 11 and Romans 12 in chapters 3 and 4). If we want to promote such activities in our eucharists today, we will have to think seriously about restructuring our liturgical spaces and times. More periods of meditative silence, more opportunities for physical movements of self-offering, and fresh modalities for expressing the renewal of our common mind in Christ may be deemed appropriate.

Practice

These thoughts guide us back to a closer consideration of what actually happened when first-century believers gathered for worship at table. Here we have to tread cautiously because the New Testament provides no church bulletins listing "orders of service"; and the Didache, which does offer directions for how to conduct a eucharistic liturgy, concedes that prophets should be allowed to lead the service as they see fit (10:7), presumably under the guidance of the Holy Spirit. We must assume a considerable diversity of practice in the early churches.

Still, we can sketch out a few details of a typical first-century table ritual with relative confidence. We have found it highly probable, for example, that prior to Paul's conversion Jewish believers in the Jerusalem congregation had developed a eucharistic meal that combined an active remembering of Jesus' last supper and post-resurrection appearances with a fervent expecting of his imminent return as messianic host at God's kingdom banquet. Moreover, it seems likely that from very early days such meals took place after sundown each week as an extension of the Sabbath. This meant that for Jewish believers the suppers occurred on what for them was early Sunday morning, close to the hour of the resurrection (see Mark 15:2). We also know that at Corinth the Lord's Supper was likewise celebrated as an evening meal, almost certainly on "the first day of the week" (1 Cor. 16:2). We have argued that due to the influence of Paul and other Jewish missionaries the weekly practice of the Jerusalem church came to prevail in a large number of Gentile congregations (see Acts 20:7–12), even though Gentiles were not typically asked to observe the Sabbath itself as a prelude to their eucharistic meals.[11] We find no evidence in the New Testament that such rituals were anything other than full meals.

This information leads us naturally to the conclusion that most worship at table took place in the dining rooms of private houses and apartments (another analogy with Sabbath meals) or, when the number of participants became large, in rented halls set up for dining. The majority of scholars today agree with this assessment, often pointing to Rom. 16:23, where Paul mentions a Corinthian patron named Gaius who acted as host to the entire church in that city. This passage indicates either that Gaius paid for space that could accommodate all of the Corinthian house churches at once or, more likely, that he put his large home at the disposal of the whole assembly once a week. Archaeological evidence suggests that some private residences of the first century would allow for up to fifty people at dinners, if rooms adjoining the dining room, including the atrium, were used.[12]

What did these spaces look like? Frescoes of Hellenistic banquets show the guests reclining on couches or floor cushions around three sides of a low table. The open side of the "C" figure or "triclinium" formed by such an arrangement was used for serving. Many New Testament passages, including several describing Jewish meals at which Jesus is present as a guest, suggest this setting (see Mark 2:15; 14:3 and parallels; Luke 7:37; 11:37; 24:30). So do the gospel depictions of the last supper (Matt. 26:20; Mark 14:18; Luke 22:14; John 13:12, 23). Nevertheless, we should not simply assume banquetlike scenes for celebrations of eucharistic meals in the New Testament churches. In smaller houses and for informal worship, higher tables surrounded by benches, chairs, or stools would have been employed.[13] In poorer houses and in tents (where we can imagine Paul lodging on some of his missionary journeys) people sat on the floor or ground to eat. The one common feature of early table worship is obvious: it took place in spaces that were more like dining rooms (or our modern living rooms) than temples and other locations officially designated for religious use.[14]

For larger gatherings that required the use of more than one room, we should envision multiple tables. On such occasions it would have been virtually impossible to provide "equal" place settings for all, so we have to guess that some participants occupied better places than others. But perhaps these spaces were rotated so that eventually everyone could enjoy them. We find plenty of material in Jesus' teachings to encourage the introduction of such a practice (Matt. 6:5; Luke 12:37; 14:7–11; 22:24–27; John 13:3ff.). It is probable that those serving the food and drink did not assume this responsibility on a permanent basis; but because Jesus referred to himself as a table servant (Luke 22:24ff.) and acted as one (John 13:3ff.), worshipers in the New Testament churches may have sought this role as a special honor.

We have no basis for positing the display of christological symbols during these early eucharistic meals. The cross, the Chi-Rho, and the fish pictogram are not attested in New Testament times. We can, however, imagine the use of a symbolic seat of authority called the *bema*.[15] In homes, a chair or high cushion might have served this purpose. According to the gospel writers, Jesus taught, healed, and prophesied while sitting (Matt. 5:1; 13:1f.; 15:29; 24:3 and parallels), which leads us to suspect that prophets and teachers in the early congregations likewise delivered their messages and led worship from this posture. Finally, we need to keep in mind that most worshipers at table could position their bodies so as to see one another face-to-face if they wished and, in smaller gatherings, converse with one another. They could also move around the house or hall with relative ease during the meal, especially between courses. No pews got in their way when they circulated to exchange the holy kiss that seems to have occurred at most gatherings for worship, at least in the Pauline churches (1 Cor. 16:20; 1 Thess. 5:26).

How did events unfold at the early eucharistic meals? Again we have to allow for much diversity of practice and a fluidity that was ensured by the Holy Spirit's guidance (1 Cor. 12:11). But the following elements of worship must have occurred regularly at congregational meetings, though not necessarily in just this order: (1) a time of assembling and mutual greeting that would have lasted a while because some church members had little or no control over their personal schedules (1 Cor. 11:33); (2) a meal with multiple courses that permitted group activities in between the courses or, if the Hellenistic symposium model was followed, after the main meal was concluded; (3) a breaking and blessing of bread in which thanksgivings for the work and presence and imminent reappearance of Jesus predominated; (4) a similar blessing and thanksgiving over wine; (5) a common partaking of the consecrated bread and wine that symbolized the unity in Christ of all worshipers present (1 Cor. 10:16f.; 11:27–29);[16] (6) an opportunity for visitors to express themselves, especially when they were led to declare their faith or an intention to be baptized (Acts 2:46f.; 1 Cor.

14:23–25); (7) one or more periods of reading from the scriptures and apostolic writings; (8) times devoted to singing, proclamations of the gospel (not yet labeled as sermons), and teaching; (9) petitions and intercessions offered by worship leaders as well as other members; (10) a confessing of sins to one another, accompanied by efforts toward reconciliation between estranged parties (Matt. 18:15–22; 26:28; see also James 5:16); (11) the commissioning of some church members to new ministries through prayer and the laying on of hands (Acts 6:5f.; 13:1–3); (12) one or more periods for ministering to one another by means of charismatic gifts — especially prophecy — all of which were expected to build up believers for their vocation as "living sacrifices" (1 Corinthians 12–14; Rom. 12:1–8; 1 Pet. 4:10f.); (13) moments of prayerful discernment that centered upon such matters as the state of one's spirit before God and the evaluation of prophetic messages claiming to disclose God's will for the congregation (1 Cor. 14:29–33; Rom. 12:1f.); (14) corporate gestures of self-offering to God that served to confirm decisions made by the community about its next step within "the work of the Lord" (Rom. 12:1; 2 Cor. 8:5; see also 1 Cor. 15:24f., 58); (15) the presentation or promise of spiritual and material resources needed to implement these decisions, including money; (16) final thanksgivings and benedictions for sending worshipers on their way.

A few comments on these features of eucharistic worship may help to fix the service as a whole more precisely in our imaginations. Here we draw on the winsome account of a visit to a Christian table ritual in Rome as told by one Publius, a fictional character in Robert Banks's well-researched little book, *Going to Church in the First Century.*[17] To begin, we cannot tell for certain whether leadership functions at the early eucharistic meals were typically performed by just one person or even by a small group of persons. Presumably those recognized in the congregation as apostles, prophets, and teachers tended to initiate activities during the worship (1 Cor. 12:28); but houseowners or patrons may well have offered the major portions of prayers over bread and wine. In any case, other church members might well have added their own words to such prayers since we have evidence that individuals in the congregation periodically lifted up their voices to acknowledge the presence of Jesus in their midst.[18] Second, the communal eating and drinking that belonged to the Lord's Supper as Paul knew it seems to have been bracketed by a blessing of bread that preceded it and a blessing of the cup that signaled its end (1 Cor. 11:23–25).[19] Yet we cannot assume that all churches followed exactly this order or that words resembling those spoken by Jesus at the last supper over the bread and wine were always recited (see, for example, Didache 9–10). Third, a great deal of bodily movement, touching, and verbal expression characterized eucharistic worship during the New Testament period. But there must have been other times when individuals just sat or reclined by themselves in silence, especially for self-examination (1 Cor. 11:27f.) and the prayerful evaluation of teachings or prophetic messages (1 Cor. 14:26–32). Even those segments of worship in which spiritual gifts manifested themselves could have been relatively quiet.[20] Congregations probably varied a great deal in expressions of exuberance

(1 Cor. 14:37–40; Eph. 5:19f.; 1 Thess. 5:16–21). Fourth, despite fluctuations in the emotional lives of worshipers, a tone of praise and thanksgiving resounded throughout the early eucharistic services. This quality of worship was not restricted to particular prayers or other utterances in which actual words of gratitude were used. Instead, the worshipers experienced it as a kind of atmosphere pervading all their activities—and as a discipline (Phil. 4:6; 1 Thess. 5:18; Eph. 5:20).

Perhaps these few observations have already set the wheels of our minds whirring toward new designs for our eucharistic liturgies, designs that might highlight their original missionary intentions. Inevitably, many questions arise here. Can we, should we, reinstate the communal meal in at least some of our table rituals? If so, do small group settings become necessary, even in larger congregations? And what kind of liturgical spaces will then be needed? Can we, should we, allow for the wide variety of activities that characterized first-century table worship? In particular, can we open ourselves to the Spirit's guidance so that a rich array of charismata can come into play? Is it possible for us to conduct some of what we now call church business within periods of eucharistic worship? Can we allow prayerful discernment to shape our decision making on these matters? Can we begin to see our eucharistic services, from start to finish, as missionary events during which visitors are brought closer to the Body of Christ and the Kingdom, whatever the level of their participation, and we so-called insiders are built up for our vocation as witnesses of the gospel?

However we answer these questions, we do well to reflect on several thoughts about the eucharist offered by two contemporary teachers. With some urgency the missiologist Anthony Gittins poses these questions for us: "How does the eucharist relate to our ongoing conversion? As regards the participants, does the eucharist we celebrate serve to reflect, endorse, and redeem — or to suppress and deny the actual person we are and the experience we bring to the assembly?"[21] And then, answering his own questions, Gittins proposes that we consider our table liturgies as a "forum both for the acceptance and for the transformation of the bodily experiences of believers and as a ritual of incorporation into the life of the community, rather than as an empty ceremony destined to remain peripheral to it."[22] Ethicist Larry Rasmussen echoes these sentiments and elaborates upon them:

> ...[S]acraments are practices supreme only if and when they embody and show forth their connectedness to the rest of life.... For Christians, the Supper of the Lamb is a central and centering event...it is this when, for example, it breaks down the barriers between races, classes, gender, and culture by welcoming all to the welcome table; when it connects with the many hungers of the world, including physical malnutrition, and moves people to alleviate them as best they can; when it celebrates the blessed creation in gratitude for life itself and recognizes God in, with, and under simple ordinary things like the fruit of the vine; when it brings judgment and a call to repentance to all the tables where the stranger is not welcomed as a partner; and when it means

new beginnings for a forgiven and refreshed people around an inclusive table community.[23]

These comments by Gittins and Rasmussen, all of them compatible with the findings of our study, take us a long way toward the formulation of concrete options for our practice of eucharistic mission today.

Abundance

By using the word "feast" in the title of our study and by exploring the lively influence of the Kingdom banquet both on the ministry of Jesus (especially at the last supper) and on the table rituals of the early church, we have been suggesting all along that abundance is a very good term, indeed, for characterizing the eucharistic meals of the first believers. We should not think here of elaborate menus — at least not regularly. Most Jews and Gentiles in the Greco-Roman world of the first century got by on simple Mediterranean diets consisting largely of grains, fruits, vegetables, olive oil, and fish, with little meat and wine served only on special occasions. Paul takes great pains to distinguish the common meal at the Lord's Supper from the overeating and drinking that typified Hellenistic banquets (1 Cor. 11:20–22). But neither should we envision early church meals as austere occasions with short rations. Sabbath suppers tended to be celebrative, perhaps with a special cake or meat dish not served during the rest of the week. Jewish believers probably continued practices of this kind in their Sunday commemorations of the last supper. In addition, the generous sharing of resources that marked the meals of the Jerusalem community (Acts 2:42ff.; 6:1–6) and those of Gentile churches as well (2 Cor. 8:1–5; Heb. 13:15f.) would have contributed to a feeling of plenty among worshipers ("God is able to provide you with every blessing in abundance, so that by always having enough of everything, you may share abundantly in every good work"; 2 Cor. 9:8). This sense of overflow must have been evident also to those who visited the church's table rituals or just heard about them (Acts 2:47).

If we were to ask a group of early believers how they experienced abundance of life during their eucharistic meals, they would almost certainly point to dimensions of their common worship like the following: praise, thanksgiving, and self-offering; clarification and renewal of vocation; sharing and exchanging of spiritual gifts; strengthening of faith through personal testimonies; mutual honoring and upbuilding of one another in love; repentance, forgiveness, and reconciliation; refreshment and healing; tastes and visions of God's kingdom; enjoyment of Jesus' presence; communion with the hosts of heaven; discernment and articulation of the boundaries between this age and the next and of God's will for the present; welcoming visitors, both believers and unbelievers. Through the centuries interpreters have repeatedly highlighted these features of the church's communal life; and we hardly want to argue that during the first century they occurred mostly in the context of table worship. Yet the New Testament witnesses we have examined do regularly associate manifestations of richness in Christ with eucharistic meals (see esp. 2 Cor. 8:9), perhaps more than with any other repeatable event known to us in the church's formative years. This suggests at the very least that practicing such rituals carelessly or infrequently or not at all would have seemed to the earliest believers a kind of mindless self-deprivation. In their minds, such laxity would not only result in the stunting of personal growth for individual believers; it would also cripple the church's universal mission.

Paul offers a happier alternative. In many ways 2 Cor. 4:15 stands as a motto for the abounding of God's work in the eucharistic feasts of the church. Writing about his apostolic ministry, Paul tells his readers: "everything is for your sake, that grace (*charis*), extended (*pleonazein*) through ever more people, may cause thanksgiving (*eucharistia*) to overflow (*perisseuein*) to the glory (*doxa*) of God."[24] The idea here seems to be that the increasing number of individuals who will be joined to Christ's Body in the near future will render more and more thanks to God, thus enlarging the divine stature for further manifestations of grace on an unprecedented scale.[25] One could object that in 2 Cor. 4:15, Paul does not think specifically of eucharistic meals when he extols the giving of thanks; but it cannot be accidental that later in this same epistle the Greek words *charis, eucharistia, pleonazein, perisseuein, doxa,* and their close synonyms multiply and combine with one another as in no other New Testament passage to describe table worship (see 2 Corinthians 8–9 and chapter 4).[26] And we must add that precisely here we find Paul also linking table worship with corporate acts of self-offering by believers (i.e., gifts of money for poor believers in Jerusalem), while interpreting the latter as manifestations and expansions of God's grace for all humanity (see esp. 8:1–5; 9:6–15). It seems best to consider 4:15 a first glimpse of this grand eucharistic mission.

A number of twentieth-century Christians have written specifically on the abundance of life that emerges from eucharistic worship and follows upon it. Many observations made by these authors seem to dovetail with the results of our study and (in my view) deserve a wider hearing in the church than they have yet received. Anthony Gittins, for example, notes that one consequence of reading 2 Cor. 4:15 eucharistically is that the church needs to see itself more intentionally as an agent for the increase of thanksgiving everywhere in the world, not just among people of faith. The ritual of the eucharist produces a eucharistic people whose mission it is to take a stand against poverties and scarcities of every sort in all their relationships.[27] J. G. Davies, writing in 1966 and also treating 2 Cor. 4:15 as a reference to eucharistic meals, boldly announces that "the goal of mission can indeed be defined as the increase of thanksgiving."[28] Then he goes on, in good Pauline fashion, to affirm that true thanksgiving always issues in sacrifice:

> Christian gratitude . . . is a confession, a laudatory heralding of what God has done and is doing in the world. That is why in the prayer written by Bishop Reynolds of Norwich (1599–1676) and usually called "The General Thanksgiving," we pray: "give us a due sense of all thy mercies, that our hearts may be unfeignedly thankful, and that we shew forth thy praise, not only with our lips but in our lives; by

> giving up ourselves to thy service." ... Thanksgiving is both a liturgical act and a direction of living.[29]

Rowan Williams echoes these thoughts when he writes that "the act of [eucharistic] praise involves a costly giving — not simply the giving up of time, but the re-orientation of hope and imagination outwards. Praise, celebration, adoration, is a direction away from self-preoccupation, anxiety, defensiveness."[30] And, we might add, the public naming of particular gifts from God in eucharistic praise actually begets an awareness of new gifts — as well as new possibilities for moving forward in God's will. It is fair to ask whether our current eucharistic liturgies allow this dialectic of thanksgiving and sacrifice to become concrete in real decisions for missionary action.

In his exquisite little collection of essays *For the Life of the World,* originally produced as a study guide for a conference of the National Student Christian Federation in 1963 and now in its sixth U.S. printing, Alexander Schmemann sets forth a view of the eucharist that has until recently seemed distinctive to the Orthodox branches of the church.[31] But if the results of our study hold up, Schmemann is also presenting accurate reflections of what many first-century believers experienced during their table worship. Perhaps most striking in his exposition of the sacrament is his insistence that eucharistic worshipers process or ascend out of "this world" to become "partakers of the world to come."[32] Here Schmemann, and the Orthodox tradition generally, are at one with the New Testament understanding of eucharistic meals as boundary events where the new creation and the kingdom of heaven intersect with everyday life in transformative ways. At the Lord's Table worshipers enter even now into something of the world renewed, the world freed from death-dealing entropies imposed by ordinary time and space. As Schmemann puts it, "This is not an 'other' world, different from the one God has created and given to us. It is our same world, *already* perfected in Christ, but *not yet* in us. It is our same world, redeemed and restored, in which Christ 'fills all things with Himself.'"[33] Schmemann's biblical reference here is to Eph. 1:23, but images of eucharistic meals from Heb. 12:22ff. and the Apocalypse also seem to be in the background as he writes.

Because Schmemann believes that worshipers, by God's mysterious grace, already sit with Christ at table "in the heavenly places" (Eph. 2:6), he can assert that joy becomes the predominant feeling-tone of the eucharist. Such joy, he writes, is the special mark "of recovered childhood, that free, unconditional and disinterested joy which alone is capable of transforming the world."[34] Schmemann finds a biblical foundation for this view in Rom. 14:17 ("For the kingdom of God is not food and drink but righteousness, peace, and joy in the Holy Spirit").[35] Readers may recall that on exegetical grounds we have taken Paul's confession here to be an intentional description of the church's eucharistic meals (see chapter 4). Is it possible for mainline Christians to allow some form of this expansive mysticism into their practice of the eucharist? By the same token one might ask members of the various Orthodox churches about the degree to which they are able to flesh out their rich heritage of eucharistic ascension in missionary outreach for the life of the world.[36]

Three contemporary authors call our attention to an overflow of discernment that occurs within table worship itself or in life situations that seem best described as eucharistic. *The Eucharist and the Hunger of the World* has become one of Catholic theologian Monika Hellwig's best-known books, and justly so. Hellwig believes that our eucharists display authenticity only when they serve to extend the redemption won through Jesus, the Bread of Life, to all people. She knows that many well-intentioned "feeding programs" in the church falter because their organizers do not recognize and address the deeper needs of humans. For her, dealing effectively with the multiple hungers of the world requires Christians to proceed from eucharistic celebration:

> What we learn from the Eucharist . . . is that the Christian mission to the hungry is to enter into their need and find ways to satisfy their hunger, to challenge the structures of the world that help keep some peoples and some populations hungry, to question the sick and inordinate desires that maintain those structures. In other words, the Christian mission to the hungry is to discern the substitute satisfactions that lead those of us in the wealthier nations to entrenched positions from which we cannot even see or hear the cries of the distressed. This in turn means the need to discern the real hungers behind the substitute satisfactions.[37]

Here Hellwig treats discernment as an essential feature of the eucharistic liturgy, and this has been confirmed by our study. What Paul would add is that such discernment always involves a real tasting of God's mercies along with our self-offering, which then clarifies further our insight into God's purposes (Rom. 12:1f.). Grace abounds in eucharistic worship, and so therefore do discernment and the courage to act boldly.

Parker Palmer stresses the vital role played by human community in the appropriation of abundance, drawing especially on the gospel stories of Jesus' feeding the five thousand. Community, he insists, is "the context in which abundance can replace scarcity." I think Palmer means that people cannot begin to share generously in circles beyond their close friends and neighbors, unless these more heterogeneous gatherings regularly become occasions for the growth of mutual trust. But that is something of a miracle.

> Even as we act to evoke community, we must remember that community itself is a gift to be received, not a goal to be achieved.... Community and its abundance are always there, free gifts of grace that sustain our lives. The question is whether we are able to perceive it and receive it. This is likely to happen only when someone takes a vulnerable public act assuming abundance but aware that others may cling to the illusion of scarcity. That is the kind of act that makes Jesus' story [the feeding of the five thousand], and ours, worthy of telling.[38]

In this writing Palmer does not refer specifically to the eucharist or to the Christ who creates holy communion with us at table. But if we have read the New Testament evidence accurately, we should expect to find especially in our meal rituals just the sort of vulnerable public acts Palmer hopes for, acts that will inspire us to discern and enter into God's abundant life.

"The Gift of Consciousness," Ann Belford Ulanov's 1998 Women in Church and Ministry lecture to the Princeton Seminary community, makes no claim to being a discourse on the eucharist.[39] As she herself notes, her observations stem largely from her practice as a Jungian analyst. Nevertheless, when we adopt the perspectives formed in the course of our study, we can hardly avoid reading some passages in Ulanov's talk as late-twentieth-century renditions of what many early believers must have thought and felt about their worship at table. For example, having cited a wealth of clinical evidence for the ultimate relativity of all human consciousness, she states:

> If we can tolerate this relativity of consciousness, its necessity and preciousness and its ephemeral nature, we can be freed from consciousness, and freed for consciousness of our ego as looked at by some other presence that makes itself known to us when we are sufficiently empty to make room for it. We see our consciousness and no longer identify with it.[40]

This sounds very much like the discernment of self and renewal of mind before God that Paul urges upon eucharistic worshipers in 1 Cor. 11:28–32 and Rom. 12:1f. Ulanov goes on to affirm that when the new consciousness of being looked at by Another is offered to us, we find space

> to behold spontaneous life given to us, through the graciousness of our Creator, the blooming flower at the bottom of the well. But we must be turned on our head to find it. In religious language, this emptiness is submission, a humble letting go of ourself, a losing of our life to find that we are found by the consciousness of a greater Subject.[41]

Ulanov suggests that many individuals experience this sort of renewal first in their dreams. But the New Testament record indicates that insofar as it occurs in community, its primary locus is the eucharistic meal. There, as in no other ritual, a corporate self-offering, joined with Jesus' sacrifice, can take place.

And this, in turn, serves to transform our everyday behavior. Near the end of her talk Ulanov puts it this way:

> If the product of going down into a different consciousness is living, and not money, sermons, recipes, fame, lectures, degrees, jobs, and all the things of this life that we reify, prize, and make into idols, then our relationship with each other changes. Ethics changes from a giving of helper to helpee to a receiving and yielding of overflow.[42]

In the language of our study, eucharistic praise and self-offering merge with eucharistic mission; and abundant life spills out into the world (Rom. 12:1–21; 15:1–13).

Archbishop Michael Ramsey's biographer Owen Chadwick reports that Ramsey once wrote his aunt Lucy that "the sacrament of the eucharist was so big he did not feel he had finished with it when he came home after the service at 8 a.m. on Sunday morning. It was many-sided — worship, praise, offering, commemoration of our Lord's life and death, sacrifice, fellowship with the faithful in the unseen, all the many sides which centre in this one act."[43] We too need more time than our formal worship permits for the immensity of the sacrament to permeate our lives. Coffee hours after the Sunday service, useful as they are, may not be enough!

Co-missioning for Redemption

On a high wall just behind the freestanding altar at St. Gregory Nyssen Episcopal Church in San Francisco hangs an unfinished icon of the risen Christ. The full-bodied figure depicted — he is three or four times life-size — appears only in outline on an all-white surface. I am told that eventually he will be polychromed like the other images adorning the sanctuary. But I have mixed feelings about this outcome, because I find it quite appropriate, on eucharistic grounds, to contemplate a Christ "in progress." One sees motion in the image itself. Unlike many Orthodox-style icons, this Christ does not sit in serene majesty but is clearly stepping forth, maybe even dancing, like the icons of the saints who look toward him from other walls of the church.[44] With one hand Christ holds a cross aloft, to show that he has co-opted the power of death. Yet he can only move forward *with* the cross, and it is hard to avoid the impression that he is calling us to follow him.

When the time for the eucharistic meal at St. Gregory's comes, the entire congregation approaches the altar en masse with a simple dance step and surrounds it as the president of the feast chants a prayer of thanksgiving over the bread and wine. After the communion, received while standing in this circular formation, the worshipers proceed around the altar a few times, dancing again and singing a hymn at the same time. Unless people close their eyes, they cannot escape an encounter with the face of the Christ icon. Whatever we may think of this unusual liturgical practice, it does help to symbolize the central meanings of eucharistic mission that have emerged from our study. The eucharistic Christ comes to us as a triumphant figure, but he still carries the cross and he has work to do. He leads our praise and thanksgiving, to the glory of God; and then, precisely in our communion with him, we are commissioned to join him as he continues with God's redemption of the world. Each eucharist, and therefore each commissioning, will prove unique.

To use the evocative title of Anthony Gittins's fine book, we are invited, through the eucharistic liturgy, to partake of "bread for the journey." The eucharist does not offer us a permanent resting place where all the comforts of domestic life are provided at the touch of a keyboard or turn of a switch. As Gustavo Gutiérrez notes, our worship at table with Jesus is more like a point of arrival and point of departure for the Christian community at work in the world.[45] Eucharistic comforts abound, to be sure, but they come to us from the dynamic presence of the Trinity for the purpose of building us up in our distinctive vocations. Above all, they are charismatic empowerments, granted by the Spirit for the enhancement of ministry and mission. John Zizioulas writes that it is from the eucharist that Christians "return into the world rejoicing and full of charisms."[46] And even prior to that return, in the very reception and initial exercising of the gifts, we hear a challenging invitation: "Get out of the boat and walk on the water!" These words, used by Gittins,[47] are based on the story in Matt. 14:28–33. But we could also cite Rev. 3:20ff., where the eucharistic Christ attempts to enter the believer's home (heart?) by knocking at the door.

Here we return to the core of our concern throughout this study. What does our eucharistic celebration today, as believers united with Jesus, really accomplish for the redemption of the world? Here we must acknowledge in all humility that we do not know the full answer to this question. At the eucharist, too, we walk by faith and promise and not by the kind of sight that will prove empirically convincing to everyone. We have to listen to the wise counsel of Old Testament theologian Samuel Terrien when he writes that in biblical faith the discernment of divine presence

> is neither absolute nor eternal but elusive and fragile, even and especially when human beings seek to prolong it in the form of cultus. The collective act of worship seems to be both the indispensable vehicle of presence and its destroyer.... When presence is "guaranteed" to human senses or reason, it is no longer real presence. The proprietary sight of glory

> destroys the vision, whether in the temple of Zion or in the eucharistic body.[48]

Terrien's thoughts are nothing other than a liturgical formulation of the classic teaching we call justification by grace through faith rather than works. Ultimately the motivation for continuing to practice our eucharistic rituals must stem not from a desire to accomplish something important but from the promising/commanding words: "This is my body. . . . This is my blood. . . . Do this in remembrance of me."

On the other hand, we do not want to miss Terrien's crucial observation that "the collective act of worship seems to be the indispensable vehicle of presence," for that is exactly what our study of eucharistic origins has indicated. From our learning about first-century beliefs and practices we can dare to posit that what we do now in our worship at table really matters, matters eternally in the cosmic plan of God through which all things are being set right.[49] In ways that we can to some degree specify, our eucharists become mission, which is to say that they enhance God's presence and power and saving purpose for all creation. How, in closing, can we best describe these streams of redemption?

We can begin by affirming, with Henri de Lubac and John Zizioulas, that "the eucharist makes the church,"[50] but only in the sense that "eucharist" means the full, complex event described by our New Testament authors and in the sense that it extends beyond the church service per se to become a force for good among all people. In the light of our study we should probably revise the de Lubac/

Zizioulas confession a bit so that it reads: "The eucharist makes the missionary church." But this revision itself calls out for further explanation.

In company with our New Testament witnesses many contemporary authors have properly emphasized the formation and equipping for mission that the eucharist provides.[51] One direct result of the learning, healing, upbuilding, forgiveness, reconciliation, renewal of mind, and prayer that takes place within the worshiping congregation is a strengthening of believers for their vocation outside the walls of the church. And this strengthening can itself be understood as redemptive mission to the world. Wherever evil is conquered by good and God's name is hallowed, the new creation grows and the kingdom comes closer. We can say the same of experiences at table that allow us to glimpse the heavenly banquet and the world renewed. To the extent that we can partake of this larger reality in our eucharists, even a little, we can choose more freely to join the Messiah's mighty labors for the fulfillment of God's reign on earth. The whole world benefits from these small decisions by ordinary saints.

In addition, the celebrative meals of thanksgiving referred to in the New Testament often drew nonbelievers to church gatherings. Verbal expressions of the good news about Jesus were of course decisive for conversion — surely no eucharist took place without them (see 1 Cor. 11:26) — but the actual turning to faith of many curious onlookers and seekers after righteousness must have come when they were able to see the gospel enfleshed in real human communities, especially during worship at table. In Jerusalem, people seem to have been attracted particularly by the first congregation's joyfulness, its healing ministry (available to all), and its radical sharing of goods. Paul expected that visitors to eucharistic meals in Corinth would be won over to the gospel by heart-penetrating messages of prophecy shared among the worshipers. William Tully rightly insists that eucharistic services in our day ought also to be considered services of evangelism. Church growth and the Lord's Table do in fact belong together.[52] On the other hand, we have found no evidence that visitors to eucharistic meals in New Testament times partook of or expected to partake of the ritual eating and drinking prior to baptism. This may have happened, but cultural studies suggest that inhabitants of the first-century Mediterranean world who visited religious observances unfamiliar to them would typically anticipate having to undergo an initiatory rite whereby a fuller entry into the community's practice was granted. All the stories of conversion in Paul's letters and Acts point to baptism as being that kind of rite.

What first enables "insiders" and "outsiders" at the eucharist to cross the boundary lines that divide them is the unifying act of praise and thanksgiving (see Rom. 15:9–13). Eating and drinking together, while hugely important and always a goal, follow upon the common offerings of gratitude to God that form the heart of our table worship.[53] Through these, gifts of the Spirit may be granted prior to baptism (Acts 10:44–48; Gal. 3:1f.). Through these, "outsiders" are brought closer and "insiders" are sent out to minister in the power of abundance. Through these, everyone present undergoes conversion (Rom. 12:1f.), whether the faith we bring is mature, immature, or virtually nonexistent. In fact, our corporate responses to God's mercy cause the boundaries between belief and unbelief to become quite porous. The same goes for boundaries between church and world or between this age and the age to come.

Eucharistia creates a sacred intersection of every time and place at which all things can be infused with grace. In praise and thanksgiving we recall the promise of Jesus at the Johannine last supper that we will do even greater works in the world than he himself was able to accomplish (John 14:12). And we are emboldened to live as if that were true. In praise and thanksgiving we find certification to celebrate our meals outside the church as the "proto-eucharists" Luke portrays in Acts, where the rule of Christ is manifested and extended (see Luke 22:30 and chapter 5). In praise and thanksgiving we become more intentional about our roles as "faithful witnesses" (the favorite name for eucharistic worshipers in Revelation), who take firm stands, in Christ, against all forms of idolatry, slavery, and oppression (see 1 Cor. 15:24–28). It does not seem artificial to call all of this "redemption." If the eucharist makes the church, especially the missionary church, it also remakes the world.

Some Christian interpreters want to go even further with this theme. From an Orthodox perspective John Zizioulas asserts that our very celebration of the eucharist "accepts and sanctifies all of creation 'recapitulated' in the one Body of the 'first born of creation' [Christ]."[54] And Pierre Teilhard de Chardin, who was mightily concerned about the fulfillment of the created order in Christ (the Omega point),

> never ceased thinking about [the] "cosmic function" and . . . "planetary dimensions" that belong to the Eucharist. In his very last essay, *Le Christique,* he is still considering how the convergence of the cosmos and the emergence of Christ "inexhaustibly react upon one another as they meet. . . . " For Teilhard, in fact, "it is the eucharistic mystery itself which is prolonged to infinity in a veritable universal 'transubstantiation' in which the words of consecration fall not upon the sacrificial bread and wine alone, but in very truth, upon the convergence of the world."[55]

This line of thought certainly challenges our everyday modes of perception, yet for all that it does not contradict the results of our study. Here, however, the last word belongs to Methodist theologian Geoffrey Wainwright, whose 1971 work *Eucharist and Eschatology* has done much to rekindle conversations between liturgists and those engaged primarily in biblical studies. For Wainwright,

> The eucharistic celebration does not leave the world unchanged. The future has occupied the present for a moment at least, and that moment is henceforth an ineradicable part of the experience of those who lived it. Where the surface has been broken from below, the ripples spread in ever-broadening circles. What has been raised to its highest destiny will not readily be content to relapse to a lower level of existence. . . . At the risk of falling into a facile doctrine of progress, it must be said that if the history of

> the individual, of the church, of the human race, and of the world bears in any way a cumulative character so that each moment of the past may become part of acquired and permanent experience, then the kingdom of God has come closer with each eucharistic celebration.[56]

Jesus seems to have known something like this already at the last supper. Now, as the Risen One who presides at our eucharists and is truly with us there in our joys and griefs, he invites us to receive our share in the (always) coming kingdom and then to do our unique part for its advancement.

What Comes Next?

Here, at the very end of our study, I am acutely aware of how much remains unstated and the degree to which the observations and conclusions offered above still fall short of our goal to clarify eucharistic origins. For example, I have said very little about the proclaimed word in the table liturgies of the earliest churches and the manner in which it may have helped church members to become preachers of the gospel themselves. Mostly undealt with as well is the relationship between the commissioning of believers inherent in baptism and the call to mission that we have found to be permeating the eucharist. In addition, some will notice that I have not placed great emphasis on the visible unity of believers at the eucharist, a force for attracting "the world" to the church specifically mentioned in the Fourth Gospel (see 17:20–23). Jesus' prayer for unity in this passage is frequently cited to good effect in ecumenical circles today, but we probably need to be more specific about the nature and quality of what was envisioned here by John — perhaps along lines proposed in this study. As for liturgical changes that might become desirable if we open ourselves to the kind of eucharistic mission assumed by our New Testament writers, I have presented only a few suggestions. I have said little about singing in the earliest meals of the church and nothing at all about the role music might play in contemporary eucharists where the missionary character of the sacrament is highlighted. Finally, while I continue to hold that the title of this study, *The Feast of the World's Redemption,* accurately mirrors what our New Testament writers were trying to say about ritual meals, I need to express some ambivalence about the first word of the title. Jesus was a Jew, and it should be obvious to us Christians that his understanding of transformative meals, both before and after the resurrection, would be shaped by the Sabbath supper and the Passover. Must we not conclude that also today the celebrating of these meals by Jews has much to do with the world's redemption? What are we all to make of our shared vocation at table?

The questions and issues just noted, along with many others that readers of this book are likely to raise, seem to me to require a larger conversation than we are currently undertaking, or at least a conversation that will more effectively engage a wide variety of theorists and practitioners, both inside and outside the church. I am no great organizer, but my guess is that somewhere theologians, Bible scholars, liturgists, missiologists, and others will hear a call to assemble those who can go forward with these matters. I truly hope that will happen, for the sake of the world's redemption.

NOTES

1: Vision and Promise at the Last Supper

1. *The Faith of the Early Fathers,* tr. W. A. Jürgens (Collegeville, Minn.: Liturgical Press, 1970), p. 55.

2. See Gerd Theissen and Annette Merz, *The Historical Jesus: A Comprehensive Guide* (Minneapolis: Fortress Press, 1998), pp. 407–414, for a short history of interpretation. On the other hand, Rudolf Bultmann, whose influence has been great, considered the synoptic accounts of the last supper to be cult legends with little historical value. See Rudolf Bultmann, *The History of the Synoptic Tradition* (New York: Harper & Row, 1976), pp. 265f.

3. A. N. Wilson, *Jesus: A Life* (New York: W. W. Norton, 1992), pp. x–xi, 193–199.

4. John D. Crossan, *Jesus: A Revolutionary Biography* (San Francisco: HarperSanFrancisco, 1994), p. 130. Something close to Crossan's view has now become the official majority position of the Jesus Seminar. See R. Funk and the Jesus Seminar, *The Acts of Jesus* (San Francisco: HarperSanFrancisco, 1998), pp. 139–142, where the historicity of both the Marcan and Pauline versions of the last supper is denied.

5. Marcus J. Borg, *Meeting Jesus Again for the First Time* (San Francisco: HarperSanFrancisco, 1994), p. 66, n. 35.

6. Marcus J. Borg, *Jesus, a New Vision: Spirit, Culture, and the Life of Discipleship* (San Francisco: Harper & Row, 1987), p. 188, n. 27.

7. See Bruce Chilton, *A Feast of Meanings: Eucharistic Theologies from Jesus through Johannine Circles* (Leiden: E. J. Brill, 1994), pp. 38–45, 63–74.

8. Ibid., pp. 75–92.

9. Ibid., pp. 93–158.

10. John's gospel contains no institutional narrative on the night of Jesus' arrest, although the evangelist does seem to know of a "sacramental" meal involving Jesus' body and blood. This data will be considered in chapter 4.

11. Gordon D. Fee, *The First Epistle to the Corinthians* (Grand Rapids: W. B. Eerdmans, 1987), pp. 548f.

12. Martin Hengel and Anna Maria Schwemer, *Paul between Damascus and Antioch: The Unknown Years,* tr. John Bowden (Louisville: John Knox Press, 1977), pp. 288–289.

13. The quoted words provide a framework in history for the bread and cup words that Paul then relates. Hengel and Schwemer, *Paul between Damascus and Antioch,* p. 147, and Jerome Murphy-O'Connor, *Paul: A Critical Life* (New York: Oxford University Press, 1996), p. 91, both argue that information about the historical Jesus formed the bulk of the Peter-Paul conversation. It might be objected that Peter would not have passed on a last supper tradition in Greek, but Hengel rightly notes that already prior to Paul's conversion, Greek-speaking Hellenist believers in Jerusalem would have translated formulas like this one from Aramaic for use in their worship. See Acts 6:1–6 and Hengel and Schwemer, *Paul between Damascus and Antioch,* p. 289. Almost certainly this kind of tradition was available to Peter, who in any case probably knew some Greek. On the other hand, Paul could have made the translation during the course of his talk with Peter in Aramaic.

14. See A. E. Morris, "Jesus and the Eucharist," *Theology,* 26 (May 1933): 256: "No one, stepping into the stream of Christian tradition between Pentecost and the proclamation of this [Lord's Supper] doctrine only about twenty years later to the Corinthians, and earlier elsewhere, could have diverted that tradition so notably yet with so little trace of disturbance. But this consideration brings us up against the necessity of allowing that the doctrine came from Jesus himself."

15. See the dates within this range proposed by Hans Dieter Betz, "Paul," in *The Anchor Dictionary of the Bible,* David Noel Freedman, Editor-in-Chief (New York: Doubleday, 1992), vol. 5, p. 191; Robert Jewett, *A Chronology of Paul's Life* (Philadelphia: Fortress Press, 1979), pp. 29–30; Rainer Riesner, *Paul's Early Period: Chronology, Mission Strategy, Theology,* tr.

Doug Scott (Grand Rapids: W. B. Eerdmans, 1998), pp. 319–322; and Jürgen Becker, *Paul: Apostle to the Gentiles,* tr. O. C. Dean, Jr. (Louisville: John Knox Press, 1993), pp. 29–31. Both Jerome Murphy-O'Connor, *Paul: A Critical Life,* pp. 7f., and Hengel and Schwemer, *Paul between Damascus and Antioch,* pp. 26f., place the year of Paul's conversion in 33, assuming a date of 30 for the crucifixion. By their reckoning, the Jerusalem trip could have been as late as 36.

16. This option is close to the theory of Hans Lietzmann, who argued in *Messe und Herrenmahl* (Leiden: E. J. Brill, 1926) that the table rituals of the first Jerusalem community were essentially love feasts evolving from the ministry meals of Jesus and celebrating his resurrection appearances. But today most scholars judge Lietzmann's thesis inadequate because it allows no room for the soteriological interpretation of the cross by Jerusalem believers in their earliest meal liturgies. See C. F. D. Moule, *Worship in the New Testament* (London: Lutterworth, 1961), pp. 21f., 25f.; John H. P. Reumann, *The Supper of the Lord: The New Testament, Ecumenical Dialogues, and Faith and Order in Eucharist* (Philadelphia: Fortress Press, 1984), pp. 16–17; and Luke Timothy Johnson, *Religious Experience in Earliest Christianity: A Missing Dimension in New Testament Studies* (Minneapolis: Fortress Press, 1998), pp. 142–145.

17. E. P. Sanders, *Jesus and Judaism* (Philadelphia: Fortress Press, 1985), pp. 116–119.

18. See Borg, *Meeting Jesus Again for the First Time,* pp. 12, 29, 103, and the critical responses to this position by D. C. Allison, "A Plea for Thoroughgoing Eschatology," *Journal of Biblical Literature,* 113, no. 4 (1994): 651–658; Bruce Chilton, *Pure Kingdom: Jesus' Vision of God* (Grand Rapids: W. B. Eerdmans, 1996), pp. 16–22, 56–101; and N. T. Wright, *Jesus and the Victory of God: Christian Origins and the Question of God,* vol. 2 (Minneapolis: Fortress Press, 1997), chapters 5–10.

19. On the authenticity of this saying, see John Koenig, *New Testament Hospitality: Partnership with Strangers as Promise and Mission* (Philadelphia: Fortress Press, 1985), pp. 20–26.

20. We should credit Jesus with enough prophetic intuition to make an accurate estimate of this approaching end. See Jürgen Becker, *Jesus of Nazareth,* tr. James E. Crouch (New York: Wal-

ter de Gruyter, 1998), pp. 336–342, and Gerd Theissen and Annette Merz, *The Historical Jesus,* pp. 428–431.

21. Sanders, *Jesus and Judaism,* pp. 77–90.

22. E. P. Sanders, *The Historical Figure of Jesus* (London: Allen Lane, 1993), pp. 252–254; see also John J. Collins, *The Scepter and the Star: The Messiahs of the Dead Sea Scrolls and Other Ancient Literature* (New York: Doubleday, 1995), p. 206; N. T. Wright, *Jesus and the Victory of God,* pp. 490f.; and Morna Hooker, *The Signs of a Prophet* (Harrisburg: Trinity Press International, 1997), pp. 43f.

23. John D. Crossan, *The Cross That Spoke* (San Francisco: Harper & Row, 1988), p. 405.

24. John D. Crossan, *The Historical Jesus: The Life of a Mediterranean Jewish Peasant* (San Francisco: HarperSanFrancisco, 1991), pp. 359f.

25. *New York Times,* 27 March 1994, A22.

26. See Raymond E. Brown, *The Death of the Messiah: From Gethsemane to the Grave* (New York: Doubleday, 1994), pp. 83, 1369, 1370–1373.

27. E. P. Sanders, *The Historical Figure of Jesus,* pp. 254–262; James D. G. Dunn, *The Partings of the Ways* (Philadelphia: Trinity Press International, 1991), pp. 47–49.

28. N. T. Wright correctly stresses the connection between 2 and 3; see *Jesus and the Victory of God,* pp. 437f., 561.

29. If there was a last supper, Mark 14:25 almost certainly belongs there and not elsewhere, contrary to the view of Bruce Chilton in *A Feast of Meanings,* pp. 38–45.

30. See John P. Meier, *A Marginal Jew: Rethinking the Historical Jesus,* vol. 2 (New York: Doubleday, 1991), pp. 304f.

31. Enrico Mazza, in *The Origins of the Eucharistic Prayer,* tr. Ronald E. Lane (Collegeville, Minn.: The Liturgical Press, 1995), pp. 36f., understands the vine in Didache 9:2 to be the Davidic kingdom. But in Mark 14:25 Jesus distinguishes between vine and kingdom. Perhaps one could say that the vine is the kingdom in its aspect of superabundance and feasting.

32. This is not stated explicitly but is implied in 1QSb 5:20ff. and "The Blessings of Jacob," both of which interpret Gen. 49:10–12 messianically. See Helmer Ringgren, *The Faith of Qumran: Theology of the Dead Sea Scrolls* (Philadelphia: For-

tress Press, 1963), p. 181; John J. Collins, *The Scepter and the Star,* pp. 45, 61f.; and John Koenig, *New Testament Hospitality,* p. 50, n. 45. Collins notes that targumic expansions of Gen. 49:10–12 were messianic, and Norman Cohn, *Cosmos, Chaos and the World to Come: How the Wait for Heaven on Earth Began* (New Haven: Yale University Press, 1993), pp. 198f., calls attention to the early-second-century "Jewish Christian" writer Papias, who prophesied that in the new age of the messiah colossal vines would bear 10,000 stems, each with 10,000 bunches of grapes.

33. John P. Meier, *A Marginal Jew,* pp. 305f.; Bruce Chilton, *A Feast of Meanings,* pp. 43f.

34. Bruce Chilton, *Pure Kingdom: Jesus' Vision of God* (Grand Rapids: W. B. Eerdmans, 1996), pp. 13f., 82.

35. John P. Meier, *A Marginal Jew,* p. 306.

36. Ibid.

37. Raymond E. Brown, *The Birth of the Messiah: A Commentary on the Infancy Narratives in the Gospels of Matthew and Luke* (New York: Doubleday, 1993), pp. 505–512.

38. Claus Westermann, *Genesis 37–50,* tr. John J. Scullion (Minneapolis: Augsburg Publishing House, 1986), p. 263.

39. John Koenig, *New Testament Hospitality,* p. 50, n. 44.

40. To my knowledge, Geoffrey Wainwright was the first contemporary scholar to emphasize this. See Geoffrey Wainwright, *Eucharist and Eschatology* (New York: Oxford University Press, 1981), p. 39.

41. See 1 Cor. 11:26 as well as the prayer "Maranatha" in 1 Cor. 16:22 and Didache 10:6.

42. See Matt. 26:29 and the stories of Jesus' interventions at table in Luke 24:29–31, 36ff.; John 17:24; 21:9ff.

43. L. Hoffman, "A Symbol of Salvation in the Passover Haggadah," *Worship,* no. 53 (1979): 519–537.

44. Ibid., p. 536; according to Hoffman, Paul seems to be drawing upon a "common imagination" among Jews when he confesses that "our paschal lamb, Christ, has been sacrificed for us" (1 Cor. 5:7).

45. Raymond E. Brown, *The Death of the Messiah,* pp. 1370–1373.

46. Ibid., 1373.

47. N. T. Wright, *The New Testament and the People of God:*

Christian Origins and the Question of God (Minneapolis: Fortress Press, 1992), p. 260, n. 3; E. P. Sanders, *Paul* (New York: Oxford University Press, 1991), pp. 420ff.; G. Vermes, *The Dead Sea Scrolls in English* (Harmondsworth: Penguin, 1975), pp. 34–38.

48. Gerd Theissen and Annette Merz, *The Historical Jesus,* p. 423, n. 15.

49. *Anchor Dictionary of the Bible,* vol. 4, pp. 238f.

50. Theissen and Merz finally adopt the position that the words "in my blood" were not spoken by the historical Jesus precisely because he, as a Jew, could not have implied any connection whatsoever between his blood and the contents of the cup. See Gerd Theissen and Annette Merz, *The Historical Jesus,* p. 423. But the Jewish Paul certainly believed that Jesus had spoken these words. And so, on our theory, did Peter and the first believers in Jerusalem. Once one presses back this far into the Palestinian milieu, the distinctions made by Theissen and Merz between what could and could not have been said about blood in first-century Judaism simply evaporate.

51. John Meier also concludes that Jesus himself said words on the order of "This is the covenant in my blood." Meier's reasoning about how the modification of the cup saying in 1 Cor. 11:25 occurred corresponds roughly to mine. See "The Eucharist at the Last Supper: Did It Happen?" *Theology Digest,* 42, no. 4 (1995): 346f.

52. The disciples seemed to know something of this scenario already, but their exact status in the age to come remained unclear. See Mark 10:35–40; Matt. 19:28/Luke 22:30.

53. Bruce Chilton sees the Ex. 24 tradition in our gospel accounts of the last supper. But he ascribes this biblical coloring of the meal to Peter and his circle, not to Jesus. See Chilton, *A Feast of Meanings,* pp. 83–86, 92.

54. In *The Partings of the Ways,* p. 54, James D. G. Dunn concludes that Jesus saw his death as "somehow vicarious." Since he apparently made intentional use of Zech. 9:9–10 in his entry to Jerusalem, Jesus could well have employed a phrase from Zech. 9:11 to interpret his impending death. There God assures Israel that "because of the blood of my covenant with you, I will set your prisoners free."

55. Bruce Chilton, *A Feast of Meanings,* pp. 117f.

56. This is well expressed by N. T. Wright in *Jesus and the Victory of God,* pp. 576–653.

2. Feasts of the Church's Founding

1. Mark 8:29; 9:2ff.; 10:35ff.; 14:33ff. and their synoptic parallels seem to reflect the precedence of these three disciples.

2. But there are also early references to communities of believers in Damascus and the regions of Judea outside Jerusalem. See Gal. 2:17, 22.

3. See James D. G. Dunn, *Jesus and the Spirit: A Study of the Religious and Charismatic Experience of Jesus and the First Christians as Reflected in the New Testament* (London: S.C.M. Press, 1975), pp. 136–156; James D. G. Dunn, *The Partings of the Ways: Between Christianity and Judaism and Their Significance for the Character of Christianity,* pp. 265–267; Martin Hengel and Anna Maria Schwemer, *Paul between Damascus and Antioch: The Unknown Years,* pp. 27–29; and Ben Witherington, *The Acts of the Apostles: A Socio-Rhetorical Commentary* (Grand Rapids: W. B. Eerdmans, 1998), pp. 129f.

4. *New Testament Apocrypha,* vol. 1, ed. Edgar Hennecke and Wilhelm Schneemelcher, English translation ed. R. Wilson (Philadelphia: Westminster Press, 1963), p. 165.

5. See *Messianic Exegesis: Christological Interpretation of the Old Testament in Early Christianity* (Philadelphia: Fortress Press, 1988), Donald Juel's useful study of the interplay between experience and scriptural study in the early church.

6. See Rowan Williams, *Resurrection: Interpreting the Easter Gospel* (New York: Pilgrim Press, 1984), pp. 33–36.

7. See Joseph A. Fitzmyer, *Luke the Theologian: Aspects of His Teaching,* vol. 1 (New York: Paulist Press, 1989), p. 561.

8. Rowan Williams, *Resurrection,* pp. 39f.

9. Thus, Peter's remorse over his denial of Jesus shows up in the synoptic tradition in a manner altogether atypical of ancient writings about notable figures. See Erich Auerbach, *Mimesis: The Representation of Reality in Western Literature,* tr. Willard R. Trask (Princeton: Princeton University Press, 1953), pp. 41–49.

10. See C. K. Barrett, *A Critical and Exegetical Commentary on the Acts of the Apostles* (International Critical Commentary, Edinburgh: T. & T. Clark, 1992), pp. 170f., on Acts 2:46.

11. Nils Alstrup Dahl, *The Crucified Messiah* (Minneapolis: Augsburg Publishing House, 1974), pp. 10–36.

12. C. F. D. Moule, *Worship in the New Testament* (London: Lutterworth, 1961), p. 21; C. K. Barrett, *A Critical and Exegetical Commentary on the Acts of the Apostles,* pp. 170f.

13. Larry W. Hurtado, *One God, One Lord: Early Christian Devotion and Ancient Jewish Monotheism* (Philadelphia: Fortress Press, 1988), pp. 111f.

14. See Bruce Chilton, *A Feast of Meanings,* p. 89, who relies on O. Cullmann, "The Lord's Supper and the Death of Christ" in *Essays on the Lord's Supper,* ed. F. J. Leenhardt (Richmond: John Knox, 1958).

15. See R. H. Fuller, "The Double Origin of the Eucharist," *Biblical Research* VIII (1963): 66ff. Fuller draws upon the earlier work of B. Lohse in *Das Passafest der Quartodecimaner* (Gütersloh, 1953).

16. Stephen G. Wilson, *Related Strangers: Jews and Christians, 70–170 C.E.* (Minneapolis: Fortress Press, 1995), pp. 236f.; James D. G. Dunn, *Unity and Diversity in the New Testament: An Inquiry into the Character of Earliest Christianity* (London: S.C.M. Press, 1990), p. 163; John Reumann, *The Supper of the Lord,* pp. 6, 17, 47f. See Alistair Stewart-Sykes, *The Lamb's High Feast: Melito, Peri Pascha, and the Quartodeciman Paschal Liturgy at Sardis* (Leiden: Brill, 1998), for a detailed treatment of the paschal liturgy at Sardis in the second century.

17. See Joachim Jeremias, *The Eucharistic Words of Jesus,* tr. Norman Perrin (London: S.C.M. Press, 1966), pp. 237–255; and I. Howard Marshall, *Last Supper and Lord's Supper* (Exeter: Paternoster Press, 1980), pp. 51–53. For a critique of Jeremias's position, see John Koenig, *New Testament Hospitality,* p. 50, n. 49.

18. To a point we can agree with Chilton (*A Feast of Meanings,* pp. 75–92) on the importance of Peter's leadership in the development of this liturgy. We diverge, however, from Chilton's view that a Petrine circle created the last supper story on which the ritual was based; see pp. 12f.; 72f.

19. See the listing of some who take this position in Stephen G. Wilson's *Related Strangers,* p. 383, n. 39. Such commentators include H. Riesenfeld (who should probably be credited with the first form of the thesis), T. Talley, and M. H. Shepherd. Wilson himself also opts for the thesis. See ibid., p. 233.

20. Ibid., p. 232.

21. Gordon D. Fee, *The First Epistle to the Corinthians* (Grand Rapids: W. B. Eerdmans, 1987), pp. 813f., implies this when he compares 1 Cor. 16:2 with Acts 20:7.

22. Bruce Chilton, *A Feast of Meanings,* pp. 75–92.

23. James D. G. Dunn, *The Partings of the Ways,* 53–70; and E. P. Sanders, *The Historical Figure of Jesus,* pp. 260–262; 272f.

24. This is not to say, of course, that the words were never remembered or mentioned.

25. Reginald H. Fuller, *Christ and Christianity: Studies in the Formation of Christology,* ed. Robert Kahl (Valley Forge: Trinity Press International, 1994), p. 57.

26. Prophets played a key role in the faith and worship life of the early communities. See Acts 7; 11:27; 15:32; 1 Cor. 11:2–16; 14; 1 Thess. 5:20; Didache 10:7.

27. C. K. Barrett, *A Critical and Exegetical Commentary on the Acts of the Apostles,* pp. 280, 302.

28. See, among others, Hans Conzelmann, *Acts of the Apostles: A Commentary on the Acts of the Apostles,* tr. James Limburg, A. T. Kraabel, and D. H. Juel, ed. Eldon Jay Epp and C. R. Matthews (Philadelphia: Fortress Press, 1987); Ernst Haenchen, *The Acts of the Apostles: A Commentary,* tr. R. McL. Wilson (Philadelphia: Westminster Press, 1971); and Richard I. Pervo, *Profit with Delight: The Literary Genre of the Acts of the Apostles* (Philadelphia: Fortress Press, 1987).

29. Martin Hengel and Anna Maria Schwemer, *Paul between Damascus and Antioch: The Unknown Years,* pp. 28f.; Bonnie Bowman Thurston, *Spiritual Life in the Early Church: The Witness of Acts and Ephesians* (Minneapolis: Fortress Press, 1993), p. 56; and Ben Witherington, *The Acts of the Apostles: A Socio-Rhetorical Commentary* (Grand Rapids: W. B. Eerdmans, 1998), pp. 39, 58–60.

30. C. K. Barrett, *A Critical and Exegetical Commentary on the Acts of the Apostles,* p. 166.

31. S. Scott Bartchy, "Community of Goods in Acts: Idealization or Social Reality?" *The Future of Early Christianity,* ed. Birger Pearson (Minneapolis: Fortress Press, 1991), p. 318.

32. There is no evidence at this early stage for excluding the unbaptized from worship at table, although it seems likely that they would not partake of food blessed at rituals commemorating the last supper.

33. John V. Taylor, *The Go-Between God: The Holy Spirit and the Christian Mission* (Philadelphia: Fortress Press, 1973), p. 134.

34. Ibid., p. 227.

3. Eucharistic Meals and Missionary Boundaries

1. Most scholars consider 1 Thessalonians to have been written about 50 C.E., which means that the church probably originated earlier, sometime in the 40s.

2. Gordon D. Fee, *The First Epistle to the Corinthians,* p. 540.

3. Joachim Jeremias, *Jesus als Weltvollender* (Gütersloh: C. Bertelsmann, 1930), p. 78; see also his *Jerusalem in the Time of Jesus: An Investigation into Economic and Social Conditions during the New Testament Period* (Philadelphia: Fortress Press, 1969), p. 131.

4. C. K. Barrett, *A Critical and Exegetical Commentary on the Acts of the Apostles,* p. 165.

5. Gordon D. Fee, *The First Epistle to the Corinthians,* p. 465; John Reumann, *The Supper of the Lord: The New Testament, Ecumenical Dialogues, and Faith and Order on Eucharist,* pp. 42f.

6. Samuele Bacchiocchi, *From Sabbath to Sunday: A Historical Investigation of the Rise of Sunday Observance in Early Christianity* (Rome: Pontifical Gregorian University, 1977), pp. 105–107; see also Thomas J. Talley, *The Origins of the Liturgical Year* (New York: Pueblo, 1986), pp. 14–16.

7. See C. K. Barrett, *A Critical and Exegetical Commentary on the Acts of the Apostles,* pp. 163f.

8. This development seems to have occurred in the sixteenth century, largely as a result of Thomas Cranmer's usage in the 1549 Book of Common Prayer. I am indebted to Prof. Alistair Stewart-Sykes for this information.

9. See T. J. Talley, "From Berakah to Eucharistia: A Reopening Question," in *Living Bread, Saving Cup: Readings on the Eucharist,* ed. R. K. Seasoltz (Collegeville, Minn.: Liturgical Press, 1982), pp. 80–101.

10. Ibid., pp. 86–89.

11. See James D. G. Dunn, *Romans 9–16* (Dallas: Word Books, 1988), p. 807.

12. Richard B. Hays, *Echoes of Scripture in the Letters of Paul* (New Haven: Yale University Press, 1989), pp. 72f.

13. It may be that the prominence of these table prayers in the church attracted the critical attention of some early rabbinic authorities. Mishnah Berakot 5:3 reads: "He who says (in a prayer) 'We give thanks, we give thanks,' is to be silenced." In examining this passage, Alan Segal recalls for us the double use of *eucharistoumen* ("we give thanks"), first over the cup of wine and then over the bread, at the beginning of the eucharistic prayer in Didache 9:2–3. Segal entertains the strong possibility that the target of the rabbinic admonition in Berakot 5:3 is a church table liturgy, presumably still taking place within a Jewish context. See *Two Powers in Heaven: Early Rabbinic Reports about Christianity and Gnosticism* (Leiden: E. J. Brill, 1977), pp. 98–103.

14. Luke Timothy Johnson, *The Acts of the Apostles,* (Collegeville, Minn.: Liturgical Press, 1992), p. 106; Eugene LaVerdiere, *The Breaking of the Bread: The Development of the Eucharist According to the Acts of the Apostles* (Chicago: Liturgy Training Publications, 1998), pp. 112f.

15. Bruce Chilton, *Judaism in the New Testament: Practices and Beliefs* (London: Routledge, 1995), p. 99; J. Louis Martyn, *Galatians: A New Translation with Introduction and Commentary* (New York: Doubleday, 1997), pp. 37, 232, 242.

16. See Wayne A. Meeks, *The First Urban Christians: The Social World of the Apostle Paul* (New Haven: Yale University Press, 1983), p. 103.

17. Ibid., pp. 159f.

18. Ibid., p. 160.

19. Ibid., pp. 191f.

20. Gordon D. Fee, *The First Epistle to the Corinthians,* pp. 541, 544, who draws upon the earlier work of Gerd Theissen in *The Social Setting of Pauline Christianity: Essays on Corinth* (Philadelphia: Fortress Press, 1982), pp. 145–174. See also John Koenig, *New Testament Hospitality: Partnership with Strangers as Promise and Mission,* p. 67.

21. Gordon D. Fee, *The First Epistle to the Corinthians,* pp. 540f.

22. See John Koenig, *New Testament Hospitality,* pp. 65–71.

23. Ibid., p. 69.

24. Wayne A. Meeks, *The First Urban Christians,* p. 190.

25. See *The Study of Liturgy,* ed. Cheslyn Jones et al. (New York: Oxford University Press, 1992), p. 206, n. 19, for a comparison of Jewish meals and Greco-Roman symposia.

26. See pp. 65f.

27. Cheslyn Jones, *The Study of Liturgy,* p. 193, recognizes this difficulty.

28. See Bernhard Lang, *Sacred Games: A History of Christian Worship* (New Haven: Yale University Press, 1997), pp. 372–378; Wayne Meeks comes close to endorsing this view when he writes, with reference to 14:23, that "the regulations set forth [here] for spirit-possessed communication . . . probably also refer to occasions at which the common meal is the central ritual"; see *The First Urban Christians,* p. 143. Allan Bouley supports our reading of 1 Cor. 11–14 more directly in that he links the prophetic utterances of chapter 14 to "eucharistic prayers." Presumably he means prayers that occurred during the commemoration of the last supper as such. See *From Freedom to Formula: The Evolution of the Eucharistic Prayer from Oral Improvisation to Written Texts* (Washington, D.C.: Catholic University of America Press, 1981), pp. 84–86.

29. Cheslyn Jones, *The Study of Liturgy,* p. 193.

30. Gordon D. Fee, *God's Empowering Presence: The Holy Spirit in the Letters of Paul* (Peabody, Mass.: Hendrickson Publishers, 1994), p. 144.

31. Bernhard Lang, *Sacred Games,* p. 372, seems to assume this distinction. So do Dennis E. Smith and H. E. Taussig, *Many*

Tables: The Eucharist in the New Testament and Liturgy Today (Philadelphia: Trinity Press, 1990), p. 65.

32. Robert Banks, *Going to Church in the First Century: An Eyewitness Account* (Auburn, Maine: Christian Books, 1990).

33. The grace after meals in Didache, which is to be spoken "after you are satisfied with food" (10:1), looks like the liturgical conclusion to a longer period of worship in which "knowledge and faith and immortality" are made known through Jesus (10:2). Here too we should probably think of an extended supper during which charismatic manifestations occurred, especially prophecy (10:7).

34. 14:29ff. does not restrict the number of prophetic expressions to two or three in total but to two or three during any one segment of the worship.

35. This statement is probably meant to affirm full participation rather than to criticize existing Corinthian practice. See Gordon D. Fee, *The First Epistle to the Corinthians,* p. 690.

36. John Koenig, *Charismata: God's Gifts for God's People* (Philadelphia: Westminster Press, 1978), p. 99.

37. Salvation is thought by Paul to be an ongoing and corporate reality. See 1 Cor. 1:18; 15:2, and L. T. Johnson, "The Social Dimensions of *Soteria* in Luke-Acts and Paul," *SBL Seminar Papers* (Atlanta: Scholars Press, 1993), pp. 530–536.

38. See chapter 2.

39. John Koenig, "Christ and the Hierarchies," *Anglican Theological Review,* supplemental series, no. 11 (March 1990): 109–113; and Walter Wink, *Engaging the Powers: Discernment and Resistance in a World of Domination* (Minneapolis: Fortress Press, 1992), pp. 83–85.

4. A Host of Witnesses: The Pauline and General Epistles

1. See James D. G. Dunn, *Romans 9–16* (Dallas: Word Books, 1988), p. 823.

2. Ibid., pp. 822f.

3. John Koenig, *Rediscovering New Testament Prayer:*

Boldness and Blessing in the Name of Jesus (San Francisco: HarperSanFrancisco, 1992), p. 188, n. 19.

4. See John Koenig, *New Testament Hospitality,* pp. 56f.

5. *Inclusio* is a Latin term used by literary critics to describe how an author sets off blocks of material on a subject by means of parallel summary statements.

6. See James D. G. Dunn, *Romans 9–16,* p. x, and Joseph Fitzmyer, *Romans: A New Translation with Introduction and Commentary,* Anchor Bible, vol. 33 (New York: Doubleday, 1993), p. xi.

7. *New Testament Questions of Today,* tr. W. J. Montague, "Worship in Everyday Life: A Note on Romans 12" (London: Fortress, 1969), p. 195.

8. See Dunn, *Romans 9–16,* p. 738, who emphasizes the permeability of church and world in these verses.

9. R. P. Martin quotes O. Cullmann and C. F. D. Moule approvingly in noting that such panoramic language about salvation was most likely to occur in eucharistic worship. See R. P. Martin, *A Hymn of Christ: Philippians 2:5–11 in Recent Interpretation and in the Setting of Early Christian Worship* (Westmont: Intervarsity Press, 1997), p. 269. The Cullmann reference is to *Christ and Time: The Primitive Christian Conception of Time* (Philadelphia: Westminster Press, 1950), p. 155, while that to Moule occurs in *The Birth of the New Testament* (London: A & C Black, 1962), p. 102.

10. " 'Anamnesis': Mémoire et Commémoration dans le Christianisme primitif," *Studia Theologica,* I, i (1947): 86; cited by R. P. Martin, *A Hymn of Christ,* p. 95.

11. Victor Paul Furnish presents convincing arguments for the literary unity of 2 Cor. 8 and 9. See *II Corinthians* (Garden City, N.Y.: Doubleday, 1984), pp. 41–43, 398–453.

12. Furnish calls attention to the liturgical character of this verse. See ibid., p. 404.

13. Hans Dieter Betz, *2 Corinthians 8 and 9: A Commentary on Two Administrative Letters of the Apostle Paul* (Philadelphia: Fortress Press, 1985), pp. 117–128.

14. Ibid., p. 121.

15. Ibid.

16. Ibid., pp. 126–128.

17. Ibid., p. 128.

18. See the balanced treatment of this issue in Raymond E. Brown's *An Introduction to the New Testament* (Garden City, N.Y.: Doubleday, 1997), pp. 610–630.

19. Gordon D. Fee, *God's Empowering Presence: The Holy Spirit in the Letters of Paul* (Peabody, Mass.: Hendrickson Publishers, 1994), pp. 637, 647, 653.

20. Rudolf Schnackenburg, *Ephesians: A Commentary* (Edinburgh: T. & T. Clark, 1991), p. 239.

21. Troy Martin argues that Col. 2:17 forms a close parallel with 1 Cor. 11:28f. and should therefore be understood as a eucharistic reference. If he is right, our hypothesis regarding 3:15f. gains some strength. See "But Let Everyone Discern the Body of Christ" (Col. 2:17), *Journal of Biblical Literature,* 114, no. 2 (1995): 249–255.

22. Most commentators do tend to identify a communal meal of some kind in Jude 12, where the term *agape* appears.

23. W. Thüsing, "'Lasst uns hinzutreten...' (Heb. 10, 22)," *Biblische Zeitschrift,* 9 (1965): 1–17. Thüsing concludes that the term "approach" focuses on the Eucharist as a paramount event for the uniting of believers with Christ's sacrifice, although it is not limited to that context. See pp. 10–12, 14, 16.

24. *Enekainesen* in v. 20 is a liturgical word roughly synonymous with the verb "institute."

25. Harold Attridge, *The Epistle to the Hebrews: A Commentary on the Epistle to the Hebrews* (Philadelphia: Fortress Press, 1989), p. 287.

26. C. F. D. Moule, *Worship in the New Testament* (London: Lutterworth, 1961), p. 37; Attridge, *The Epistle to the Hebrews,* p. 396, n. 85.

27. *The Epistle to the Hebrews,* pp. 395, 397. Attridge seems inclined toward the position that v. 9 is meant to repudiate a certain kind of eucharistic theology; however, he does not press this point.

28. See Moule, *Worship in the New Testament,* p. 40, who calls attention to parallels between texts in Hebrews and 1 Clement. Emphasizing the eucharistic character of the latter,

he concludes that Heb. 13:10 may refer to, but is not limited to, the Eucharist.

29. Ernst Lohmeyer, *Theologische Rundschau* (1937), p. 296.

30. E. G. Selwyn, *The First Epistle of St. Peter: The Greek Text with Introduction, Notes and Essays* (London: Macmillan, 1947), pp. 294f.

31. Ibid., p. 296.

32. Ibid., pp. 295f.

33. Ibid., p. 297.

34. The textual evidence for *agape* in 2 Pet. 2:13 is not strong.

35. Jesus' presence can also be discerned in the remembering of his teachings (12:14–21) and in his readiness to clothe believers with himself (13:14). This second passage (literally: "put on the Lord Jesus Christ") points not to baptism but to what Paul hopes will be a renewed commitment by the Romans to a spiritual transformation. See J. D. G. Dunn, *Romans 9–16,* pp. 790–794. Here we are dealing with a clear parallel to Rom. 12:1f.

36. On this subject see Hans Dieter Betz, *2 Corinthians 8 and 9,* pp. 118–120.

37. See J. H. Elliott, *1 Peter* (Augsburg Commentary on the New Testament, Minneapolis: Augsburg Publishing House, 1982), p. 83.

5. A Host of Witnesses: The Gospels, Acts, and Revelation

1. Eugene LaVerdiere, *The Breaking of the Bread: The Development of the Eucharist According to the Acts of the Apostles* (Collegeville, Minn.: Liturgy Training Publications, 1998), p. 190.

2. Richard Bauckham, *The Theology of the Book of Revelation* (Cambridge: Cambridge University Press, 1993), p. 3.

3. John Koenig, *New Testament Hospitality: Partnership with Strangers as Promise and Mission* (Philadelphia: Fortress Press, 1985), pp. 85–123.

4. We are not trying to show that the historical Jesus

purposely gave hints or made prophecies about eucharistic practices that he planned to establish for his followers — apart from the last supper itself. He may have done so, but the evidence for making this case is too scanty. On the other hand, we have argued (together with Bruce Chilton) that throughout his ministry, Jesus' words and acts were shaped by a lively sense that the festal abundance of God's kingdom was close at hand and already at work in the present (see above on Is. 25:6–9 and its effect on Matt. 8:11).

5. See Matt. 11:18f. and John Koenig, *New Testament Hospitality*, pp. 20–26.

6. Bernd Kollmann, *Ursprung und Gestalten der frühchristlichen Mahlfeier* (Göttingen: Vandenhoeck & Ruprecht, 1990), pp. 191–195.

7. Eugene LaVerdiere, *The Eucharist in the New Testament and the Early Church* (Collegeville, Minn.: Liturgical Press, 1996), p. 54.

8. There is no evidence to suggest that unbaptized people actually partook of eucharistic meals, but everything indicates that such people were expected to be present (see 1 Cor. 14:23ff.).

9. See John Koenig, *Rediscovering New Testament Prayer: Boldness and Blessing in the Name of Jesus* (San Francisco: HarperSanFrancisco, 1992), p. 184, n. 14.

10. Martin Hengel, *Studies in the Gospel of Mark* (Philadelphia: Fortress Press, 1985), p. 37.

11. Ibid., p. 44.

12. Gordon Lathrop, "Eucharist in the New Testament and Its Cultural Setting," *Worship and Culture in Dialogue*, ed. S. Anita Stauffer (Geneva: Lutheran World Federation, 1994), p. 80.

13. Bernd Kollmann, *Ursprung und Gestalten der Frühchristlichen Mahlfeier*, pp. 182–184.

14. See the translation and explanation of this passage by J. Neusner in *Torah from Our Sages: Pirke Abot* (Chappaqua, N.Y.: Rossel Books, 1984). The sayings are dated by Neusner from 70 to 132 C.E.

15. See especially Matt. 5:23, 43–48; 6:12; 9:5; 18:21–35.

16. In her book *Jesus the Meek King* (Harrisburg: Trinity

Press International, 1999), my colleague Deirdre Good does not take up the question of whether Matt. 11:28f. might be a eucharistic reference. But she does establish that the beckoning Jesus in this vignette is primarily a royal (messianic) figure whose behavior is characterized by meekness (i.e., compassion, humility, charity, etc.). She also shows that 11:27, which sets the context for our passage, exhibits a natural connection with the teaching commandment in the Great Commission (28:20). See pp. 61–64; 82–88. In other words, disciples are to join Jesus' mission, first by learning through an intimate relationship with him what the Father has revealed to him (11:27–29) and then by going out into the world to baptize and teach, assured of his royal presence in their evangelistic activity.

17. See John Koenig, *New Testament Hospitality*, pp. 86–91.

18. Eugene LaVerdiere, *Dining in the Kingdom of God: The Origins of the Eucharist According to Luke* (Collegeville, Minn.: Liturgy Training Publications, 1994); Eugene LaVerdiere, *The Breaking of the Bread* (see note 1).

19. LaVerdiere, *Dining in the Kingdom of God*, p. 24; see also pp. 7–23.

20. *Luke and the People of God* (Minneapolis: Augsburg, 1972); see especially "The Twelve on Israel's Thrones," pp. 85–96. Jervell supports his proposal by stressing the distance noted in Acts between Israel's official rulers and the apostles; only through the message and ministrations of the latter are the people renewed. Jervell does not address the issue of whether Luke thinks the twelve, upon Jesus' return from heaven (Acts 3:20), will also act authoritatively in the final judgment of God's people. Given such passages as Luke 21:25–28, that is probable.

21. This group involves more than the twelve.

22. LaVerdiere, *The Breaking of the Bread*, pp. 32–33.

23. For the view that Luke is writing to strengthen the missionary vocation of residential believers, see John Koenig, *New Testament Hospitality*, pp. 103–110, 119f.

24. See LaVerdiere, *The Breaking of the Bread*, pp. 45–65.

25. Ben Witherington III, *The Acts of the Apostles: A Socio-Rhetorical Commentary* (Grand Rapids: W. B. Eerdmans, 1998), p. 773.

26. See David Rensberger, *Johannine Faith and Liberating Community* (Philadelphia: Westminster Press, 1988), pp. 64–77.

27. Ibid., 76–78.

28. See especially J. Louis Martyn, *History and Theology in the Fourth Gospel* (New York: Harper & Row, 1979).

29. Barnabas Lindars, *Behind the Fourth Gospel* (London: SPCK, 1971), pp. 23, 47, 61.

30. See Teresa Okure, *The Johannine Approach to Mission: A Contextual Study of John 4:1–42* (Tübingen: J. C. B. Mohr, 1988), pp. 198f., for the missionary meaning of *kosmos* in John's gospel.

31. Note the correlation between the healing work which "we" do (9:4ff.), where the reference is to Jesus and his disciples, and the greater works that his disciples will accomplish when he is gone (14:12). J. Louis Martyn calls attention to the prominence of healing ministries in the Johannine church. See *History and Theology in the Fourth Gospel,* pp. 30–36.

32. David Rensberger, *Johannine Faith and Liberating Community,* p. 78. See also Barnabas Lindars, "Word and Sacrament in the Fourth Gospel," *Scottish Journal of Theology,* 29 (1976): 58–63.

33. Rensberger stresses the boundary quality of Johannine eucharistic practices. They mark the community off from the unbelieving world. See pp. 77–81. But given John's missionary concerns, we should probably think of these boundaries as expanding, on the model of the Pauline churches.

34. Richard Bauckham, *The Theology of the Book of Revelation* (Cambridge: Cambridge University Press, 1993).

35. See G. K. Beale, *The Book of Revelation: A Commentary on the Greek Text* (Grand Rapids: W. B. Eerdmans, 1999), pp. 174–76, 312.

36. Ibid., pp. 200ff.

37. Jürgen Roloff, *The Revelation of John,* tr. John E. Alsup (Minneapolis: Fortress, 1993), p. 253.

38. See G. K. Beale, *The Book of Revelation,* pp. 1155f.

39. Ibid., p. 305.

40. Bauckham, *The Climax of Prophecy: Studies in the Book of Revelation* (Edinburgh: T. & T. Clark, 1993), p. 106.

41. See G. K. Beale, *The Book of Revelation,* p. 309.

42. S. E. Allo, *Saint Jean, l'Apocalypse* (Emerson, N.J.: Ocker & Trapp, 1999), p. 45; G. B. Caird, *A Commentary on the Revelation of St. John the Divine* (London: Black, 1966), p. 58; Wilifred Harrington, *Revelation* (Collegeville, Minn.: Liturgical Press, 1993), p. 75; Bernd Kollmann, *Ursprung und Gestalten der Frühchristlichen Mahlfeier,* p. 225; Gerhard Krodel, *Revelation* (Minneapolis: Augsburg, 1989), p. 145; Paul Minear, *I Saw a New Earth: An Introduction to the Visions of the Apocalypse* (Washington, D.C.: Corpus Books, 1968), pp. 57–58; Jürgen Roloff, *The Revelation of John,* p. 65.

43. For a similar view of the vital connection between eucharistic worship and mission in Revelation, see Bruce Chilton, *A Feast of Meanings: Eucharistic Theologies from Jesus through Johannine Circles* (Leiden: E. J. Brill, 1994), pp. 144f.

6. The Call to Eucharistic Mission

1. See especially *Baptism, Eucharist and Ministry (BEM),* Faith and Order Paper no. 11 (Geneva: World Council of Churches, 1982); *Being Anglican in the Third Millennium,* compiled by J. M. Rosenthal and N. Currie (Harrisburg: Morehouse, 1997); and A. Schmemann, *For the Life of the World* (originally published in 1963, Crestwood, N.Y.: St. Vladimir's, 1998). Other recent works in which one finds the concerns of this study paralleled include R. Fabian, *Worship at St. Gregory's* (San Francisco: All Saints', 1995); G. Lathrop, *Holy Things: A Liturgical Theology* (Minneapolis: Fortress Press, 1993) and *Holy People: A Liturgical Ecclesiology* (Minneapolis: Fortress Press, 1999); J. Vanderwilt, *A Church without Borders: The Eucharist and the Church in Ecumenical Perspective* (Collegeville, Minn.: A Michael Glazier Book of the Liturgical Press, 1998); and J. Zizioulas, *Being as Communion: Studies in Personhood and the Church* (London: Darton, Longman and Todd, 1985).

2. *Baptism, Eucharist and Ministry,* pp. 14–15.

3. Some Presbyterian churches make use of short speeches by congregants called "Moments for Mission." These occur

during the worship and usually place some challenge before the community. I have seen effective adaptations of this practice in Episcopal churches.

4. See D. Aune, *The Cultic Setting of Realized Eschatology in Early Christianity* (Leiden: E. J. Brill, 1972), pp. 96–98, 126–135, and various passages in chapters 13–17 of the gospel. The first chapter of Revelation also contains a vision of Christ that seems closely connected with eucharistic worship.

5. See "The Real Absence: A Note on the Eucharist," in *Living Bread, Saving Cup: Readings on the Eucharist,* ed. R. K. Seasoltz (Collegeville, Minn.: Liturgical Press, 1982), pp. 190–196.

6. See Bonnie Thurston, *Spiritual Life in the Early Church* (Minneapolis: Fortress Press, 1993), pp. 53, 104f.

7. See John Polkinghorne, *The Faith of a Physicist: Reflections of a Bottom-Up Thinker* (Princeton: Princeton University Press, 1994), p. 158.

8. Ibid., pp. 168–170. Polkinghorne derives some of his ideas here from G. O'Collins's *The Easter Jesus* (London: Darton, Longman and Todd, 1987).

9. See J. Koenig, *New Testament Hospitality,* p. 69.

10. But we should not imagine a rigid sequence of events here. Simultaneity may be closer to the truth.

11. But we can hardly doubt that they were aware of the Sabbath's importance to Jews, and, to the extent that they themselves had had positive associations with Judaism, they probably borrowed from its Sabbath practices.

12. See James D. G. Dunn, *Romans 9–16* (Dallas: Word Books, 1988), p. 911.

13. Joachim Jeremias, *The Eucharistic Words of Jesus,* tr. Norman Perrin (London: S.C.M. Press, 1966), pp. 48f.

14. As far as we can tell, most synagogue congregations of the first century also met in private homes.

15. New Testament writers understand the *bema* as a judicial bench. But other sources from the first century indicate that it could also be a "throne-like speaker's platform." See p. 140 of *A Greek-English Lexicon of the New Testament.* This is W. Bauer's fifth edition of his *Wörterbuch,* tr. W. F. Arndt and

F. W. Gingrich; revised and augmented by Gingrich and F. W. Danker.

16. But this was not absolutely necessary. In Romans 14 and 15, Paul takes the position that the presence of all believers together is more important than a common partaking of food and drink. One can give thanks at this meal even by fasting (14:6).

17. Robert Banks, *Going to Church in the First Century: An Eyewitness Account* (Auburn, Maine: Christian Books, 1980).

18. It seems that people offered many short prayers out loud to their Lord. See J. Koenig, *Rediscovering New Testament Prayer: Boldness and Blessing in the Name of Jesus* (San Francisco: HarperSanFrancisco, 1992), pp. 135–139.

19. See J. Koenig, *New Testament Hospitality,* p. 67. My views are based on G. Theissen's *The Social Setting of Pauline Christianity: Essays on Corinth* (Philadelphia: Fortress Press, 1982), pp. 151–68.

20. Prophetic messages and other utterances inspired by the Spirit — including glossolalia — can be quite subdued. So can the laying on of hands for healing.

21. Anthony J. Gittins, *Bread for the Journey: The Mission of Transformation and the Transformation of Mission* (Maryknoll, N.Y.: Orbis Books, 1998), p. 45.

22. Ibid., p. 49.

23. Larry Rasmussen, "A People of the Way," *Auburn Views* (Auburn Theological Seminary), 1, no. 1 (Fall 1993): 5.

24. I find this translation by V. P. Furnish to be the most accurate. See *II Corinthians,* Anchor Bible 32A (Garden City, N.Y.: Doubleday, 1984), p. 252.

25. For the provocative conviction that the giving of thanks by humans actually adds to God's substance and power, see V. P. Furnish, *II Corinthians,* p. 287, and H. D. Betz, *II Corinthians 8 and 9,* pp. 118f. Both commentators rely on an earlier work by G. H. Boobyer, *Thanksgiving and the Glory of God in Paul* (Dissertation, Heidelberg; Borna-Leipzig: Noske, 1929). Something close to Paul's view was already expressed in Ps. 22:3.

26. The piling up of these terms is stunning. See 2 Cor. 8:1, 4, 6, 7, 9, 15, 16, 19, 23 plus 9:8, 11, 12, 13, 14, 15.

27. Anthony Gittins, *Bread for the Journey,* p. 76.

28. See J. G. Davies, *Worship and Mission* (London: SCM Press, 1966), p. 120. Davies draws upon the earlier work of exegete Paul Minear, especially his "Gratitude and Mission in the Epistle to the Romans," *Basileia* (1959): 47.

29. Ibid., p. 121.

30. Rowan Williams, *Eucharistic Sacrifice: The Roots of a Metaphor* (Bramcote, Notts.: Grove Books, 1982), p. 29.

31. Alexander Schmemann, *For the Life of the World.* (Geneva: World Council of Churches, 1963).

32. Ibid., p. 42.

33. Ibid.

34. Ibid., p. 30. But he also accents the cross; see pp. 23f.

35. Ibid., pp. 43f.

36. Schmemann himself is quite clear about the missionary character of the Eucharist. See *For the Life of the World,* pp. 22f.

37. Monika Hellwig, *The Eucharist and the Hunger of the World* (Kansas City, Mo.: Sheed & Ward, 1992), p. 87.

38. Parker Palmer, "Scarcity, Abundance, and the Gift of Community," *Community Renewal Press,* 1, no. 3 (January 1990): 4f.

39. A written form of the talk appears in the *Princeton Seminary Bulletin,* 19, no. 3, new series (1998): 242–258.

40. Ibid., p. 253.

41. Ibid., pp. 253f.

42. Ibid., p. 258.

43. See Owen Chadwick, *Michael Ramsey: A Life* (New York: Oxford University Press, 1990), p. 47.

44. This and other striking features of the church's architecture and worship are described in Richard Fabian's *Worship at St. Gregory's* (San Francisco: All Saints', 1995).

45. See Gustavo Gutiérrez, *We Drink from our Own Wells: The Spiritual Journey of a People* (Maryknoll, N.Y.: Orbis Books, 1984), p. 134. The quotation appears in Gittins, *Bread for the Journey,* p. 153.

46. See "La vision eucharistique du monde et l'homme contemporain," *Contacts,* 19 (1967): 91. The quotation appears in P. McPartlan, *The Eucharist Makes the Church: Henri du*

Lubac and John Zizioulas in Dialogue (Edinburgh: T. & T. Clark, 1993), p. 278.

47. Gittins, *Bread for the Journey,* p. 159.

48. Samuel Terrien, *The Elusive Presence: Toward a New Biblical Theology* (San Francisco: Harper & Row, 1978), p. 476.

49. This is a paraphrase of what I have written earlier about prayer. See J. Koenig, *Rediscovering New Testament Prayer,* p. 160.

50. Apparently de Lubac coined this sentence in 1938. But Zizioulas, who drew upon de Lubac's thought, offered a fuller exposition of it in *Being as Communion.* See McPartlan, *The Eucharist Makes the Church,* pp. xiii–xxii.

51. We find this focus especially in *Baptism, Eucharist and Ministry* and *Being Anglican in the Third Millennium.*

52. William Tully, "Is Church Growth Compatible with Anglican Spirituality?" *The Anglican,* 26, no. 3 (July 1997): 7. But our study places a big question mark behind Tully's assertion that "to be eucharistic and evangelical at the same time is virtually without precedent in Christian history." If this remark is meant to include the New Testament period, it seems inaccurate. For an earlier view of the inherent connection between the sacrament of the altar and evangelism, see A. Schmemann, *For the Life of the World,* pp. 32f.

53. This is what Paul seems to be getting at in Rom. 14:6.

54. See "L'eucharistie: quelques aspects bibliques," in J. Zizioulas, J. M. R. Tillard, and J. J. von Allmen, *L'eucharistie* (Marne, 1970), p. 71. The quote appears in McPartlan, *The Eucharist Makes the Church,* p. 290.

55. G. Martelet, *The Risen Christ and the Eucharistic World,* tr. R. Hague (London: Collins, 1976), p. 173. Martelet notes that as of 1976 *Le Christique,* from which he quotes, has gone unpublished.

56. Geoffrey Wainwright, *Eucharist and Eschatology* (New York: Oxford University Press, 1981), p. 150.

INDEX OF ANCIENT TEXTS

ANCIENT JEWISH LITERATURE

ANCIENT CHRISTIAN LITERATURE

INDEX OF SUBJECTS

Page references enclosed in parentheses
indicate textual references to the endnote.